The Book of Princes and Princesses

The Book of Princes and Princesses

Andrew Lang and
Leonora Blanche Lang

MINT EDITIONS

The Book of Princes and Princesses was first published in 1908.

This edition published by Mint Editions 2021.

ISBN 9781513281766 | E-ISBN 9781513286785

Published by Mint Editions®

 MINT
EDITIONS

minteditionbooks.com

Publishing Director: Jennifer Newens
Design & Production: Rachel Lopez Metzger
Project Manager: Micaela Clark
Typesetting: Westchester Publishing Services

Contents

PREFACE

All the stories about Princes and Princesses in this book are true stories, and were written by Mrs. Lang, out of old books of history. There are some children who make life difficult by saying, first that stories about fairies are true, and that they like fairies; and next that they do not like true stories about real people, who lived long ago. I am quite ready to grant that there really are such things as fairies, because, though I never saw a fairy, any more than I have seen the little animals which lecturers call *molecules* and *ions*, still I have seen people who have seen fairies—truthful people. Now I never knew a lecturer who ventured to say that he had seen an ion or a molecule. It is well known, and written in a true book, that the godmother of Joan of Arc had seen fairies, and nobody can suppose that such a good woman would tell her godchild what was not true—for example, that the squire of the parish was in love with a fairy and used to meet her in the moonlight beneath a beautiful tree. In fact, if we did not believe in fairy stories, who would care to read them? Yet only too many children dislike to read true stories, because the people in them were real, and the things actually happened. Is not this very strange? And grown-ups are not much wiser. They would rather read a novel than Professor Mommsen's "History of Rome!"

How are we to explain this reluctance to read true stories? Is it because children are *obliged*, whether they like it or not, to learn lessons which, to be sure, are often dry and disagreeable, and history books are among their viiilessons. Now Nature, for some wise purpose probably, made most children very greatly dislike lesson books. When I was about eight years old I was always reading a book of true stories called "The Tales of a Grandfather": no book could be more pleasant. It was in little dumpy volumes that one could carry in his pocket. But when I was sent to school they used this book as a school book, in one large ugly volume, and at school I never read it at all, and could not answer questions in it, but made guesses, which were not often right. The truth seems to be that we hate doing what we *must* do; and Sir Walter Scott himself, who wrote the book, particularly detested reading or writing what he was obliged to read or write, and always wanted to be doing something else.

This book about Princes and Princesses is not one which a child is *obliged* to read. Indeed the stories are not put in order, beginning with the princes who lived longest ago and coming down gradually to people who lived nearest our own time. The book opens with the great Napoleon Bonaparte, who died when some very old people still living were alive. Napoleon was not born a prince, far from it; his father was only a poor gentleman on a wild rough little island. But he made himself not merely a king, but the greatest of all emperors and generals in war. He is not held up as a person whom every boy should try to imitate, but it is a truth that Napoleon always remained a boy in his heart. He liked to make up stories of himself, doing wonderful things which even he was unable to do. When he was a boy he played at being a general, making snow fortresses and besieging them, just as many boys do. And when he was a man he dreamed of conquering all the East, Asia, and India, and Australia; and he tried to do all that, but it was too much even for him.

He used to think that he would write a new religious book, like Mahomet, and ride on a dromedary to conquer ixIndia, with his own book in his hand. Can anything be more like a boy's fancy? He even set out in the direction of India, but he stopped to besiege a little weak ruinous town called Acre, in the Holy Land, and the Turks and English, under Sir Sidney Smith, defeated him, and made him turn back, so that, later, he never came nearer India than Moscow, whence he was driven back to France by the snow and frost and the Russian army. After that he never had much luck, though he had won so many battles, and made himself an Emperor, and married an Emperor's daughter, like a poor young man in a fairy tale. I am sure that no fairy prince ever did such extraordinary things of all sorts as Napoleon; but another story shows how his only son was very unfortunate, and had a very short and unhappy life, always longing to be like his famous father. No doubt he might have been happy and fortunate if Napoleon—like the great boy he was—had not tried to do more than was possible even for himself. It was like a great boy to take no trouble to learn difficult languages, and to write such a bad hand that his marshals and generals could not read his notes written on the battlefield, and could not be certain what he wanted them to do. Now the Duke of Wellington, though not so wonderful a general as Napoleon, wrote a very good hand, when shot and shell were falling all round him, and there could be no mistake as to what he meant.

In fairy stories the princes and princesses are not always fortunate and happy, though they are always brave, good, beautiful, and deserving. If they were always happy and fortunate, nobody would care to read about them; the stories would be very dull. For example, Prince Meritorio was the eldest son of Meritorio III, King of Pacifica. He was born healthy, brave, and clever. At the age of twenty-one years, all of them spent serenely in learning his lessons, including fencing and fortification, Prince Meritorio married the eldest daughter of King xBenevolo, of the happy island of Crete. The two kingdoms were always at peace; on the death of Meritorio III and Benevolo II Prince Meritorio came to the throne of both countries. He had eleven sons, who used to play the Eleven of the island of Crete and beat them; and when Prince Meritorio died, at a great age, beloved by all his subjects, he was succeeded by his eldest son, Prince Sereno.

No doubt Prince Meritorio was happy and fortunate, but as he never had any troubles or sorrows, as he married his first and only love with the full consent of the dear and royal parents of both, never was changed into a rabbit by a wicked magician, never had to fight a dragon or giant, never was a starving, banished man, but continually had his regular meals, why, the Life of Prince Meritorio is not worth reading. Nobody cares a penny about him, any more than they care about George II, who was a brave man, and as fortunate as a king can be, and yet we prefer to read about Prince Charlie, who was nearly as unfortunate as King George was lucky.

Even Napoleon himself, with all his wonderful victories, is more interesting because he was defeated at last, and died like an imprisoned eagle, a captive on a little island, than he would be if he had been constantly fortunate and enormously fat.

It cannot be said that the princes and princesses in this book were too happy. The Princess Jeanne was perhaps the luckiest, and she had troubles enough while still a little girl, with being nearly forced to marry a prince whom she did not want. Indeed all young princesses and princes were much to be pitied, when they were being vexed with marrying before they were out of the nursery or the school room. They were obliged to marry first, and fall in love afterwards if they could, which is quite the wrong arrangement. Think of King Hacon's mother, too, who was obliged to prove that she was good by carrying a red-hot iron in her hands without being burned. The xibest little girl now alive will be wise not to try this experiment, if she is accused of breaking anything which she did not break. Then poor Marie Louise was obliged to marry a king who was little better than an idiot; and no amount of diamonds, nor all the gold of Peru, could console her for living such a strange life as hers was in a foreign country with such a very foolish king. However, he was fond of her, at least, whereas Henry VIII was not fond of his many wives for more than a very short time, and then he cut their heads off, or sent them away. It was a wise princess who said, when he asked her to marry him, that if she had two heads he would be welcome to one of them, but as she had only one she would prefer some other monarch. The Princess Henriette, too, after all her wanderings, when she was as poor as a goose girl in a fairy tale, found a very unsatisfactory prince to marry her at last, and perhaps was not sorry to die young. Truly they all had strange adventures enough; even Henry VII, though, when once he was king, he took good care to have no more adventures.

The story of Mary, Queen of Scots, who had so much unhappiness, is not told here, because very little is known of her childhood. But there are two tales of her childhood worth remembering. When she was a very little girl in Scotland, the Governor of the country was Cardinal Beaton. He was a Catholic, and Henry VIII, being a Protestant, was always at war with Scotland, and often tried to seize Mary when she was a little child. Now she had been told a fairy tale about the Red Etin of Ireland, a kind of red ogre, who stole a king's daughter, "the flower of fair Scotland," and beat her every day. So when Mary, being about three years old, first saw Cardinal Beaton in all his scarlet clothes, she thought that *he* was the Red Etin of Ireland, and was terribly frightened, crying, "Kill Red Etin! Kill Red Etin!" They *did* kill him, presently, but not because of her command.

The other story is merely that when she was about ten years old, or not so much, she was taken across the sea with her four little friends, the four Maries, to France, to marry the king's son. They had a very stormy voyage, and she was the only one of the company who was not sea-sick. So she was very merry at the expense of all the others. No doubt a saintly little princess would have been sorry for their sufferings; still, perhaps many little girls would have laughed. Many princes have had disagreeable uncles, like Crookedback Richard; indeed one might think, like a little girl who had read history books, that "all uncles are *villains*." But perhaps no prince ever had such a terrible ogre of a father as Prince Frederick of Prussia, who became the great king and general. Though his father was very particular about making Frederick clean and neat, we do not find that he ever had a bath, or did more than wash his hands and face. Indeed Frederick's father was a horrible ogre in every way, though perhaps it was not unnatural that he did not like the prince to be perpetually playing the flute, even when out hunting!

After all, when a child thinks of his own father and mother, and his excellent uncles and aunts, he may be glad that he was not born to be a prince, and be hidden from his enemies in a bundle of hay, like Duke Richard, or dressed as a little boy, when she is a little girl; or locked up for a year in a cold sanctuary; or be smothered in the Tower; or run all the many uncomfortable risks of all these poor royal children. The greater a man or woman is, the more terrible are the falls from greatness, as in the case of the most unhappy of all queens, Marie Antoinette. To be a good king a man must be far better and wiser than other men, far more clever too; if he is not, he does more mischief, and probably has to bear more misfortunes, like Richard II, than any ordinary person. When we read about kings like Charles II, who only lived to amuse himself; or Charles VII of France, who was little better—and not xiiinearly so amusing—and think how many people far fitter to be kings died for these unworthy princes, we begin to wonder at kingship, at making a man king merely because he is his father's son. However, to consider thus is to consider too curiously, and certainly the lives of princes and princesses have been full of great adventures, and are rather more interesting to read about than the lives of the sons and daughters of the Presidents of Republics. Nobody tries to run away with them; they have not to be dressed up as beggar boys, or hidden in bundles of hay, and their fathers never burn their books, break their flutes, shut them up in prison, and threaten to cut their heads off.

Thus we learn that there is a good side to everything, if we know where to look for it, which is a very comforting reflection. But only a truly sagacious person knows where to look for it, if the misfortune happens to himself.

Meanwhile let British children remember that their forefathers were loyal even to kings not of the best—"at least, as far as they were able"— and that we have in our time been blessed with the best Queen who ever lived. So, as the old song says:

> *Here's a health unto his Majesty!*
> *And he who will not drink his health,*
> *We wish him neither wit nor wealth,*
> *But only a rope to hang himself!*

I

Napoleon

If you look out of your window in a clear dawn on the French Riviera you may, if you are fortunate, see, far away to the south, a faint mountain range hanging on the sea, and if you *do* see it, it is a sight so beautiful that you will never forget it. The mountain range belongs to Corsica, and under its shadow was born the most wonderful man the world has ever seen—Napoleon.

In the year 1769 two babies were born in widely distant places, both destined to spend the best years of their lives in a life and death struggle with each other. The birthday of Arthur Wellesley, afterwards Duke of Wellington, was on May 1, and his home was an Irish castle; while Napoleon Buonaparte saw the light in a small house in the little town of Ajaccio, in Corsica. Napoleon's ancestors came over from Tuscany early in the sixteenth century, and found in the island a large number of colonists like themselves, some Italian and some Greek, but all of them seeking refuge from the foreign armies which for fifty years had been trying to parcel out Italy among themselves. Though distant only a few hours' sail from its coasts, the inhabitants of the island were as different from those of the mainland as if the whole world lay between them. In Italy men were lazy, yet impulsive, lovers of beauty, of art, of literature, and of luxury; in Corsica they were gloomy, silent, watchful, living hardly, careless of everything which had not to do with their daily lives.

Their hatreds were not only deep and strong, but lasting. As in old Rome, it was the rule that he "who slew the slayer" should himself be slain, and these blood feuds never died out. No wonder that a traveller was struck with the sight of nearly the whole population wearing mourning. Almost everyone was related to the rest, and in almost every family one of its members had recently fallen a victim to a *vendetta*— what we call a "blood feud." Periods of mourning were long, too, often lasting for ten years, sometimes for life. So the country was dismal to look at, with the high bare mountains shadowing all. While in Italy things moved fast, and new customs seemed best, in Corsica they seldom altered. The father was in some ways as absolute over his wife and children as in ancient Rome. He gave his orders and they were obeyed, no matter how hard they might be or how much disliked. His wife was not expected or wished to be a companion to her husband or a teacher to her children. Even if a lady by birth, like the mother of Napoleon, she worked as hard as any servant, for there was little money in Corsica, and people cultivated their ground so that they might have produce to exchange with their neighbours—olive oil for wine, chestnuts for corn, fish for garments woven by the women, from the hair of the mountain sheep or goats.

The life led by both boys and girls in Corsica made them grow old early, and Charles Buonaparte, Napoleon's father, married at eighteen the beautiful Laetitia Ramolino, four years younger than himself. Charles had studied law in the University of Pisa, and, unlike his fellow-countrymen, was able to talk French, so that his friends looked up to him with awe, and often consulted him about their affairs, which greatly pleased him, as he loved to think himself a person of importance. He was both restless and ambitious, and in the disturbed state of the island he saw his chance for advancement. The Corsicans had lately risen against the rule of Genoa, under the leadership of Paoli, who wished to form a Republic. But his party was not powerful enough of itself to drive out the Genoese, so Paoli sent over to Paris to beg the help of France. It is curious that his common-sense did not tell him what would be the consequence of this step. The French arrived, and by their aid the islanders got the upper hand, but when the Genoese had sailed away the newcomers refused to follow their example. Charles Buonaparte had at first been one of the strongest partisans of Paoli, but he was not proof against the offer of the title of "Conseiller du Roi," and of some small legal appointments that were given him by the French governor. He forsook his former leader and took service with the French. Henceforward he was no longer "Buonaparte," after the Italian manner, but "Bonaparte."

So Napoleon, who was born a few months after this event, was a Frenchman. He was the fourth child of his parents, but only Joseph, a year older than himself, was living; and though by-and-by Napoleon completely ruled his elder brother, for a long while the two stood apart from the younger children, Joseph sharing Napoleon's affections with Marianna, his next sister, who died at the age of five. The others who lived were all much younger, Lucien, the next, being born in 1775. Madame Bonaparte was so much occupied after Napoleon's birth with trying to put things straight which had been upset by the war that she was forced to get a nurse for him. This woman, Camilla Ilari, was the wife of a man who picked up a living on the seashore, and all her life was devoted to her nursling, whom she always addressed as "my son."

Napoleon, on his part, fully returned her affection, and was never too great or too busy to give her proofs of it. Thirty-five years later, when the world was at his feet, she sent to say that she wished to be present at his coronation in Nôtre Dame. "There is no one who will be more welcome," was his reply, and when she had made the journey and braved the perils of the sea, and weary days of travel that seem so strange and so long when you do not understand a word of what is being said around you—when all this was over, and the Tuileries was reached, she found Méneval, the Emperor's own secretary, awaiting her, saying that he was to place himself at her orders and to show her everything she wished to see. Oh, how happy that old woman was, and what stories she had to tell when she got back to Corsica! She had long talks with "Madame Mère," as the Emperor's mother was now called, and with all her children, one by one. Even Marianna—or Elise, to give her the new name she thought more elegant—and Caroline, the youngest, forgot for a few minutes how grand they had become, and laughed as Camilla reminded them of the old days and the scoldings she had given them, while Paulette, who gave herself no airs, but only wanted admiration and petting, asked fifty questions all at once, and never waited for the answers!

Of course, Camilla had no intention of going home without seeing the wife of "mon fils," and Napoleon's wife, Josephine, sent for her into her rooms, and, though she could not make out a word that Camilla said, smiled and nodded in reply, and presented her with two beautiful diamonds. Most wonderful of all, His Holiness Pope Pius VII announced that he wished to give her an audience! Camilla was the proudest woman in the world when she received that message, but at the same time she was rather frightened. Why, she had never spoken to a bishop, and how was she to behave to a Pope? However, M. Méneval, who was the messenger, suggested that obedience was her first duty, so Camilla rose up and followed him meekly into the apartments of His Holiness.

"Be seated, my daughter," said a gentle voice; and Camilla, who had knelt down at the threshold, got up slowly, and sat very upright in the chair which Méneval placed for her. For an hour and a half the audience lasted, the Pope putting to her all sorts of questions as to Napoleon's infancy and childhood. To begin with she only answered in as few words as possible, but gradually she ceased to remember where she was and to whom she was speaking, and poured forth a torrent of recollections about the nursling whom she loved better than her own son.

"Ah, the Signora Laetitia was a grand lady, and beautiful as an angel! Yes, there were many children to be sure, and much work needing to be done for them, but the Signora Laetitia saw to their manners and never suffered them to lie, or be greedy or rude to each other. Punished? Oh yes, they were punished; in Corsica punishments were many, but the children loved their mother none the less for that; and had not her Napoleone told her only last night how much he had all his life owed to the advice of his mother? How the poor darling had suffered when he had gone, at five, for a few months to a girls' school, and how the horrid little creatures had laughed at him because his stockings would not keep up! Did they make him cry? Napoleone? She could count on one hand the tears he had shed since he was born! Well, it was true she *had* heard he had wept a little when Joseph, whom he loved better than anyone in the world, was separated from him at that French school where they were together; but then, as everyone knew, one tear of Napoleone's was worth bucketsful of Joseph's! What friends they were, those two, though they *did* quarrel sometimes! And how, big and little, they *did* love water! If ever you missed them, you might be certain they were bathing in one of the streams that came down from the mountains, and even when they were being driven in state to see their noble relations the boys would be sure to wriggle out of the carriage and jump into the river with their clothes on!"

Not since he was a boy himself had the Pope been so well amused, but all kinds of important people were waiting to see him, and very unwillingly he must put a stop to Camilla's interesting talk. So, reaching some chaplets and rosaries from a table beside him, he held them out to her, and signing her to kneel before him, he gave her his blessing. A few days after the great ceremony Camilla returned to Corsica laden with gifts, and richer by a pension and many vineyards from "Napoleone."

LIKE OTHER CORSICAN LADIES LAETITIA Bonaparte knew nothing of books, probably not even as much as her friend, the mother of Madame Junot, who had only read one in her whole life, and that was the "Adventures of Telemaque," which perhaps accounts for her never wishing to read another! She wrote very badly, and could not speak even her own language, which was Italian, without making many mistakes, and in this Napoleon resembled her. In spite of all his wars, of his reading, of the people he came in contact with, he never succeeded in learning either German or English, and was forced to speak Spanish through an interpreter.

It was this inability to "pick up" languages which made him feel so dreadfully lonely when, in 1778, he and Joseph were taken by their father to France, and placed at school at Autun. Neither of them knew a word of French, but Joseph soon managed to learn enough to make himself understood, while Napoleon was tongue-tied. For five months they were left together, and then the younger boy, who was nine, was removed to the great military school of Brienne, in Champagne, for which the King had given his father a nomination. It was on this occasion that he shed the "few tears" of which Camilla had told the Pope. Poor little boy! he had no one he could speak to, and hated games unless they had to do with soldiers. His schoolfellows did not like him, and thought him sulky because he spent most of his time by himself. Occasionally he wrote home, but letters to Corsica cost nineteen sous apiece, and he knew that there was not much money to spare for postage.

Now and then he sent a letter to Joseph, in which he begs him to do his work and not be lazy; and once he writes to his uncle pointing out that it would be a pity to make Joseph into a soldier, for he would be no good in a fight. And as to this Napoleon could speak with certainty, for in all their boyish quarrels Joseph was never known to return a blow. One friend he did have, Bourrienne, in after-years his military secretary, who entered Brienne only a month after he did, and has written memoirs of his own life. But the rest of the boys stood aloof, though Napoleon seems to have got on better with the masters. When he had been at Brienne four years, his father again returned to France to place Marianna, who was six, at school at St. Cyr, near Paris, and Lucien, who was eight, at Brienne. Napoleon was glad to see his father, who died about fifteen months later; but he and Lucien were, of course, far apart in the school, and, what was more important, they never got on together, so that Napoleon was not much less lonely than before. Besides, he was fourteen now, and would soon be going to the military school in Paris.

That winter it was very cold, and snow fell heavily in Champagne. In England it would have been welcomed heartily by the boys, who would have spent hours in snowballing each other; but the masters at Brienne never thought of this, and gave orders that exercise was to be taken in the big hall of the college. Now the hall, which only had a fire at one end, looked very dreary, and nobody felt inclined to play. The older boys stood round the chimney and the younger ones peered disconsolately out of the windows, hoping in vain to catch a glimpse of blue sky. Suddenly young Bonaparte left the fireplace where he had been leaning, and touched Bourrienne on the shoulder.

"I am not going to stay here," he said. "Let us go and make a snow castle, and besiege it. Who will come?"

"I," and "I," and "I," they all shouted, and in a moment they were all gathered round Napoleon in the courtyard, begging him to tell them what to do.

"Get as many shovels as you can find in the tool house, and we will make a castle," he answered. "A proper castle with a keep, and a donjon and battlements. Then we must dig some trenches for cover. When we have finished we must garrison the castle, and I will lead the attacking party." Unfortunately, the spades and shovels left by the gardeners only numbered about one to every fifteen or twenty boys, so they had to take them in turns, the others using any tools they could find, or even their own hands. All the afternoon they worked without a moment's pause, and at sunset, just before the bell for lessons sounded, the castle was finished. That night, when the lights were put out in their cold dormitory, they asked each other anxiously, before they went to sleep, if they were *quite* sure that it did not feel any warmer. It would be dreadful to wake up and to find that their beautiful castle had crumbled away! Never before had there been so little difficulty in getting out of bed as when the boys woke up the next morning. No, it was certainly not warmer; in fact, it was a good deal colder, and their fingers were so frozen that they could hardly fasten the buttons of their uniforms, but their faces were rosy and smiling as they trooped down the stairs. At the classes they were more attentive than usual, and no pranks were played; nothing must be done which could earn them a punishment, or risk their being deprived of that glorious sport. So when the hour of recreation came the whole school filled the courtyard.

It was wonderful, if anyone had cared to notice, what a change had taken place in the feelings of the boys towards the gloomy, masterful youth who stood apart, and was disliked and shunned by the rest. Now it was to *him* that they looked for orders, and a word from *him* made them glow with pleasure. For fourteen happy days the siege went on, sometimes one party getting the better and sometimes the other, the faults on both sides being pointed out clearly by Bonaparte himself. At the end of that time the snow had wasted, and the snowballs had a way of getting mixed with the small stones of the courtyard, so that the wounds were no longer imaginary. Then the principal of the college stepped in, and commanded the fort to be dismantled.

After this the young cadets looked on Napoleon with different eyes. As to the professors, they had long ago made up their minds about him, and their opinion agreed in most points with that of M. de Kéralio, who came to inspect the school in 1784. The inspector found that he was backward in Latin, in all foreign languages, and wanting in grace of manner, but that he was distinguished in mathematics, and fond of geography and history, especially of Plutarch. In conduct he was obedient and well-behaved, except when his temper got the better of him. In fact, that he would make an excellent sailor! But Napoleon did *not* make a sailor; indeed, except on his voyages to Corsica, Egypt, and St. Helena, he never went to sea. Instead, one day he climbed to the top of a heavy lumbering old coach, and travelled slowly to the great military school in Paris, to which he had a nomination as "King's Cadet." The school was a beautiful building in the Champs Elysées, and had been founded by Louis XV for the sons of the nobles. Everything was on the grandest scale, and the cost was enormous. An immense number of servants were attached to the institution, besides a quantity of grooms to attend to the horses in the large stables. There was a private hospital on the premises, with doctors, surgeons, and four nursing sisters, and a staff of seven servants. The food was abundant, and consisted, even on fast days, of soup, two kinds of vegetables, eggs, fish, and three sorts of fruit for dessert. Two suits of uniform were allowed the cadets in the year, and these were put on punctually on the first of May and on the first of November, while their linen was changed three times a week. Of course, officials of all sorts were necessary to superintend these departments, and they were legion. The overseer of the kitchen, with its seven cooks and numerous scullions, was called "the controller of the mouth," and seven porters kept the seven doors. In all, counting the priests, who said mass daily at half-past six in the morning and prayers at a quarter to nine at night, a hundred and eleven people were employed about the school, and this without reckoning any of the professors. For there were, of course, professors for everything—riding, fencing, dancing, gunnery, mathematics, artillery, languages, history, geography, fortification, drawing, and many other things, besides a professor for special training in all that was then considered essential to good manners, which included being able to write a well-expressed letter and to move in society without awkwardness.

At the time that Napoleon Bonaparte entered the Ecole Militaire by far the greater number of the cadets were young nobles belonging to rich families, whose reckless waste of money was one of the causes of the coming Revolution. The luxury of the school was to them a necessary part of life, but it bore hardly on the King's Cadets—Elèves du Roi—who, like Napoleon, were all poor. Soon after his arrival he wrote to M. Berton, the head of the school at Brienne, describing the state of things he had found in Paris, and the indignation he felt on the subject. "It is specially harmful," he says, "to the King's Cadets, who have no money, and, in order to foster their vanity and be on the same footing as their rich comrades, run into debt, besides rendering them discontented with their homes. It would be far better only to give them all a dinner of two courses, and to teach them to wait on themselves, to brush their clothes, to clean their boots, and to groom their horses." And when, years after, he founded his military school at Fontainebleau, the ideas he had held at sixteen were carried out to the letter. As for his companions, the effect of the life of luxury was less harmful than he thought. After the Revolution, now so soon to break out, almost all of them became *emigrés*, to avoid the vengeance of the Republican leaders on the whole class of the nobility. Numbers fled to England, having lost everything they possessed, and we all know with what splendid courage and gaiety they bore the worst hardships and supported themselves by teaching their own language and the dances they had learned in the Ecole Militaire. It is strange that out of the hundreds of youths who were Napoleon's comrades in Paris only one was destined to fight by his side, and this was a boy whom he hardly knew by sight, so recently had he come—Davoust, the future Duke of Auerstädt.

Stern and solitary, yet outspoken when he was strongly moved, Napoleon was no more a favourite in Paris than he had been at Brienne, yet the cadets, as well as the greater part of the professors, felt that in some way or other he stood apart. The director of studies, Valfort, was struck by the weighty words and keen insight of this boy of sixteen when he thought it worth his while to speak, which was not often. "His style is granite melted in a volcano," says the professor of grammar about his exercises, and the phrase may be applied to his life-long character. M. de l'Esguille, on reading his historical essays on Plutarch, Cæsar, Rousseau, Tacitus, Voltaire, and a score of other famous writers, declared that he had a great future before him if he was helped by circumstances—perhaps not seeing that men like Napoleon fashion their circumstances for themselves. "He is the best mathematician in the school," replies a student to a question of the German professor, driven to despair by the dense stupidity of Napoleon over the language; for, as we have said, neither then nor later could he ever make himself understood in any foreign tongue; neither could he learn to dance, although he took lessons. But when he was not at his classes, or engaged in working for them, the boy might have been found in the great library, forgetful of cold or hunger, poring over the histories of the past. It may have been there that he first dreamed the dream of his life—that some day he too, like Alexander, would march across the desert at the head of an army, and, entering India on the back of an elephant, would restore the broken French Empire in the East.

It was the custom of the cadets to remain for three or even four years in the Ecole Militaire, but Napoleon had only been there ten months before he passed for the artillery, and was given a commission in the regiment of La Fère, then quartered in the town of Valence, with pay amounting to 45*l.* a year. He left Paris at the end of October, the only Corsican who had ever been admitted to the great military school, and, accompanied by his friend Des Mazis, arrived at Valence on one of the early days of November. Here lodgings had been found for him in the house of a certain Madame Bou, who looked after him and made him comfortable. The pale sad-looking youth was grateful for her kindness, and fifteen years later, when he passed through the town on his way from Egypt, he sent a message that he wished to see her, and gave her a beautiful Indian shawl that a queen might have envied, and a silver compass that still may be seen in the Museum at Valence.

Madame Bou's house was the only home he had known for nine years, and while there he grew for a time younger and happier in the society of some of her friends. Not that his work gave him much leisure. For three months he studied hard, for he had to learn drill and to study gunnery and fortifications. His ardour and quick mastery of all that was most difficult drew attention and praise from his commanding officers, but from his equals, as usual, he held aloof. For one thing, he had no money to enable him to share their pleasures, though he was too proud to confess it; and for another, his interests and ambitions were widely different from theirs. To the end he remained the "Spartan" that the boys at Brienne had called him. The pomp and glory of his later life was only put on for purposes of state—an ill-fitting garment, in which he never felt at ease.

Having once satisfied his colonel as to his knowledge of drill, Napoleon applied for leave in order to see after the affairs of his family in Corsica. Charles Bonaparte had died in France of a most painful illness about six months earlier, and had left behind him many debts, not large in themselves, but more than Laetitia could pay, and Joseph, who had been with his father, does not seem to have been able to help her. So in September, shortly after his seventeenth birthday, Napoleon crossed the sea once more, and remained in Corsica, with only a short interval, till 1788. He found many changes in the home that he had left eight years before: Louis, who had then been a tiny baby, was now a big boy, and there were besides Paoletta, Nunziata (afterwards known as Caroline) and Jerome, the youngest of them all. Joseph was still his friend and companion, with whom everything was discussed, for their mother had become poorer than ever, and was obliged to look closely after everything, and it was no easy matter to provide such a family with food. She was heartily glad to see her son again, though like a true Corsican she said little about it; but was a little disappointed that he had almost forgotten his Italian, and had become, in everyone's opinion, "so *very* Frenchified." How the cadets of the Ecole Militaire would have laughed if they had heard it! Bonaparte, who could never learn to dance, or to bow, or to turn a graceful compliment! But though Joseph was perhaps pleasanter, and more popular, and made more friends, there was something about Napoleon which gave his mother rest. She felt that whatever he undertook would be done, and done thoroughly.

Meanwhile Napoleon began for the first time to enjoy games, even though his playfellows were only his little brothers and sisters. Paoletta, or, as he called her, Paulette, was very pretty, with little coaxing ways, strange indeed to find in Corsica, and when he was not talking seriously with Joseph of the disturbed state of the island, he was generally to be seen with Paulette on one side and Louis on the other. For from the first he was very fond of Louis, and all the time he was at home he taught him regularly part of every day. He had some books with him that he bought by denying himself things that most young men would have thought necessaries. Among them were mathematical treatises, Corneille's and Racine's plays, which told stories of old Rome and her heroes, the Gallic wars of Cæsar, translated, of course, or Napoleon could not have read it, and Rousseau's "Social Contract"; but Louis was as yet too young for that, being only eight. In his spare moments Napoleon studied politics and made notes about the history of Corsica, hoping some day to make them into a book, and chattered French to the little ones, who picked it up much more easily than their teacher had done. It seems strange that he should have been allowed to remain at home for nearly two years, but in France events were rapidly marching towards the Revolution, and rules were in many cases relaxed. Anyhow, it was not till June 1788 that he returned to his regiment, then quartered at Auxonne. His superior officers, especially Baron du Teil, all interested themselves in the young man for whom no work was too hard as long as it bore on military subjects, and encouraged him in every possible way. His men liked him, and felt the same confidence in him that his mother had done; but from his own comrades he still held aloof, and the walks that he took round the city, pondering how best it could be attacked or defended, were always solitary ones. In general he was left pretty much alone—there was a feeling among them that he was not a safe person to meddle with; but sometimes their high spirits got the better of them, and when he was trying to puzzle out a problem in mathematics that had baffled him for days, his thoughts would be put to flight by a sudden blast of trumpets and roar of drums directly under his window. Then Napoleon would spring up with a fierce burst of anger, but before he could get outside the culprits were nowhere to be seen.

As time went on, and the Revolution drew nearer, Napoleon's thoughts turned more and more towards Corsica, and when, in July 1789, the taking of the great prison of the Bastille seemed to let loose the fury of the mob all over France, he felt that he must play his part in the liberation of his native island. So in September he applied for leave and sailed for Ajaccio. On his arrival he at once began to take measures for enabling the people to gain the independence which he hoped would be formally granted them by the National Assembly in Paris. The White Cockade, the Bourbon ensign, was to disappear from men's hats; a guard must be enrolled; a club, composed of all who

ANDREW LANG AND LEONORA BLANCHE LANG

wished for a new order of things, must be founded. Even when the French governor puts a stop to these proceedings, Napoleon is not to be beaten, but turns his attention to something else, taking care always to keep his men well in hand and to enforce discipline.

In this way passed the winter and spring, and in 1790 the exiled Paoli was, by virtue of decree of the National Assembly, allowed, after twenty-two years, to return to the island. From Napoleon's childhood Paoli had been his hero of modern days, as Hannibal was of ancient times; but when they actually came face to face Napoleon's boyish impatience chafed bitterly against the caution of the older man. It was their first difference, which time only widened.

When Napoleon went back to Auxonne in February 1791 he was accompanied by Louis, then thirteen years old. They travelled through a very different France from that which Napoleon had beheld in 1778. Then all was quiet on the surface, and it seemed as if nothing would ever change; now, women as well as men met together in large numbers and talked excitedly, ready at a moment's notice to break out into some deed of violence. Everywhere the tricolour was to be seen, the "Marseillaise" to be heard. Napoleon's eyes brightened as he listened to the song, and Louis watched and wondered. But not yet had the poor profited by the wealth of the rich. Napoleon's lodging, which he shared with Louis, was as bare as before; his food was even plainer, for now two had to eat it. Masters were costly and not to be thought of, so Napoleon set lessons to be learned during the day, and to be repeated at night when military duties are over. And Louis was as eager for knowledge as Napoleon himself had been. "He learns to write and read French," writes the young lieutenant to his brother Joseph. "I teach him mathematics and geography and history. The ladies are all devoted to him" (probably the wives and daughters of the officers), "and he has become quite French in his manners, as if he were thirty. As for his judgment, he might be forty. He will do better than any of us, but then none of us had so good an education." So wrote Napoleon; and Louis on his side was deeply grateful for the pains and care bestowed on him. "After Napoleone, you are the one I love most," he says in a letter to Joseph, whose tact and good nature made him everybody's favourite, though his stronger brother always looked down on him a little. Louis was a good boy, with generous feelings and a strong sense of duty, which in after-years, when he was King of Holland, brought him into strife with Napoleon. But in 1791 that was a long time off, and soon after this letter he writes another to Joseph, in which he says, "I make you a present of my two cravats that Napoleone gave me." Did he keep any for himself, one wonders?

Deeply though he loved his military duties, Napoleon could not rest away from Corsica, and in the autumn he again asked for leave from his long-suffering colonel. He found the island in even a worse condition than when he had last left it, for parties were more numerous and hatred fiercer. More than once Napoleon narrowly escaped with his life, which, by all the laws of war, he had really forfeited as a deserter by long outstaying his leave. But this did not trouble Napoleon. With France upset, with "Paris in convulsions," and with the war with the allied Powers on the point of breaking out, no one was likely to inquire closely into the conduct of an unimportant young soldier. Besides, rumours had reached the island that the school of St. Cyr would shortly be closed, and his mother was anxious about Marianna, who was still a pupil there. Clearly his best plan was to go to Paris, and to Paris he went in May 1792, hoping to be allowed quietly to take his old place in the regiment. Scarcely had he arrived when, walking in the street, watching all that passed and saying nothing, he came upon his old friend Bourrienne, from whom he had parted eight years before. The young men were delighted to meet, and spent their time making plans for the future. "He had even less money than I," writes Bourrienne, "and that was little enough! We formed a scheme for taking some houses that were being built, and subletting them at a higher rate. But the owners asked too much, and we were forced to give it up. Every day he went to seek employment from the Minister of War, and I from the Foreign Office."

Towards the end of June they both visited Marianna at St. Cyr, and from her Napoleon learned that the school was almost certain to be closed or totally changed in its institutions, and the girls returned to their relations without the present of 3,000 francs (120*l.*) usually given to them when they left. It is curious to think that at that time, when girls grew up so early and married so young, they were expected to remain at St. Cyr till they were twenty. Marianna was at this time sixteen, "but," says Napoleon in a letter to Joseph at Ajaccio, "not at all advanced for her age, less so, indeed, than Paoletta. It would be impossible to marry her without having her at home for six or eight months first, but if you see any distant prospect of finding her a suitable husband, tell me, and I will bring her over. If not, she had better stay where she is till we see how things turn out. Still, I cannot help feeling that if she remains at St. Cyr for another four years she will be too old to adapt herself to life in Corsica, while now she will glide into its ways almost without noticing them." In the end St. Cyr was closed, and Marianna threw off the white cap which the girls so hated because its fashion dated back to the time of the foundress, Madame de Maintenon, and set out with her brother for Corsica. She was a dull and rather disagreeable young lady, with a great notion of her own importance, and a bad temper. Some of the new ideas, especially those of the superiority of women over men, had reached her ears in a confused way, and had readily been adopted by her. She spent hours in talking over these with Lucien, her next brother, a youth of rather peculiar disposition, who did not get on with the rest.

But all this happened in the autumn, and meanwhile Napoleon stayed in Paris, observing the course of events and roaming the streets with Bourrienne. One day they saw collected near the Palais Royal a crowd of five or six thousand men, dirty, ragged, evil-faced, and with tongues as evil. In their hands were guns, swords, knives, axes, or whatever they could seize upon, and, shouting, screaming, and gesticulating, they made their way towards the Tuileries. "Let us follow those brutes," said Bonaparte, and, taking a short cut, they reached the garden terrace which overlooks the Seine, and from there they watched terrible scenes. "I could hardly describe the surprise and horror they excited in him," writes Bourrienne, "and when at length the King appeared at a window, wearing the Red Cap of Liberty which had been thrust on his head by one of the mob, a cry broke from Napoleon:

"Why did they ever let these beasts enter?" he exclaimed, heedless of who might hear him. "They should have mown down five hundred of them with the guns, and the rest would have run away." "They don't know what they are doing," he said to Bourrienne a few hours after when they were sitting at dinner in a cheap restaurant. "It is fatal to allow such things to pass unpunished, and they will rue it bitterly." And so they did; for the 10th of August was soon to come, and after that the September massacres of nobles and great ladies.

With feelings like these—feelings often quite different from the doctrines which he held—Napoleon must have had hard work to keep his sword in its sheath on that very 10th of August when the Tuileries was attacked and the Swiss Guards so nobly died at their post. He was standing at a shop window in a side street, and his soul sickened at the sight of the struggle. At last he could bear it no longer, and, dashing into the midst of the fray, he dragged out a wounded man from the swords of the rabble, who by this time were drunk with blood. "If Louis XVI had only shown himself on horseback," he writes to Joseph that same evening, "the victory would have been his." But, alas! Louis never did the thing that was wisest to do. Eager as he was to get away, Napoleon had to linger on amidst the horrors of the September massacres till he gained permission to take his sister back to Corsica. Here the state of affairs seemed almost as desperate as in France, and no man could trust his neighbour. Napoleon now fought openly against Paoli, whom the execution of Louis XVI threw into the arms of England, and fierce battles and sieges were the consequence. Once he was imprisoned in a house, and sentinels were placed before the door, but he contrived to escape through a side window, and hurried back to Ajaccio. Here his arrest was ordered, but warned by his friends Napoleon hid himself all day in a grotto, in the garden of one of his Ramolino cousins. Still, as it was clear that Ajaccio was no longer safe for him, he got on board a boat and rejoined Joseph at Bastia.

Furious at his having slipped through their hands, the partisans of Paoli turned their wrath upon Laetitia and her children. With the high courage she had shown all her life "Madame Mère" wished to stay and defend her house, but was at last persuaded to fly, taking with her Louis, Marianna, and Paoletta, with her brother Fesch to guard them, leaving the two youngest children with her mother. Hardly had she gone when her house was pillaged and almost destroyed. It would have been burned to the ground but for fear of setting fire to the houses of the Paolistes. It was only on June 11, after perils by land and perils by sea, that the fugitives, now joined by Napoleon, set sail for Toulon. The voyage lasted two days, and as soon as they touched land Napoleon's first care was to find a lodging for his mother and the children, where they might rest in peace till he could decide what was best to be done. He then made his way to Nice, where a battery of artillery was quartered, and found that by great good luck the brother of his old general Baron du Teil was in command. In happier times he would most likely have been put under arrest at once, before being shot as a deserter; but, as in earlier days, the Republic was in need of every man it could get, and he was at once employed to inspect the defences along the coast and to collect guns and ammunition. In all this the warfare he had carried on in Corsica stood him in good stead. It had taught him how to deal with men, and his eye had learned to discover the strong and weak points of a position, while his mind had grown rich in resource. As in the case of many of the greatest men, he had been trained for victory by defeat. It was at the siege of Toulon he gained the name at which for eleven years "the world grew pale." Revolted by the cruelties of the Convention in Paris, the town, like others in different parts of France, had declared for Louis XVIII A friendly fleet of English and Spanish ships had cast anchor in the bay, and the French army which besieged the city was undisciplined and ill commanded. All that it had in the way of artillery was in so bad a condition as to be useless, the powder and shot were exhausted, Dommartin, the artillery officer, was wounded, and there was no man to take his place.

"Send for young Bonaparte," said Salicetti, one of the commissioners of the Convention, who had known him elsewhere; and from that moment the tide began to turn. Messengers were despatched at once to bring in horses from miles round, while an arsenal was built on one of the surrounding hills. Day and night the men kept at work, and before a week had passed fourteen big guns and four mortars were ready, and a large quantity of provisions stored up. Day and night the men laboured, and day and night Bonaparte was to be found beside them, directing, encouraging, praising. When he could no longer stand, he wrapped himself in his cloak and lay down beside them, present to guide them in any difficulty, to repair any blunder. And the representatives of the Convention noted it all, and one morning handed him his brevet of general of battalion. Armed with this authority Napoleon's task became easier. He had aides-de-camp to send where he would, and forthwith one rode along the coast to bring up cannon from the army of Italy, and another set out for Lyons to gather horses and food. But whatever he did, his eyes were fixed on the key of the city—the Fort Mulgrave which, it was plain to all, must be the first object of attack. Close underneath the fort a French battery was erected and manned—only to be swept clear by the guns from the English ships. Another set of volunteers slipped out from the ranks, and fell dead beside their comrades. For the third time Bonaparte gave the word of command, but there was silence. "Call it the Battery of the Fearless," he said, and in an instant every man had sprung forward. The battery was never without its gunner till the fort was taken.

With the fall of Toulon we must bid farewell to Napoleon, whose youth was over and whose manhood was now begun. You all know the story which ended at last in Waterloo, and there is no need to repeat it. "He was not a gentleman," is said by many. Well, perhaps he was not *always* a gentleman, but the hold he obtained on France, and particularly on the men who followed him, was true and deep and lasting, for it endures even to this day. Listen to a soldier standing in the Invalides, where his body was laid when it was brought from St. Helena, with his hat and his sword placed beside him.

"Ah! c'est Lui! c'est son chapeau! c'est son épée!" he cries, the glorious memories of the past rushing over him, till he too feels that he has fought at Austerlitz and at Marengo.

And when they asked for rights, he made reply

> "Ye have my glory." And so, drawing round them
> His ample purple, glorified and bound them
> In an embrace that seemed identity.
> "He ruled them like a tyrant." True. But none
> Were ruled like slaves. Each felt Napoleon.

II

HIS MAJESTY THE KING OF ROME

At nine o'clock on the morning of March 20, 1811, the boom of a cannon sounded through Paris. Peace reigned throughout France, yet the roar of the gun had a magical effect on the hurrying passers-by. Every man, woman, and child, whatever might be their business, stopped where they stood, as if a fairy had waved her wand over them. No one moved; no one spoke; not only did their feet seem enchanted, but their tongues too. Silently they all remained in their places while the thunder of the cannon still went on, but their faces wore a strained, intense look as if they were counting something. Nineteen! twenty! twenty-one! one and all they held their breath. Twenty-two! and a cry as of one man rung out. The spell was broken, handkerchiefs were waved, hats flew into the air, old soldiers embraced each other with tears in their eyes. The King of Rome was born.

And who was this King of Rome, the only bearer of a noble name, and why was his birth so dear to the citizens of Paris? He was the son of Napoleon and the Archduchess Marie Louise, destined, so it was hoped, to carry on the work of his father and to bear the eagles triumphant through many a field of battle. And yet, if they could have looked forward twenty-one years, they would have seen a youth dying of consumption far from the country which he loved, after one of the saddest lives that perhaps any child ever knew.

But now, on the day of his birth, nobody dreamed of the doom that lay on him! Instead, he seemed the most fortunate baby in the whole world! He had a lady-in-waiting in charge of him and his numerous nurses, and chief attendant, the Comtesse de Montesquiou, "Maman Quiou" as he called her in after-days; his room was hung with soft green silk curtains, with palm trees and golden lizards embroidered on them. He slept all night long, and part of the day too, in a cot shaped like a boat, with a gilded prow, and the green, myrtle broidered curtains that shaded him from the light were caught together by a wreath of golden laurels. In the room there was another cradle, more beautiful, given him by the City of Paris, which was to go with him by-and-by into exile, and can still be seen at the Palace of Schönbrunn. This cot had been the work of famous artists; Prud'hon had drawn the designs, and the most skilful sculptors and goldsmiths had carried them out. The curtains at his head were of lace, sprinkled with golden stars, and an eaglet, with outstretched wings, hovered over his feet.

When His Majesty the King of Rome was a month old, he was driven out to the palace of St. Cloud, where he lived with Madame de Montesquiou in rooms opening straight on to the gardens. Here, in the green and quiet, he grew strong, and able to bear the fatigues of his christening, which was celebrated in the Cathedral of Nôtre Dame, on June 9, with all the pomp suitable to the occasion. Once again the bells rang out, and all along the way troops took up their places. At five o'clock the Tuileries gardens were filled with carriages, and the procession began to form. The escort of troops rode first, and were followed by the gay-coated heralds and the officers of State, these last in carriages drawn by four horses. The Emperor's brothers and sisters came next, and after them was a pause, till the Imperial carriage, drawn by eight horses, hove in sight, containing Madame de Montesquiou, holding on her knees the King of Rome. His long robe was of white satin covered with lace; a little lace cap was on his head, and across his breast lay the red ribbon of the Legion of Honour. "Long live Napoleon Francis Charles Joseph, King of Rome!" cried the heralds when the baptismal ceremony was over, and the Emperor, snatching the child from the arms of its mother, held him out to the crowd who thronged the church. "Long live the King of Rome!" it cried in answer: then the procession re-formed, and returned to the Tuileries in the same order.

Marie Louise does not seem to have had the boy much with her, though Isabey, the famous artist, was constantly ordered to paint his picture, and it was his father whom he first learned to know. Napoleon had always been fond of playing with children; and before the birth of his own son, his nephews and nieces were constantly about him. Best of all, he had loved the little Napoleon Charles, son of his brother Louis, King of Holland, and Hortense Beauharnais, and Charles was never happier than when trotting about at "Nanon's" side. Nanon was the pet name of Napoleon. Together they would go and feed the gazelles with tobacco—which (if strong) was very bad for the gazelles, and made them ill for a whole day after—or the Emperor would take him to parade, and Charles would cry, "Long live Nanon the soldier!" And how proud Nanon was one day when Charles, who had been lost at a review held at Boulogne, was found wandering between the line of fire of the two armies, not a bit afraid of the guns.

Charles was a very nice little boy, and had been taught good manners by Queen Hortense. When he went into Nanon's dressing-room he did not pull about the things that were lying on the dressing-table, but sat still while he chattered to his uncle, or repeated some fable of La Fontaine's which he had learned the day before. He was a generous little fellow, and would readily give away his toys or sweets, and only laughed when Napoleon pulled his ears, instead of getting angry like his cousins, the little Murats. Every day he did his lessons, and was allowed sometimes, as a great treat, to copy out the "Wolf and the Lamb," or the "Lion and the Mouse," or the "Goose with the Golden Eggs," to show to Nanon. But by-and-by he had to say good-bye to Nanon and go back to his father and mother in Holland, where he fell ill and died, at the age of four and a half, in May 1807.

After Charles's death Napoleon made a pet of the dead child's younger brother, Napoleon Louis, though he never took the elder child's place in his uncle's heart. Still, the Emperor liked to have Louis about him, and swung him on to his knee at breakfast, and gave him bits of omelette or cutlet on his fork. Louis, of course, wanted to do everything his uncle did, and one day insisted on sipping his coffee, but he did not like it, and made a face. "Oh, Louis!" cried the Emperor, "your education is certainly not finished, as you have not learned how to hide your feelings." The boy stared and grew rather cross, for he felt he was being laughed at, though he did not understand why. His temper was never as good as his brother's, and he often flew into a rage when Napoleon teased him, as he was very fond of doing. One morning, when Louis was three years old, he was breakfasting with the Emperor, and was just going to eat an egg, when Napoleon caught it up, and held it out of his reach. "Give me my egg, or I will kill you," said Louis, picking up a knife. "Would you really kill your uncle?" asked Napoleon.

"Give me my egg, or I will *kill* you," repeated Louis, louder than before; and Napoleon laughed and gave it back to him, and patted his head, saying, "Ah, some day you will be a fine fellow!"

But now that he had a son of his own, who would by-and-by inherit the Empire he had created and tread in his footsteps, Napoleon could not make enough of him. He, too, came to breakfast, and, much to Madame de Montesquiou's disgust, the Emperor would dip his fingers in the red wine he was drinking, and give it to the baby to suck. The

King of Rome would shrink away in terror from the bunch of nodding plumes on his mother's bonnet, but he smiled and crowed when his father lifted him in the air. Sometimes, however, the play got too rough, and the child would screw up the corners of his mouth and begin to cry. Then the Emperor would stop and look at him gravely, and say to him:

"What, Sire! are you crying? A king, and yet you cry! Oh, that is very bad! Kings don't cry!" and he would begin to make faces, which the baby loved, and it would break into smiles directly. The boy grew quickly, and at eight months old he was already trying to walk, but, on the other hand, he was very backward in talking. As he got older, he would often manage to escape from the nursery, and, running along the passage, knock with his fists on the door of the Emperor's study.

"Open! I want papa," he would say to the sentry, who always answered:

"Sire, I must not let in your Majesty."

"Why not? I am the little king."

"But your Majesty is alone!" replied the sentry, who had been ordered not to admit the boy unless Madame de Montesquiou was with him. The child's eyes filled with tears, but hearing "Maman Quiou's" voice behind him, he took hold of her hand and looked at the man, saying:

"Now open it. The little king desires it."

"His Majesty the King of Rome," announced the usher, and the little fellow ran straight up to his father, sure of his welcome. No matter how occupied the Emperor might be, the child was never sent away. His father would hold him on his knee while he signed State papers, or walk up and down the room with the boy on his back as he dictated despatches to his secretaries, or, greatest joy of all, he would allow his son to play with the little wooden soldiers that he kept on the table when planning his campaigns. In face the little king grew daily more like an Austrian, though his father tried in vain to see some resemblance to himself. But in many ways he showed his Corsican blood, and chiefly in the sudden bursts of temper to which he was liable. These were always stopped at once by his governess, who never spoilt him herself or suffered anyone else to do so. One day, when something had displeased him, he stormed and raged till Madame de Montesquiou feared he would fall into convulsions, as his cousin, Achille Murat, had done only the week before. Finding that the child would listen to nothing, she ordered an attendant to close all the shutters. The boy, astonished at the sudden darkness, ceased crying at once, and asked why the sun was shut out.

"So that nobody might hear you, Sire. The people would never want you for their king if they knew how naughty you could be!"

"Did I scream very loud?" he inquired in rather a small voice.

"Very," replied the governess.

"Do you think they heard?"

"I am afraid so."

At this answer his tears began to fall again, but quite silently. He made a violent effort to check them, and when he could speak, he stretched up his arms to his governess, and whispered, "I'll never do it again, Maman Quiou. I am very sorry."

By the time he was two years old the little king had a whole roomful of toys of every sort: there was a drum, mounted in silver, that Napoleon had given him on his first birthday, before the ill-fated army started for Russia; there was a top in an ivory frame, and a Polish lancer who could move his legs; there was a wonderful pearl and enamel box, with a locket inside, and out of the locket a bird jumped and sang. The King of Rome cherished them all; but best he loved a woolly sheep with a velvet collar and golden bells. He would play with this sheep for hours together, pretending it was the lamb that the wicked wolf was trying to catch, as told in his favourite story. When he went out, he had two real white sheep to draw him, in a beautiful little carriage given him on his birthday by his aunt, Caroline Murat, and in this he drove along the riverside terrace of the Tuileries, dressed in white muslin and lace, with the red ribbon of the Legion of Honour peeping out of the folds. And the Parisians were always delighted to see him, and at the bidding of his governess he smiled and waved his hand, for the Emperor was most particular about his manners. He was also anxious that the child should grow up as strong and hardy as he himself had done, so every day, whatever the weather, the little prince drove out in his carriage, with a merino pelisse over his muslin frock, and a pink or blue loose coat on top. The Empress thought it a pity, and feared her son might catch cold, but in this matter Napoleon had his way.

Long before this the château at Meudon had been prepared as a sort of school for the Imperial children; if indeed the King of Rome should have any brothers or sisters. It was a rest for Napoleon to turn from the thoughts of war, and to plan every detail of the education that was to be given to his son. He collected a library of 6,000 volumes, which it would be years before the boy could read or understand. After the fashion of the day he ordered a dinner-service to be made at the manufactory at

Sèvres, and each of the seventy plates contained a lesson. Eleven of them were painted with scenes from Roman history, thirty-two with famous victories of the French; while the rest were covered with pictures of sun, moon, and stars, or birds, beasts, and fishes. His rooms were hung with blue velvet, and the backs of the chairs and sofas, as well as the walls, were covered with drawings of the most celebrated Roman buildings. It was in the same spirit that Madame de Genlis desired to teach Roman history to her two pupils, Louis Philippe and his sister, only she wished to have the events woven into tapestries, which would have taken even longer to make than the dinner-set and have been still more costly.

So the little prince was sent, with his governesses and his nurses and his own staff of servants, to Meudon, and Madame de Montesquiou wrote constant reports of him to his parents at the Tuileries. At fourteen months he had for dinner soup, beef, chicken, and pudding; at least these things appeared on his table, though most likely he was not allowed to eat them all. Directly the dinner was ready, the dishes were placed in a large box, which was carefully locked by the head cook, who gave it to a footman, and by him it was carried to the prince's apartments, where the box was unlocked by Madame de Montesquiou with a second key. These precautions dated back from many centuries, when poison, or rather the fear of it, played so large a part in the life of Courts. Certainly nobody wanted to poison the poor little King of Rome, and if they had, they would hardly have liked to face the consequences! Instead, he was adored by all his attendants, as a good-tempered, healthy baby generally is. They loved to stand and peep through the door, when "Maman Quiou" was not looking, and watch him staggering and tumbling about on the mattresses, three feet thick, that were spread in his rooms, so that he might learn to walk without hurting himself; and they would wait behind the curtains to see him start for his drive, with his two white sheep beautifully combed and curled, the golden bells of their collars tinkling as they went.

For some months the baby and his household remained at Meudon with his governess, while the Emperor had begun the fatal war with Russia, and the Empress was enjoying herself at Dresden with her father, Francis II Madame de Montesquiou writes her reports to the Emperor as usual, and no matter how busy he is, he never fails to answer. Sometimes these letters are accompanied by a bust or a miniature, and by-and-by Marie Louise herself sends a full-length portrait of him by Gérard, which arrives on September 6, 1812, the day of the battle of the

Moskowa. For an instant Russia ceases to exist for Napoleon: the world holds nothing but a little boy in a white frock. "Summon my generals," he says, and they come crowding into his tent, where the portrait of the King of Rome stands upon a rough table. As they look the Emperor turns to them with a wave of his hand. "Gentlemen, if my son were fifteen years old instead of eighteen months, it is not only in his portrait that he would be present to-day." Then, steadying his voice, which had trembled as he spoke, he added, "Take it away; it is too soon for him to look upon a field of battle."

It was on December 18 that the Emperor, ill and dejected, returned to France, leaving the remnant of his army behind him, to struggle with the horrors of the retreat. He knew too well that at the first sign of weakness and defeat the hatreds that his despotism had sown all over Europe would spring in scores from the earth, armed to the teeth, and for the first time in his career the thought entered like iron into his soul that the star in which he so firmly believed might be setting. Could anything be done, he wondered, in case, in case—it was as well to be prepared for everything. Yes, that was it! His son must be crowned Emperor by Pope Pius the Seventh, who was still a prisoner at Fontainebleau, and then, if abdication was forced upon himself, his dynasty would still sit on the throne of France. But though the Pope did not refuse when Napoleon arrived unexpectedly at Fontainebleau, and even allowed the day for the ceremony to be fixed, he made various difficulties, and in the end retracted altogether the consent which had been unwillingly wrung from him.

While his father was thus mapping out his future career, the little prince was living happily at St. Cloud with Madame de Montesquiou. In April, just after he had passed his second birthday, a great event happened—he put on his first pair of trousers, and though they were only made of muslin, his nurses were as proud as if they had been a pair of jack boots! Nobody, they said, and it was quite true, would have taken him for less than three, or even four, but still it was strange that so quick and lively a child should be so slow in talking.

"Maman Quiou" agreed with them. It was very strange, but perhaps he needed a friend of his own age, to play and even quarrel with. So she made inquiries among the prince's attendants and chose the son of a Madame Froment, about a year older than the prince, a good-tempered and well-behaved boy who knew nothing about rank, only that they were two little boys together. What fun they had on their ponies, those two! and though of course they never went out without grooms to lead them, they both felt as great as ever Napoleon had done after Marengo or Austerlitz! Did they not wear the uniforms of Mamelouks or Turkish guards; and did not the people smile and bow as they passed, and the children look after them with envy? In the company of little Froment the King of Rome soon found his tongue, and when on Sundays ministers and marshals flocked to pay their court, he was able to stammer a few polite words taught him by his governess. On these occasions he was always dressed in a smart uniform, which soon became his daily costume. He was either a Lancer, or a Grenadier, or a National Guard, and every Sunday he drove round the park and looked at the waterfalls which were always a joy to him. Once, as a special favour, a girls' school was allowed to stand in the hall of the palace and watch him go by! They gazed silent and awe-stricken at the fortunate baby, but when they got out into the air once more, they chattered like magpies about his golden hair and his lovely clothes, and his pretty manners. "Oh! how nice to be a king," they said.

Of course he was much too little to read any of the books his father provided for him, but he soon learned to know his letters, and to point out which was Cæsar and which Henri IV Fairy tales were strictly forbidden to him; they were "useless," his father said, and the boy who had begun his life like a fairy prince ended it early in the grimmest of realities.

At the moment that the King of Rome was born Napoleon's power was at its height. One by one he had forced the nations of Europe to bow to his yoke, or to accept his alliance, except England, which still defied him, and Spain and Portugal that with her help were shaking themselves free of the chains that bound them. But soon there were signs that the vast Empire was about to crumble. Russia was the first to rebel, and the campaign against her in 1812 was full of disasters. The people did not hesitate to set fire to their beloved city of Moscow, rather than allow it to fall into the hands of the invaders, and its stores were destroyed and its fire engines broken. In November began the retreat amidst the winter snows. Thousands of French soldiers died from cold and exposure, while, to add to the horrors, the Russian army hung on the rear, and harassed them at every step. At the news of each check to the French arms the hearts of Napoleon's many enemies beat faster, and soon it grew plain that he would have to fight not only Prussia and Russia, but his present ally Austria, and England, Portugal, and Spain:

and that on the victory depended, not his supremacy in Europe, but his hold over France. Still, he had faith in his star, and in his soldiers, and shut out all doubts from his mind as he made his preparations.

It was on January 23, 1813, that, wearing the uniform of the National Guard, the King of Rome was carried by Madame de Montesquiou into the Salle des Maréchaux in the Tuileries, which was filled with the officers of the regiment. The Emperor signed to the governess to put the child on the ground, and, placing him by his side, advanced with the Empress into the middle of the room. "I am on the eve of starting to lead my army to fresh victories," he said, "and I leave my wife and son to your care. Will you defend them? Say! will you defend them? Can I trust you; will you defend them?" A great shout answered him; then, snatching up the boy, he carried him down to the Place du Carrousel where the privates were assembled, crying, "Long live the Emperor! Long live the King of Rome!" The boy waved his hand and smiled, and Napoleon smiled also. "He knows you are my friends," he said, and the shouts grew louder than before.

All that year, while Napoleon was desperately fighting the allied army in order to retain the Empire that was slipping from him, his son was living quietly with "Maman Quiou," who did her best to train him for the position she was beginning to doubt that he would ever occupy. In spite of the care which she had exercised to treat him as an ordinary child, and the blows that had been given and taken by little Froment, it had naturally proved impossible to prevent foolish people from flattering and indulging him. "As papa is away I am master," he once said, not knowing that the "master" was no longer himself or his father, but the Allies, for Napoleon's star had set at last. He was beaten.

Marie Louise and her son were sent to Blois, where they remained for a short time, the Empress, who was wholly Austrian at heart, nourishing hopes of a kingdom to be created for her by her father, Francis II In vain did Méneval, the Secretary, and Madame de Montesquiou urge her to join her husband at Fontainebleau, and stand by him when he signed, on April 13, the act of abdication. To take her share in any trouble was never the way of Marie Louise; but she seems to have been satisfied when she learned that she was still to be called "Empress," and to have the duchies of Parma, Piacenza, and Guastalla as her dowry. As for accompanying Napoleon to the island of Elba, which had been chosen for his prison, it never so much as occurred to her. The "General," as she henceforth called him, had passed out of her life. Scraps of conversation and anxious looks caused the little boy, "King of Rome" no more, but "Prince of Parma," to feel that something terrible was in the air, something that had to do with himself and his father and mother, and he soon found out what it was. "Blücher is my enemy," he said one day to his governess, and on his way to Vienna he remarked to one of his attendants, "Louis XVIII has taken papa's place, and has kept all my toys, but he must be made to give them up," while another time he added sadly, "I see that I am not a king any more, as I have no pages."

It was at the château of Rambouillet, not far from Pau, that Marie Louise met her father, whom she welcomed with pure delight, as if the visit had been only one of pleasure. The arrangements for the journey to Vienna were soon made, and her son's attendants chosen. They were to be Madame de Montesquiou, who left her family behind so that the little prince might not feel himself forsaken; Madame Soufflot, and her daughter Fanny, a girl of fifteen, who, the boy thought, made a better playfellow than his friend Froment, from whom he was now parted; Madame Marchand, his nurse; and Gobereau, the valet, with his wife and little son. Most of his possessions were, as he said, left behind for Louis XVIII, but he was allowed to take with him to the country palace of Schönbrunn the wonderful cradle given him by the City of Paris, and some of his favourite toys, selected by himself. How hard it was to know what to choose out of those multitudes of beautiful things. "Oh! I can't leave *that!* I must take *that!*" he would cry, as his nurses and governesses pulled out one toy after another, and it was very difficult to make him understand that he could not take them all. At length, after many tears, a few were put aside: two wooden horses, a stable, a grenadier, a hussar, a cow and a milkmaid, a Turk playing on a mandoline, a grocer's shop—these and a few others were what he took with him, but dearer than all were his little carriage drawn by the sheep, and a hundred and fifty pebbles which he had collected himself.

He travelled in a carriage with Madame de Montesquiou, as his mother soon grew tired of him, and much preferred the company of her lady-in-waiting, Madame de Montebello. It was a long journey, and they did not travel fast, so that it was the end of May before they reached Schönbrunn. There the child began to feel as if he was a king again, so warm was the welcome of the people, who were charmed with his fair hair and merry smile. Indeed, though he did not forget his father, and often asked about him, he was quite happy for a few months, surrounded by his French friends who so dearly loved him. By this time he could read, and every morning after he got up and had had some coffee and rolls, he learned a little history and geography, with Gobereau, the valet's son, as a companion in his studies. When these were finished, an Italian master came and taught him the Italian names of the things in the room and short sentences, and *he* was followed by a German, whom the child did not like as well. After the German took leave of him, his playtime began, and he had great games at soldiers with himself and Fanny Soufflot on one side, and his little uncle the Archduke Francis and Gobereau on the other. From his earliest years war had been a passion with him; guns never frightened him, and military music made him dance with excitement. Little though he knew of his father—for his Austrian tutors did not encourage conversation about Napoleon—he was at any rate aware that he had been a great general, and the older the prince grew, the more ardently he longed to tread in his footsteps. But the Revolution, which had given Napoleon his chance, was past and gone, though perhaps if the Eaglet (as the prince was called) had inherited his father's genius, he would have made an opportunity for himself. But he had not genius, only ambition; and the circumstances of his life were against him.

One March morning the news flashed through Europe that Napoleon had landed in France from Elba, and that with every fresh day many thousands joined his standard. Not for one moment did Marie Louise think of joining him, or of watching with any feeling but that of dismay the struggle which was yet to come. Her child was hurriedly removed from Schönbrunn into Vienna itself, so that he should run no risk of being carried off by his father's friends. To make all safer, his grandfather, Francis II, ordered Madame de Montesquiou to deliver the boy to him, and to return at once to her own country, though as a matter of fact she was kept in a sort of confinement till the battle of Waterloo had decided the fate of Napoleon and his son.

Madame de Montesquiou heard the command with a feeling of despair. For four years her life had been absorbed in that of the prince as it had never been absorbed in that of her own children. From seven in the morning, when he got up, to the time that he went to bed, he was scarcely out of her presence for half an hour. During these four years he had been of more importance to her than anything in the world, not only from duty, but from love, and he knew it, and came to her for everything. It would have been hard enough to have parted from him had they still been in France—had Napoleon been there to watch over and protect him—but it was a thousand times more bitter to leave him alone, for he *was* alone, though his mother and his grandfather were both in Vienna.

Sorely though the boy wept at parting with "Maman Quiou" there still remained the Soufflots and Marchand, the nurse, to console him, and they did their best. New games were invented for him and wonderful stories were told him, and when he grew tired of them he would go to Méneval, who knew all about soldiers, and could show him how they advanced to cross a river or besiege a fort. But by-and-by there came about him a strange lady whom he did not like, and who did not seem to like him either. She gave orders to Madame Soufflot and to Fanny, who curtsied and turned red, and said as little as possible; but though after she had gone they went back to their games, they did not enjoy them as heartily as before.

At last, one dreadful day, Méneval entered the room when the lady was present, and, with a low bow, he informed "his Imperial Highness the Prince of Parma" that he was about to quit Vienna for France, and wished to know whether he had any messages for his father. The prince, grown dull and silent during the last few days, did not answer, but walked slowly down to the furthest window and looked out. Méneval followed him to take leave, when the child whispered quickly, "Tell him that I always love him, Monsieur Méva."

He not only loved him, but thought about him, and listened eagerly to what his elders might let fall, though, as long as he had his French attendants with him, he rarely put any questions to his German tutors. But soon he noticed that both Madame Soufflot and Fanny had red circles round their eyes, and could hardly look at him without crying. The prince did not need to be told the reason; by this time he understood many things. As usual he said nothing, but went straight to his room and brought out all his treasures, the treasures that had come with him from France a year and a half before. There was his little gun, his Order of the Legion of Honour, his soldiers, the veil that he had worn at his christening, the medals that had been struck at his birth. "Take them," he said to Fanny Soufflot; "take them back to France."

Now there was only Marchand left, in whose presence he had slept every night since he was born. She was only a peasant woman, and surely could not be suspected of plotting against the Austrian Court! No, but she might talk to him of his father, and keep alive memories which were better let die. She put him to bed one night as usual, in the spring of 1816, but in the morning there stood at his bedside, not Marchand, but an Austrian officer. Once more the boy understood. He turned a shade paler, but asked no questions, merely saying, "Monsieur Foresti, I should like to get up."

It had not been without a struggle that the friends of Napoleon had allowed his son to be set aside. An effort was made to proclaim him Napoleon II when his father, for the second time, abdicated the French throne. But the attempt met with no response, and was, indeed, quite ignored by the Chamber of Deputies. The only result to the prince was to surround him more strictly than before with German tutors and attendants, and to discourage him to speak in French. Henceforth he was to be an Austrian, and an Austrian only, and as he was not yet five years old the task did not seem difficult. They were soon undeceived; the child did not talk much about his former life to these strangers, but every now and then he would put inconvenient questions.

"Why was I called 'King of Rome?'" he asked his tutor one day.

"Because at the time you were born your father ruled over many countries," was the reply.

"Did Rome belong to my father?"

"No; Rome belongs to the Pope."

"Is not my father in India now?"

"Oh dear no, certainly not."

"Then he is in America?"

"Why should he be in America?"

"Where *is* he, then?"

"That I cannot tell you."

"I heard someone say that he was in great misery."

"Well, you must have known that that was not likely to be true."

"No, I thought it couldn't be," answered the boy, with a smile of relief.

All his teachers found that he was quick at his lessons, when he chose to take the trouble to learn them, which was not always, and, like many other little boys, he would listen for hours to what was read to him, though at first he was not fond of reading to himself. However, when he was about six he suddenly changed in this respect, and was often found poring over the Old Testament, delighting in the descriptions of the wars with the Amalekites or the exploits of Samson. As for his amusements, sometimes he acted in theatricals at the Court, and in spite of his age was present at the State balls, where everyone was struck with his grace, for, unlike his father, he always loved to dance. His tutors were quite kind to him, and did their best to bring him up in a way that was suitable to the grandson of the Emperor of Austria, but by trying to make him forget the country of his birth they went the wrong way to work. His recollections and feelings refused to be stifled; he was alone, and knew he had no place in the world; he had not a title, for the Congress of Vienna had deprived him of the succession to his mother's three duchies, and now even his name was taken from him. He was no longer "Napoleon," but "Prince Francis Charles." As his custom was, he kept silence about it, but this hurt him more than all the rest. After a time, however, Francis II, who was really fond of him, saw that it was not for his own dignity to leave his grandson in this position, and created him Duke of Reichstadt, with coat-of-arms, and lands, and a palace at Vienna.

Early in the year 1821, when he was ten years old, the Duke of Reichstadt began his studies in a public school, which were to end in a commission in the Austrian army. In spite of all his teaching he does not seem to have had a much greater talent for languages than his father, whose dislike of Latin he shared cordially. Great pains had been taken at first to force him to forget French, and to make him speak only the tongues used in the Austrian Empire, which were German and Italian, but as he grew older his lessons in French were begun again. After eleven years of study he was unable to write an Italian letter without mistakes, while his French compositions show that he thought in German, and then translated his ideas, so that it did not seem like real French at all. Like Napoleon, again, he was fond of mathematics and loved history, but best of all his drill. However idle he might be in other things, he worked hard at this, and how proud he was when he earned his promotion as a sergeant, and was allowed to mount guard before the room of his grandfather.

The prince was at Schönbrunn with his tutors, when on a hot summer morning a messenger arrived from Vienna, and desired to speak with Monsieur Foresti. Their talk was long, and when they parted Foresti's face was unusually grave, but he said nothing till the evening, when he told the boy in a few words that the father of whom he thought so much had died at St. Helena on May 5. Notwithstanding his occasional bursts of temper, the duke's silence and reserve about his feelings had won him the reputation of coldness of heart, and Foresti was amazed at the torrent of tears which broke from him. Now indeed he was alone, with only his shadowy recollections for company, and the stories of the Emperor's greatness which he had heard from his French governesses five years before. And during these five years his thoughts had never ceased to hover round his father, all the more persistently, perhaps, from the ignorance in which he had been kept concerning him. But well he remembered how the portraits and miniatures of himself had from time to time been sent to his father to Elba, to Fontainebleau, and some to St. Helena—though exactly where St. Helena was he did not know. *That* he was to learn later, when his tutor bade him look it out on the map, and gave him a lesson on its size and produce. Meanwhile he was put into mourning, which Foresti and Collin wore also; but they had strict orders not to go near any public places, where their black clothes might be seen and noticed, as neither the Emperor nor his Court had made the slightest change in their dress. The young duke's heart must have burned within him at the double affront to himself and his father, but what must his feelings have been if he ever heard of the conduct of his mother! The letter which she wrote to her son must have sounded cold and trifling even to a child; but perhaps the news may have been kept from him that she declined to allow Napoleon's name to be inserted in the prayers for the dead, and had refused his dying wish to have his heart buried in Parma. "It would be a fresh shock to me," she wrote to Francis II.

So the years passed on, and outwardly "Napoleon, King of Rome," disappeared more and more completely, and in his place stood "Francis, Duke of Reichstadt." At twelve he became a cadet; at seventeen he was nominated captain in the regiment of Chasseurs. "The spur of honour, and the wish to merit such a distinction, have completely changed me," he writes to Foresti on this event, which he calls "the happiest in his life," and adds, "I wish to shake off everything that is childish in me, and become a man in the best sense of the word." But he was not allowed to join his regiment, though the Austrian army was full of young officers of fewer years than his, and for the present he was forced to remain idle, and employ himself in riding fiery horses, an exercise for which he had a passion. Yet his loyalty was no whit behind that of his friends, and for the time being his military ardour made him more Austrian than the precepts of his tutors could ever have done.

For the first time since he had crossed the French frontier the Duke of Reichstadt had become a person of importance. In France Louis XVIII had been succeeded by his brother, Charles X, and a large party of discontented people were sowing afresh the seeds of revolution. The eyes of the Bourbons turned uneasily to Vienna, where the young Napoleon stood by his grandfather's side. If the Emperor chose to send him with an army across the Rhine, who could tell what fires might not be lighted in Paris? In Vienna rumours began to be heard of plots to kidnap or assassinate the young duke, and measures were taken to guard him carefully. There was some talk of making him king of the newly formed kingdom of Greece, but neither Francis II nor his minister Metternich would listen for a moment to the proposal that a Catholic prince should forsake his religion and become a member of the Greek Church. Then came the news that the Bourbon dynasty had been expelled from France. Who was to be king? Was it to be Louis Philippe, Duke of Orléans, or Napoleon II ?

As if by magic fifteen years were blotted out by the Parisians, and the remembrance of the great Emperor sprang into life. Pictures of Napoleon leading his army to victory, portraits of his son at every age, beginning with his childhood, when he was a fair-haired, white-skinned boy with eyes whose keen, far-seeing glances were never a heritage from his Austrian mother, were sold in the streets, while the backs of gloves were adorned by his image. In the young man himself all his early instincts and his worship of his father's memory stirred strongly. But the moment passed, and for eighteen years Louis Philippe sat on the throne of France.

As early as the year 1828 the Duke of Reichstadt began to show signs of delicacy. Always tall for his age, of late his growth had been very rapid, and he was now over six feet—seven inches taller than his father had been—but he became always thinner and thinner. The doctors carefully examined him and found great weakness in his chest and lungs, and reported the fact to Neipperg, Marie Louise's second husband, and to Dietrichstein, the prince's governor, a strict and stern though just man, who was not likely to encourage fancies. But with the coming winter the state of the prince's health gave rise to great anxiety. "I am forbidden to dance this carnival," he writes to a friend in January; yet though dancing was prohibited he was ordered a course of swimming and cold baths. One can only suppose that this was intended to strengthen him, but the intense cold of an Austrian winter seems an odd moment to begin such treatment. It is hardly surprising that it failed, and that his weakness increased as the spring advanced, and a summer spent in camp did not improve matters. At last, in 1830, a fresh doctor was tried, one who had attended several of the Bonapartes, and he was horrified at the condition in which he found his patient. The duke scarcely ate anything at all, and coughed continually, and when at length his dearest wish was about to be fulfilled, and he was to accompany his regiment into camp, his hopes were dashed to the ground by the statement of the doctor that only the greatest care could save his life.

The disappointment was bitter. As long as he could remember he had dreamed dreams, and they were all of military glory. He was to prove himself his father's son, was to carry on worthily the name and traditions that had been left him, and now—But once again he practised the concealment of his feelings which he had so early learnt, and bore his pain in silence. It was during this time that the Revolution in France took place which caused the downfall of Charles X, and caused the dying prince to become of such sudden importance. By the Emperor's orders an establishment was formed for him, and in the spring, when he reached his twentieth birthday, his tutors were dismissed. His health was no better, perhaps even worse, but it did not suit Metternich, the Emperor's chief Minister, to notice this; in spite of the remonstrances of the doctor, the prince was again allowed to join his regiment and take part in the manœuvres.

Ill though the duke felt, at last he was happy. His military duties were well done, and, like his father, he had the genius to make himself loved by his soldiers. For a time his strong will carried him along, but one day in giving orders to his troops his voice failed him. He made light of it, and said he had strained it unnecessarily, and that he would soon learn to manage it better; but a bad attack of fever which followed shortly after obliged him unwillingly to quit the camp, and to go for a change to Schönbrunn. Here, in the country, his health improved, but in a short time the fever returned, and left him too weak to care about anything. So passed the summer and autumn; but in the early spring his health began to mend, and with renewed strength came a sudden longing for the old pleasures. The doctor, thinking it would do the prince more harm to thwart him than to let him have his way, gave him permission to take a quiet ride; but the moment he once more felt a horse under him, he threw prudence to the winds and galloped madly round the park, till both horse and rider were quite exhausted. And as if this was not enough, he insisted, wet though it was, in going for a drive in the evening. Unfortunately the carriage broke down, and no other was at hand. He had only one attendant with him, and the officer did not dare to leave him alone in the cold, shelterless place. There was therefore nothing for it but to walk back to Vienna, but it was quite plain that the prince scarcely had power to drag himself there. It was really a very short distance, but to the invalid the way seemed endless, and he had hardly reached the first houses when he staggered and fell.

From this period his state was practically hopeless, though he would sometimes surprise his doctors by sudden if short-lived improvements. When the warm weather came he was taken to Schönbrunn and fed at first on asses' milk. But his cough prevented his sleeping; he ate almost nothing, and it was evident to all who saw him that the end could not be far off. Then, and only then, did his mother consent to come to him, and the Viennese, who had always loved the ill-fated boy, said bitter things about her indifference. But the young Napoleon said no bitter things; he only smiled and welcomed her. Even at this time, though every symptom showed that death was close at hand, his mother could not bring herself to remain with him. Short visits in the day and one before she went to bed were all she thought needful. Another woman would have known that for her own sake it would have been well to have pretended, if she did not feel, a little more motherly love, but from first to last Marie Louise had been too stupid to guess how people would judge her.

In the night of July 22, 1832, he awoke from a feverish sleep crying out, "I am dying," and directly after he added, "Call my mother." He was past speaking when she came, followed by her brother, but he looked at her and feebly moved his head. Then the prayers for the dying were said, and at five o'clock his sufferings were over.

In the chapel of the Capuchins at Vienna his body lies amongst the tombs of the Hapsburgs, parted from his father in death as he had been in life. Yet, faithless and cold-hearted as she was, his mother did not dare refuse him at the last the name she had so hated and disgraced, and he stands forth to the world, not as the "son of Marie Louise" alone, as he had been called hitherto, but as the "Son of Napoleon."

III

THE PRINCESS JEANNE

It was a cold day in January 1528 when Jeanne de Navarre was born in the royal castle of Fontainebleau. Most of her relations were remarkable people, famous even then for their cleverness and strong wills, and her mother, Marguérite d'Angoulême, sister of Francis I, was distinguished above them all for her learning. But Marguérite was better than learned, she was wise, and she thought that her little daughter would be much happier away from Court, with other children to play with, than in travelling about the rough roads and small mountain towns that formed a large part of the kingdom of Navarre, or in crossing the wide rivers that lay between the Pyrenees and the city of Paris. For Paris was the home of Francis I, whom Marguérite loved better than her husband, her mother, or her little girl. So in a few days the baby was quietly christened in the private chapel of the château, and when she was a month old was very warmly wrapped up, and taken in a big heavy carriage drawn by eight horses to a place near Alençon where lived her mother's great friend, Madame de Silly, wife of the Bailiff of Caen. Here, in company with Madame de Silly's own children, Jeanne left her babyhood behind her. She was very strong, and very lively and mischievous besides; it was she who led the others into mischief, who would tuck up the long silk frock worn by little girls in those days, and climb trees after rosy apples, or persuade one of the boys to get up very early and go with her for hours into the woods on the hills, till Madame de Silly and everybody else were frightened out of their wits. Nothing ever frightened Jeanne, and she only laughed at the punishments dealt out to her.

"Oh, yes, I promise not to do it again—not till next time," she would say; and her eyes looked up so merrily into the eyes of Madame de Silly that the scolding suddenly stopped.

The only thing that ever made Jeanne really sorry for her naughty tricks was when Madame de Silly talked to her about her mother, whom the child loved deeply, though she saw her so seldom. To grow up like her was Jeanne's great wish, even when she was quite a baby; and as her mother loved the king, her uncle, so much, why, of course, she must love him too. Every now and then Francis I sent for her to the palace of St. Germain, to play with her cousins, Princess Madeleine, who was afterwards to be queen of Scotland, and Marguérite, the future duchess of Savoy. The two little princesses were both delicate, and could not ride and jump and run like Jeanne, who was besides the prettiest of the three, so she was petted and spoilt and flattered by all, and when she went back to Lonray, she gave herself all sorts of airs, till you would have thought she was not made of flesh and blood at all, or just a child like the rest.

By-and-by Jeanne's father, King Henry of Navarre, grew tired of dangling about the French Court, where nobody took much notice of him, and proposed going for a time to live in his own kingdom in the south of France. Marguérite was herself weary of tournaments and pageants and constant banquets, and pined for leisure to read books, and to write poetry. So she gladly gave her consent, and wished to take Jeanne with her, that they might get to know one another. But to this Francis would not agree. He knew—or guessed—that the Emperor Charles V, King of Spain, desired to bring about a marriage between his son Philip, prince of the Asturias, and the heiress of Navarre, and such a marriage would mean that the King of Spain would also be lord of a great part of France. If Jeanne even approached the frontier who could say what might happen? Therefore, to the grief of her mother and the great wrath of her father, she was to remain in France as the ward of the king. However, to make things as pleasant as he could, Francis announced his desire to betrothe the princess to his second son, Henry, Duke of Orleans, a boy of twelve, even then showing signs of the silent and melancholy character which distinguished him in later years.

The prospect of this alliance delighted both the king and queen of Navarre, but in spite of it Marguérite refused to allow Jeanne to live at the Court and be brought up with her cousins. After much talk, it was arranged that the gloomy castle of Plessis-les-Tours should be her residence, and here she was to dwell in state under the care of Madame de Silly, with a bishop, two chaplains, and a poet, to look after her education, and some other children, probably the daughters of great nobles, for her to play with.

Considering how many large and beautiful castles were owned by Francis, it seems strange that he should have chosen such a dismal place as Plessis for a child to be brought up in. The thick forests by which it was surrounded kept out the sun, and even Jeanne's high spirits were awed by the dark memories of Louis XI which filled every corner—by the deep holes, or *oubliettes*, through which a man might be thrust—and forgotten; by Cardinal La Balue's iron cage. She was still, in spite of her strength and cleverness, a very little girl, and she often lay awake at night half afraid and half fascinated, wondering what *she* would have thought about all day long in that iron cage, and making plans how to get out of it.

As has been said, Jeanne desired in all things to resemble her mother, and worked hard at her lessons; she learned several languages, besides the history of France, and Navarre, and Spain, and a little about that strange country England, whose king, Henry VIII, had stirred up the Church and disobeyed his Holy Father the Pope, in his refusal to allow Henry to put away his wife Katharine of Aragon, and marry somebody else. In after years Jeanne disobeyed the Pope in other ways, and taught her son to do so also; but at Plessis her sharp little ears picked up all that was said about Henry VIII and his three wives, and her sharp little mind was horrified at the bare idea of revolting against the Holy Father. She came to know many of the poems of Monsieur Pierre Ronsard and Joachim du Bellay by heart; but best of all she liked the songs of Louis, Duke of Orleans. She even struggled to write poems herself; but she had sense enough to see that they were not good enough to waste her time on. On wet or cold days, when the wind whistled through the forest and the old towers, she and her friends would dance in the hall, or sing songs together in the firelight.

Sometimes the castle was turned upside down by the news that the king was coming to pay his niece a visit. Poor Madame de Silly rather dreaded these grand occasions, for Jeanne was apt to have her head turned by her uncle, who encouraged her to say what she liked, and only laughed when she answered him pertly. He was amused, too, by the way in which she stuck to any plan she had formed, and, if he refused his consent one day, would begin all over again the next. Very often she got her own way through sheer obstinacy, and Madame de Silly would sigh as she looked on, for she knew that it would take some time after the king's departure to get Jeanne into order again.

And when Jeanne was tiresome she could be very tiresome indeed. She not only had a quick tongue, but a quick temper, and would despise and even ill-treat anyone who was not so determined as herself. When she was ten years old her aunt, the Vicomtesse de Rohan, came to live at Plessis with some of her children, for her husband had lost so much money that they had almost nothing to live on. The eldest girl, Françoise, had already gone to live at Pau with Queen Marguérite, which made Jeanne bitterly jealous, so that when she heard from Madame de Silly that her cousin was to be left at Plessis while the Queen of Navarre went to Court, she was thoroughly prepared to dislike her and everything she did. If only Mademoiselle de Rohan had behaved to Jeanne as Jeanne behaved to *her* they would soon have made friends; but, unluckily, she was easily frightened, and would give up anything sooner than quarrel about it. She was lazy, too, and preferred sitting over her embroidery to joining in the rough games in which Jeanne delighted. Of course she was not allowed to have her way, and was forced, little as she liked it, to go with the rest; but Jeanne, who played as earnestly as she did everything else, was speedily provoked by the listless Françoise, and even went so far as to give her a hard slap as a punishment for her indolence. Mademoiselle de Rohan did not slap her back, but she had weapons of her own which stung as well. When Marguérite returned to fetch her on her road to Pau, a poem of "Farewell to Plessis" was left behind, each lady in the queen's suite writing one verse. The stanza composed by Françoise, whose poetical gifts were greater than her cousin's, ran as follows:

> *Farewell, dear hand, farewell, I say,*
> *That used to slap me every day;*
> *And yet I love the slapper so,*
> *It breaks my heart that I must go!*

No doubt Queen Marguérite heard all the story from Madame de Silly, and scolded her daughter, and no doubt also that when Jeanne recovered her temper she felt very much ashamed of her rudeness. All her life she was absolutely truthful, whatever it might cost her, and when she had done wrong, and knew it, she never made excuses for herself, but accepted manfully the punishment that was given her. But though Jeanne was pleased enough to say good-bye to Françoise, she was extremely sorry to part from Mademoiselle de Grammont, who was three years older than herself, and a very clever and decided young lady, who at thirteen thought herself a woman, and wrote some pretty lines to Jeanne on her departure from Plessis, assuring the princess that she would never cease to love her all her life, and that when they were both married, which would probably be soon, they would crave their husbands' permission to meet often.

After all the excitement was over, and everyday habits were resumed, Jeanne began to feel very dull indeed. Her lessons ceased to interest her, and she no longer cared for games, but would listen eagerly to the dark tales of cruel deeds done by Louis XI more than fifty years before, which you may read about in "Quentin Durward," by Sir Walter Scott. Her mind seemed to brood over them, and Madame de Silly would gladly have welcomed some of the mischievous pranks, which had formerly been Jeanne's delight, rather than watch her growing pale and thin, gazing out of the narrow windows into the dripping forest, yet seeing nothing that was before her. When this had gone on for many weeks Madame de Silly became really frightened, and told Jeanne that if she was unhappy where she was she had better write to the king and her mother and tell them so, and perhaps they would allow her to leave. Jeanne brightened a little at the thought of getting away, and Madame de Silly, who noticed this, added letters of her own both to Francis and to Marguérite, pointing out that if the princess was kept there much longer her health would probably break down altogether.

Jeanne was, as usual, standing at the window when the two men-at-arms rode out through the great gate of the castle. Many days would pass, she knew, before they could come back again; but still—surely her mother would listen to her prayers, and not leave her in that horrible place, where she would soon die, and *then*, perhaps, they would be sorry they had treated her so unkindly! And Jeanne burst into tears at the sad picture she had made for herself. About three days later the messenger who had ridden to Francis at Amboise returned to Plessis, and handed Jeanne a letter. Her heart beat with excitement as she cut the strings wrapped round it, and so eager was she to know her fate that the words seemed to dance under her eyes. Then she looked up with the face of the old Jeanne once more. "I'm going! I'm going!" she cried, tossing the king's letter in the air. "I'm going to Pau at last. To *live* there—do you understand, Madame? But first the king is coming to see me, for he has not been here for a long time, and he fears I may have forgotten him. I wonder if I have any dresses fit to welcome him, for I have grown so tall—nearly as tall as *you*, Madame la baillive de Caen."

Madame de Silly smiled at her pleasure; yet she was a little uneasy also, for she too had heard from the king, and he had told her something which he had hidden from Jeanne. He spoke of a marriage he wished to arrange between his niece and the young Duke of Clèves, a Lutheran prince, part of whose duchy had been seized by the emperor. If, said the king, Jeanne were once wedded to the Duke of Clèves there would be an end to the project of her marriage with the Prince of the Asturias—and there would be an end, he might likewise have added, of the long-talked of match with his own son, the Duke of Orléans! But this had conveniently slipped from his mind, and he only remembered that by this alliance he would get the better of his life-long enemy, the King of Spain. If Francis had forgotten the early betrothal of Jeanne and her cousin, the King of Navarre most certainly had not, and great was his rage on receiving his brother-in-law's letter, which had arrived some time before Jeanne's. He was naturally angry at the hardly veiled contempt with which the King of France always treated him, and felt very sore with his wife for suffering it, and for always taking her brother's part against himself. Then, for reasons of state, he thought the marriage a very undesirable one, and when he laid the matter before his council they entirely agreed with him. Unluckily, however, Jeanne was in the power of the King of France, who made hardly any secret of his intention to invade Navarre should her father, Henri d'Albret, refuse his consent. In case of war, the country would inevitably fall to the lot of either France or Spain, and with a sullen face and heavy heart Henri desired his wife to inform her brother that he might do as he willed in the matter. Of course, when once he got his way, Francis was all smiles and gracious words again, and he instantly replied that as soon as the betrothal ceremony had been performed Jeanne should join her mother and remain with her till she was fifteen. For, said he, he considered that she was at present of too tender years to take on herself the cares of the married state. And with that prospect, Henri who passionately loved his daughter, had to be content.

It was on a brilliant spring morning that Francis set out from the castle of Amboise to hunt in the forests on the banks of the river. For a while he seemed, as usual, eager for the chase, then suddenly he let it sweep past him, and, signing to two or three of his most constant attendants, galloped down the road to Plessis-les-Tours, and was pealing at the great bell before Jeanne had any time to think of her clothes.

"Oh, Sire, what happiness to see you!" she cried, throwing her arms round his neck. "And look, am I not tall? And a woman grown, though my twelfth birthday is not long past!"

"A woman indeed, and beautiful withal! A woman ready for a husband! Is it not so, Jeanne?" And as he spoke Francis gazed at her steadily, and

Jeanne dropped her eyes and blushed, though *why* she did not know. The story was soon told; the Duke of Clèves, rich, young, handsome, accomplished, brother of the lately wedded Queen of England, was to be the bridegroom of the heiress of Navarre, just half his age. There was no time to be lost, and she must make ready to join her mother at Alençon, where the contract was to be signed. The king expected some astonishment, perhaps a little hesitation; but he certainly did not expect the burst of tears which greeted his news, still less her "humble petition" to the king's grace that she might not be forced into the marriage.

"Why, what do you mean? he is a cavalier in a thousand," Francis exclaimed angrily, and Jeanne could give no answer. The duke *sounded* all that a maiden could dream of, but—she did not want him for a husband. So her tears flowed afresh, and the king, finding her still silent, bade her remember that he should expect to see her in Paris on her way to Alençon in a week, and returned to Amboise in a very bad temper.

Left to herself, Jeanne continued to cry for some time; then she dried her eyes, and wondered why she so hated the thought of marrying the duke. It was not any love she had for her cousin, though like her father she felt a rush of indignation when she thought of the way she had been used and thrown aside—no, it was something quite different. What could it be? In a moment the answer came to her: Oh, no! no! she could never leave France; "France," which was more to her than anything in the world except her mother! And after all, she reflected, holding up her head, they could not marry her against her will—her, the heiress of Navarre, and a person of great importance. With that smiles came back to her face, and she went quite cheerfully to give orders to her maids, not knowing, poor little girl, that it was exactly *because* she was "a person of great importance" that it was so difficult for her to be happy.

Quite firm in her resolve, Jeanne rode out from Plessis two days after, accompanied by Madame de Silly, and followed by the chief officers of the household and a guard of soldiers. Her spirits rose as they left the gloomy woods and gloomier towers behind them, and passed into the spring sunshine, and the lovely gardens of the valley of the Loire. Much too soon for Jeanne's wishes they reached Paris, and went straight to the palace of the Louvre. After she had changed her riding dress for a beautiful garment of blue velvet, with a chemisette and high collar of fine lace, she was summoned to the king's apartments, where he stood with the Duke of Clèves. If Jeanne had not been so determined to hate him, she would have been forced to admit that he was very handsome and manly, and that he moved and spoke with the ease and grace so highly prized in the Court of France. As it was, she stared at him rudely, and would scarcely answer any of his pretty speeches, and altogether (if she could only have known it) behaved more like the naughty little girl she *was* than like the grown-up woman she thought herself to be. As was natural, nothing came of this conduct, except that the king became extremely angry with her, and Madame de Silly was obliged to give her a scolding, and show her that she would not advance her cause with her uncle, whose mind was set on the marriage, and only make her future husband to despise and dislike her.

"I certainly fail to see what I am to gain by leaving France and my own kingdom in order to marry a duke of Clèves," Jeanne answered contemptuously; and her governess, knowing that in this mood nothing was to be done with her, left her to herself. Later in the day, Madame de Silly was sent for by Francis, whom she found much enraged by Jeanne's obstinacy.

"You will both set out for Alençon to-morrow morning," he said sternly, "and you will inform the Queen of Navarre of what has happened. I will see the princess no more till she has learned to obey me." The news of her daughter's behaviour and her brother's displeasure sorely grieved Queen Marguérite. Giving Jeanne no time to rest after her long ride, she went at once to her chamber, and begged the girl to tell her all that had happened from the very beginning. The queen listened with anger and surprise to her daughter's account of her first interview with the king, whose lightest word had always been law to *her;* but Jeanne no more feared her mother than she did her uncle, and could not be induced either to express any regret for what she had done or to promise obedience for the future. So, with a troubled countenance, the queen left the room, and sat down to write to Francis.

To our eyes her letter seems rather slavish, and as if she possessed no rights in her own child. She assures the king that Jeanne's parents "had no will but his," and that her father was "more indignant at his daughter's conduct than he had ever been about anything." This was hardly the truth, as Marguérite could scarcely have forgotten her husband's wrath when the marriage was first proposed, and even if he now thought it wiser to change his tone so as not to irritate his brother-in-law further, she was too clever a woman to be deceived in this, and must have guessed that, strong-willed though Jeanne was, she would not have dared to withstand them all if she had not been sure of the approval of her father.

The visit to Alençon must have been rather unpleasant for everyone, for when the queen was not employed in trying to persuade her daughter to comply with her uncle's desire, she was engaged in teaching her some of the principles of the Reformed religion, professed, as has been said, by the Duke of Clèves. As Jeanne was at this time a devout Catholic, these lessons only served to exasperate her further, and it was probably a relief to all three when the Bishop of Séez, to whom the queen had entrusted the letter, returned with the answer.

It was very short, merely stating that the Queen of Navarre was to arrange without delay the ceremony of betrothal between her daughter and the Duke of Clèves, and this being over they were to go at once to Châtelherault, where the actual marriage would publicly take place. As to Marguérite's assurances of grief and abasement, scant notice was vouchsafed to *them*. Though Jeanne was her own daughter, and only twelve years old, the queen felt very uncomfortable as she walked up the narrow winding turret staircase which led to the girl's rooms. Jeanne turned first red and then white as she glanced at the letter in her mother's hand, but she listened without interruption while it was being read out to her. The queen was a little surprised at this, and felt she was getting on better than she expected; but when she had ended, and raised her eyes to Jeanne's face, what she saw there froze her into silence. In a moment more the storm broke, and such a torrent of reproaches flowed from the princess—reproaches as to the sacrifice that was to be made of her, of the misery to which they wished to condemn her, and of her firm resolve never to utter the vows which would make her the duke's wife—that for a while the queen felt quite stunned. It was seldom indeed that a mother of those days listened to such words from her daughter. At length she recovered her presence of mind.

"Cease, Jeanne," she said, laying her hand on the child's shoulder, "is it thus you have learned your duty to me? Be quiet instantly, or I shall have to whip you as if you were a little girl again."

The outburst of fury had somewhat exhausted Jeanne, and she felt rather ashamed of her anger. Not because, as she told herself eagerly, she retracted anything—it was all quite true; but perhaps she had behaved in an undignified way, and in a manner unbecoming a princess. So she made no reply, but began to think out another plan, and the result was a paper protesting at being forced against her will into this marriage. If she really composed it—it is certainly written in her own hand—it is surprisingly clever for a child of twelve; but it is possible that she may have been helped by one of the three officials who were witnesses of her signature. In any case, however, it was of no use, for the betrothal took place as arranged, and the public marriage at Châtelherault followed it. Outwardly, Jeanne had resolved to accept the fate which she could not escape, but before leaving Alençon she wrote a second protest, declaring that as her vows were only made under force and not freely, they were null and void, and the marriage no marriage.

Francis I was much relieved when he saw his niece ride up to the gate of the castle. Powerful though he was, Jeanne's opposition had caused him to feel uneasy as well as irritated; he could not have told *what* he feared, but he was aware that a burden rolled off him as she dismounted from her horse and walked towards the great door. He left the windows at once, in order to welcome her, so he did not notice the bridegroom hold out his hand to lead her up the steps, nor the air with which the bride repulsed him. Poor bridegroom! he was having a very unpleasant time, and it was well for him that he had a charming mother-in-law to talk to, who more than made up for the loss of her sulky daughter.

By the king's orders the marriage festivities were to be on the grandest possible scale, and Marguérite had given special care to Jeanne's dress. The jewels on her long robe of cloth of gold dazzled the eyes of the spectators, and her velvet mantle was broidered with ermine. No wonder that on a hot July day the weight of these clothes felt enormous, and Jeanne had some show of reason on her side when she told her uncle, who came forward to lead her to the altar, that she really could not move from her chair. Francis was naturally very much provoked, but not deigning to notice such childish behaviour, he turned to the constable, M. de Montmorency, and bade him carry the bride into the chapel. The constable fulfilled his orders, and set down Jeanne in her place by the side of the duke, the royal family feeling truly thankful that she had not kicked or struggled, as they fully expected her to do.

After the quiet life she had led at Plessis the splendid ceremonies of her marriage, and particularly the banquet and ball that followed it, interested Jeanne very much, though she would have died rather than show it. She even contrived to keep all her eagerness out of her eyes, and sat there, like a little wooden image, till the Queen of Navarre would gladly have given her the whipping she deserved. When the ball was over, and she was alone with her mother (in whose care she was to spend the next two or three years) she was scolded severely for her childishness, but all in vain. Not one smile could be detected on her face as she occupied the place of honour at the tournaments that were held during eight days and nights in the great meadow adjoining the castle, or walked among the tents of twisted branches where dwelt hermits clad in velvet, green as the trees, who undertook the charge of any strange knights till they could fight in the tourney. All this she enjoyed secretly, and better still did she like the fairies and water sprites who peopled the woods and hovered on the banks of the stream, though she resolutely kept silence, instead of speaking to them graciously, as she knew quite well it was her duty to do. In fact Jeanne was as tiresome and perverse as a little girl could be, but in her own heart she thought herself very grand and dignified, and the more she saw everyone put out by her conduct the better she was pleased.

At length it was all over; the bridegroom took his leave and returned to fight against the emperor, and the king and queen of Navarre took theirs also, and started for Béarn. For the first time in her life Marguérite was thankful to part from her beloved brother. She had passed a miserable fortnight, never feeling sure what her daughter might do next, and generally being much ashamed of what she *did*. But when they had left the Loire behind them, and were entering the country which "Madame la Duchesse de Clèves" had never visited since she was a tiny child, Jeanne threw off her injured airs and became the eager, observant girl she naturally was. Oh, how happy she felt to see Nérac again, and to spend the autumn in the free wild country where the sun shone, and the wind blew fresh from the mountains! She forgot at times (in spite of her title) that such a being as the Duke of Clèves existed, and she behaved so well, both at Nérac and at Pau, during the following winter, that Marguérite used to wonder if those terrible festivities had *really* only taken place a few months ago. During part of the day Jeanne was taught many things by her mother, and learned all the quicker for having the queen's maids of honour to share her lessons. In the evening she talked with some of the members of the Reformed religion, to whom the Court of Navarre was always open. Gradually she began to feel drawn to their doctrines, and probably would have adopted them altogether but for the fact that the Duke of Clèves had long ceased to be a Catholic.

So two years slipped happily by. Jeanne, without becoming less truthful, had grown more gentle, and more humble also. She no longer dwelt with pride on the thought of her behaviour on her wedding-day, but if she was alone her cheeks even flushed red at the recollection of it.

She was kind and pleasant to everyone she met with, and would chatter to the people in the curious *patois* which they spoke. She felt as if she had lived in Béarn for ever, and that Plessis and Alençon were a dream. Then, one morning, the Cardinal du Bellay rode into Pau, and craved an audience of Madame la Duchesse de Clèves. When admitted to her presence he delivered a letter from the King of France bidding Jeanne set out at once under the Cardinal's escort, and join him at Luxembourg, from which he would take her to Aix, where the Duke of Clèves then was. A frantic burst of tears was the only answer the cardinal received; but at last Jeanne found words, and declared that she would die if she was dragged away from her beloved Pau. Her mother, whom she hastily summoned, as usual took the side of the king; but her father wept with her, and assured her that if she was forced to go on this journey he would go with her. Henri was powerless to deliver her, as Jeanne well knew; still his presence was a comfort, and in two days the sad little procession took the northern road.

Meanwhile events across the Rhine had marched rapidly, and, unknown to Francis, the Duke of Clèves had done homage to the emperor, who had invaded his duchy. It was not until the treaty was actually signed by the duke that notice was sent to Francis of the matter, and with it went a letter requesting that the princess Jeanne might be sent immediately to Aix to take up her position as Duchesse de Clèves. The terms of the letter were of course dictated by the emperor, and were not intended to soothe Francis. The king's first act was to despatch a messenger to Soissons, to meet Jeanne, who was to rest there for a day or two, after her long journey. At midnight she was awakened from a sound sleep by a clatter in the courtyard beneath her windows, and a few minutes later one of her maids brought a message that the cardinal would feel greatly honoured if the princess would see him for a few minutes. Wearily Jeanne suffered her ladies to dress her, and dropping into a chair, waited to hear what the cardinal had to say. Nothing pleasant it *could* be, for did not every hour bring closer her farewell to France, and her life among people that she hated. Bowing low, the cardinal entered, bearing the despatch, which he presented to Jeanne.

"Read it," she said, in a tired voice, waving her hand; and the cardinal read it. As he went on her fatigue suddenly disappeared; she leaned eagerly forward, her eyes bright and her cheeks glowing. "What is it you say? That the king will see that my marriage—my *hateful* marriage—shall be set aside, and that I am to go at once to Queen Eleanor at

Fontainebleau? Oh, what joy! what a deliverance!" Jeanne's rapture was shared by her father, and next day they travelled, with very different feelings, over the road they had just come.

To judge by her letters, Queen Marguérite seems to have been more angry at the way in which her daughter—and her brother—had been treated than relieved at the princess's escape from a husband whom she detested. Steps were at once taken, not only by the King of France, but by the Duke of Clèves, to implore from the Pope a dispensation setting aside the marriage contracted on July 15, 1540. And as the reason given for the appeal was the fact that the marriage had been forced on the bride against her will, the "protests" were produced as evidence, and Jeanne felt with pride they had not been drawn up for nothing. Indeed, she was bidden by Francis to write a third one, which was sent straight to Pope Paul III But royal marriages are neither made nor marred in a day, and a year and a half dragged by before Jeanne was a free woman again. After some months spent with her mother at Alençon, she returned to Plessis, with Madame de Silly, to await alone the decision of the Pope. Here in the chapel, on Easter Day, Jeanne addressed the bishops and nobles assembled to hear High Mass, and read to them a short statement of the events relating to her marriage five years before, begging that the Cardinal de Tournon might be sent to Rome without delay. This time Pope Paul III paid more attention to the matter than he had done before, and by Whitsuntide the contract was annulled, and Jeanne and her bridegroom henceforth were strangers.

Strange to say, even after she was set free, Jeanne appears to have spent a considerable time at Plessis—which, as we know, she hated nearly as much as she did the Duke of Clèves—for she was still there when she heard of the death of Francis I in the spring of 1547. She at once joined her father, but does not seem to have tried to console her mother, who was broken-hearted, and henceforth gave up the life and studies, in which she had so much delighted, for the service of the poor. Many years previously Francis had married his son Henri to the young Catherine de Medici, who now sat on the throne of France, where the King of Navarre had thought to have placed his daughter. Henri was a very different man from Francis: he was shy and gloomy, and he had not the gay and pleasant manners of his father, and his affections were given to a wholly different set of friends. But on hearing of the fresh advances made by the Emperor Charles to the King of Navarre for a union between Jeanne and the young widower, Philip of Spain, Henri bethought him of the danger from Spain which was so prominently before the eyes of his father, and summoned Jeanne, then nearly twenty, to Fontainebleau. So seldom had the princess been at Court that she was almost a stranger, but her high spirits and quick tongue made her a favourite with most people. Queen Catherine, however, did not like her; she could not understand Jeanne, or the bold way in which she set forth her views. Speech, according to Catherine, was given you to hide your thoughts, and not to display them; while Jeanne thought the queen's elaborate compliments and constant reserve very tiresome, and avoided her as much as possible. "How cold Catherine was, and how stingy," said Jeanne to herself. "She did not seem to care for anybody, even her own children, while as for gratitude"—and, with her head held high, Jeanne sat down to write a letter respecting the care of her old nurse.

Of course, no sooner did the handsome young heiress appear at Court than suitors for her hand appeared also. The king favoured the claims of François, duke of Guise, afterwards the captor of Calais; but Jeanne declared that her husband must be of royal blood, and asked Henri how she could suffer the Duchesse d'Aumale, who now thought it an honour to bear her train, to walk beside her as her sister-in-law? Perhaps, being a man, the case might not have seemed as impossible to Henri as it did to Jeanne; but one thing was quite clear to him, and that was that he could never obtain the consent of the lady, so he wisely let the matter drop. The other suitor was Antoine de Bourbon, eldest son of the Duc de Vendôme, and nephew, by her first husband, of Marguérite. Antoine was now about thirty, a tall, handsome man, and a leader of fashion; but, had she known it, Jeanne would have been much happier as the wife of Francois de Guise. For the Duc de Vendôme, though brave and fascinating, was absolutely untrustworthy. His word was lightly given, and lightly broken; his friends were always changing, and only his love of pleasure and love of ease remained the same. As to the king and queen of Navarre, *their* opinions were, as usual, divided. Henri d'Albret did not like his proposed son-in-law—he was too thoughtless, and too extravagant; while Marguérite, on the contrary, was prepared to overlook everything, seeing he was the first prince of the blood, and, like his brother Condé, an advocate of the Reformed religion. She did not pause to ask herself how far his life gave evidence of any religion at all! However, also as usual, the wishes of the King of Navarre were once more thwarted, and Jeanne, her mother, and Henri II proved too much for him. The marriage took place at the town of Moulins, at the end of October 1548, when the bride was nearly twenty-one, the King and Queen of France being present at the ceremony. The King of Navarre did all he could to prevent his daughter's dowry from being wasted by declaring that it should only be paid in instalments, while the queen stipulated in the contract that Jeanne should have absolute control over the bringing up of her children till they were eighteen years of age.

The future life of Jeanne, married to a man like the Duc de Vendôme, was certain to be unhappy, and the state of France, with its perpetual religious wars, could only increase that unhappiness. As far as possible she stayed in her own kingdom, and kept her son, afterwards Henri IV, living a free, hardy life among the mountains. But there were times when policy forced her to visit the Court of Catherine, whom she hated and mistrusted, and, what was infinitely worse, to leave her son there. His tutors were men of the Reformed religion, but Henri had too much of his father in him for any faith to take root, and when he had to decide between Calvinism and a crown, it was easy to tell what his choice would be. But Jeanne was spared the knowledge of that, and of much else that would have grieved her sorely, for she died in Paris, whither she had gone to attend the marriage of Henri and the Princess Margot, a few days before the Massacre of St. Bartholomew.

IV

Hacon the King

When little Hacon, son of the dead king Hacon, and grandson of Sverrir, was born at Smaalen, in Norway, in the summer of 1204, the country was divided into two great parties. In the south were gathered the Croziermen, or churchmen, supported by the King of Denmark, while further north lay the followers of old Sverrir, who had been nicknamed "Birchlegs" from the gaiters of birch-bark which they always wore. In those days men needed a king to keep order, and after the death of Hacon, son of Sverrir, the great council, called the Thing, met to consult about the matter. The first king they chose died in a few months, and then Ingi, his kinsman, was put in his place. But when the child of Hacon and Inga proved to be a boy the Birchlegs declared that he and none other should rule over them. Now the Croziermen were spread all over the south and east of Norway, and, as Smaalen was right in the middle of them, a few Birchlegs went secretly to Inga, the child's mother, and told her that for a time the baby must be hidden away so that no man should know where he was; for they feared King Ingi.

So Thrond the priest took the boy and gave him the name of his father, and his wife cared for him as her own, and no one knew he was a king's son, save only herself and her two boys. And Inga his mother abode close by.

In this manner a year passed over, and when Christmas was coming for the second time whispers reached the ear of Thrond the priest, and he made a plan with Erlend, kinsman of Sverrir, that Hacon should leave the country of the Croziermen and go north. Then they two took the child and Inga his mother and journeyed by night through strange places till on Christmas Eve they reached a place called Hammar, where they met some Birchlegs, who told them that news of their flight had spread abroad, and that Croziermen were spread over the mountains. Worse than all, Ivar the bishop was at Hammar, and he, as everyone knew, was a sworn enemy to the race of Sverrir. Thrond and Erlend looked at each other as the Birchlegs spoke. It was what they had dreaded, and little surprised they felt when next day arrived a messenger from Ivar the bishop claiming kinship with the boy—which

ANDREW LANG AND LEONORA BLANCHE LANG

was true—and inviting Inga and her son to spend the feast of Yule, for so Christmas was called, with him. But, by counsel of the Birchlegs, an answer was sent saying that the child and his mother needed rest after journeying, and would stay where they were till Yule was past, and after that they would come to the bishop's house. When Ivar's messenger had ridden out of sight, the Birchlegs rose up swiftly and hid Hacon and his mother in a farm among the hills, while they bade all the Birchlegs that were scattered for many miles round to hold themselves ready. On Christmas night Inga wrapped the baby warmly up in furs, and, giving him to Erlend to carry, they set out from the farm, and took a path that led eastwards through mountains and forests, and on each side of Hacon walked Thorstein the fighter and Skerwald the Shrimp, swiftest of all men on snow shoes, so that, should the Croziermen try to capture him, he might be borne away out of their reach.

For many nights and days they tramped forwards, lying in caves or scooping themselves huts in the snow. Not a house was to be seen anywhere; and, though Inga had a brave heart, she sometimes wondered if the guides knew the way any better than she did. At length they came to a barn, and here they kindled some wood by means of a fire-stick, but that only melted the snow on the broken roof till it was more uncomfortable inside than out. Their food had all been eaten that morning, and they had nothing to give little Hacon except the water of the snow. But he did not seem to mind, and only laughed when the drops fell on his nose. He was ever the merriest baby. A day after leaving the barn they struggled through snow so hard that it had to be broken with the spears of the Birchlegs, and before them lay a farm, where they received a hearty welcome, and were given good food to eat and soft beds to lie on. Then the farmer set them on horses and gave them guides, and they turned northwards towards Drontheim. On the journey many Birchlegs joined them, and some of them brought news that the Croziermen had started in pursuit, but the snowdrifts through which Inga and Hacon had won their way proved too deep for *them*, and they went back to Erling Stone-wall, whom they had chosen king.

Now INGI, KINSMAN OF LITTLE Hacon, lay at Drontheim with a large army, when one day a man entered his hall and told him that his brother, who had been hunting bears in the mountains, had seen from afar a body of men marching towards the city, and the people of the hill country whispered that a king's son was with them. "What king's son?"

the young man had asked, but that no one could tell him. There were also tales of another force from further east; but all was uncertain, so Ingi the king waited for the return of his messengers, and spread tents for himself and his bodyguard, till the men came back.

"Well, what tidings?" said Ingi, as they entered his tent.

"Here are two guides who have travelled far," answered the messengers pointing to the Birchlegs, "they will tell you their story;" and so they did from the beginning, and that the child in their company was Hacon, grandson of Sverrir the king. Then Ingi gave thanks that the boy had come safe through such perils of winter and wild beasts, and bade the men sit down to eat and drink, and said that he himself would tarry where he was till Hacon his kinsman was brought to him. And when the boy hove in sight Ingi strode out to meet him, and took him in his arms and kissed him, bidding him and his mother welcome, and he was good to them both all the days of his life. Perhaps, when he grew older, Hacon may have heard the tale of another little boy across the seas named Arthur, like himself the heir to a kingdom, who, only a year before the birth of Hacon, had been done to death by John, his uncle, who coveted his crown. But no such thought ever entered the mind of Ingi.

It was strange for Hacon to wake up to find himself lying on soft cushions, and broad beams over his head instead of the stars, or the brilliant, rushing, Northern Lights. Sometimes he would raise himself on his elbow and listen with bent head, dreaming that he heard the soft pad of a wolf's foot, or that if he looked he would see a pair of bright eyes staring at him from behind a bush, as he had often done in the mountain forests. Then he remembered that wolves did not come into palaces, and, curling himself up comfortably, went to sleep again. All that winter and the next he stayed in Drontheim, and every day the Birchlegs visited him and told him stories of his father and grandfather, which the boy liked to hear, but sometimes found beyond his understanding. But in the second spring after his coming, earl Hacon, brother of Ingi, took him to his castle at Bergen, and he loved him greatly, and would say to his men that little Hacon was in truth king of Norway. That summer, while earl Hacon was away, the Croziermen under their new king Philip besieged Bergen, and the boy fell into their hands, and some thought of making him king instead of Philip. Most likely Philip knew of this, and it would have been quite easy for him to kill Hacon, as King John across the seas would have done. Yet the Norsemen, though fierce in battle, were not apt to slay children, so he treated Hacon kindly, and in three days yielded him up to Thorir the archbishop. With him Hacon lived till his kinsman the earl came back from fighting; then he went again to his house, and remained with him always either on land or sea.

Of the two, Hacon loved best being on the sea, and when he was four the earl built a splendid ship, larger than any which had sailed in those waters. Its prow was high out of the water and carved with a raven's head, and inside there were thirty-one benches for the rowers to sit on, who wielded the great long oars. Of course it was very important to find a good name for such a splendid vessel, and Hacon and the earl consulted daily about it, but at length they agreed that none was so fitting as Olaf's Clinker. So "Olaf's Clinker" it was called, and in the autumn the two Hacons sailed in it to the Seljar Isles, and lay there all through the great frost. Food they had in plenty, but it was very hard to use it; their drink was a solid lump of ice, and their butter was frozen so tight that many a knife broke its blade in two before it could cut off a morsel for little Hacon to eat, for the men gave him of the best always. One day the earl bade the cook bake the child a soft, thick cake of flour, and it was brought to him where he stood listening to the tales of the king's guard. They also were eating their food, and he watched them biting morsels of the hard bread and after of the frozen butter.

"Give me some butter," he said with a laugh, and the soldier chopped off a piece and handed it to him. "Now let us fettle the butter, Birchlegs," laughed he, and took the butter and folded it up in the hot cake so that the butter melted.

"So little and so wise," they murmured to each other, and Hacon's saying was told throughout the army, and became a proverb in the land. All men loved him, for he always had merry words on his tongue and took nothing amiss. But for his years he was small, and often the Birchlegs would take him by his head and heels and pull him out, "to make him grow taller," they said, but he never grew above middle stature.

When Hacon was seven years old the earl told him it was time he learned something out of books, as his father had done. Hacon was willing, and spent some time every day with the priest who was to teach him. For many months the boy worked at his lessons, or at least so the earl thought, as he no longer trotted at his heels like the big blue boarhound. One evening, when the earl had come in weary from a day's hunting, and had stretched himself in front of the huge hall fire, waiting for the skald or poet to come and sing to him the mighty deeds of his fathers the Vikings, Hacon ran in.

"Come hither, boy," said the earl, "and tell me what you are learning."

"Chanting, lord earl," answered Hacon.

"That was not the sort of learning I wished you to know," replied the earl, "and you shall not learn it any more, but how to read and write, for it is not a priest, nor even a bishop, that I mean you to be."

It seems strange that though both Ingi the king and Hacon the earl loved the boy truly, and that, as has been told, the earl often said in the hearing of all men that if everyone had his rights the grandson of Sverrir, and not Ingi, would rule over them, yet in this very year Hacon the earl and Ingi the king agreed together that whichever of them lived longest should reign over the whole of Norway, and that Hacon the child should be set aside. A Thing was called, where the archbishops, and bishops, and other men were present, and they declared that compact to be good. For, said they, did not Solomon speak truly when he wrote, "Woe to the land whose king is a child," and how should Hacon, Sverrir's grandson deliver us from the hands of the Croziermen and the Danes and keep order in the land?"

Now it happened that on the very day on which this matter was determined by the Thing, little Hacon had been sent by request of his mother to visit Astrida, his kinswoman, and an old Birchleg went with him. Though it was evening when he returned, the sun was quite high in the heavens, it being summer, and Hacon sought at once his old friend Helgi the keen, saying that there was yet time to play one of the games they both loved. But at the sight of him Helgi's face grew dark, and he roughly bade him begone.

"What have I done to anger thee, my Helgi?" asked Hacon wonderingly; but Helgi would have none of him. "I know of nought that can have vexed thee," repeated Hacon; and Helgi answered:

"Why do I bid thee begone? Because to-day thy kingdom was taken from thee and given to another man."

"Who did this deed, and where?" said Hacon.

"It was done at the Thing," returned Helgi, "and those who did it were thy kinsmen, Ingi and Hacon."

"Ingi and Hacon," repeated the boy and was silent for a moment. Then his face brightened and he added, "Well, be not wroth with *me*, Helgi. None can tell if the deed will stand, for no spokesmen were there to plead my cause."

"And who are your spokesmen?" inquired Helgi.

"God and Saint Olaf," answered Hacon, "and to them I leave it."

"Good luck be with thee, king's son," said Helgi, taking him up and kissing him.

So Hacon the child lived on in the house of the earl his kinsman, who loved him greatly, and spurned in anger the evil counsel of one Hidi, who offered secretly to do him to death.

"God forbid," cried the earl, "that I should in this manner buy the kingdom for my son," and he bade Hidi begone from his presence and keep his treachery to himself. And the better to preserve the boy from harm he had him always in his company, even when he fell sick of the illness that was to end in his death. Hacon, who by now was ten years old, mourned him sorely; but in the spring Ingi the king came south to Bergen, and carried the boy northwards to Drontheim, where he sent him to school with his son Guttorm, two years younger than himself. The boys were good friends, and treated alike in all things. Guttorm, being most easily moved to wrath, and often finding himself in trouble, came to Hacon to make him a way-out, which Hacon did, many times with a jest or a laugh, for he was gentle and slow to anger, and all men loved him.

In this year Ingi the king fell sick also, and Skuli, his brother, urged upon him to place the crown on the head of his son Guttorm. Some men agreed with Skuli, and the Birchlegs feared for Hacon, and desired to bear him away with them and gather an army and fight and see who should be king; but Hacon would not listen to the old Birchlegs, and said it was "unwise to set those at one another who ought to fight under the same shield, and that he would wait, and for the present let things be." After all Ingi the king got well, and for two more winters he ruled as before. But when Hacon was thirteen and Guttorm eleven a sore weakness fell upon Ingi, and he knew that he would go out no more to battle. Grievous was it for a man who had spent his life in faring to and fro to be tied down to his bed; but he uttered no words of wailing, and lay listening to the merry jests of Hacon and his steward Nicholas till he laughed himself, and his illness felt lighter. Skuli, the king's brother, likewise watched by him, and his friends were gathered there also, and they pressed Ingi sore to give the kingdom into Skuli the earl's hands. And Ingi had no strength to say them nay, and he let them have their will, and soon he died, leaving the rule to Skuli. But the men of Norway did not all agree as to this matter. Some wished that Guttorm, Ingi's son, should be king, others declared that Hacon had the best right; while the rest said that the throne of Norway was no place for a boy, and they would have a man such as Skuli to reign over them. For Skuli, though filled with ambition and a man whose word and promises were swiftly broken, was tall and handsome, generous with his gold, and pleasant of speech. Therefore he had a large following and a powerful one; but to Hacon he was ever a bad friend, seeking his throne, and met his death hereafter in strife against him.

It happened that Guttorm the archbishop was away in the far north, and Skuli would fain have waited till his return, for many canons and learned clerks desired him for their lord, and the earl hoped that the archbishop might gain over others also. So he went to work secretly, seeking by sundry devices to put off the choice of a king, and so cunning he was that he seemed to have succeeded. But one day when he was asking counsel of a friend the blast of trumpets was heard.

"What means that?" cried the earl, starting up from his seat, and, striding out of his chamber, he went quickly down the narrow stairs and entered the great hall, which was crowded with men.

"Lord earl," said one of the bodyguard, an old man with scars about his face, "Lord earl, we have waited long enough for the archbishop, and we are minded to wait no longer. A meeting shall be held this morning in this very place, and Hacon, Sverrir's grandson, shall sit by your side on the high seat, and king shall he be called till the great Thing be got together. If you say nay to this, then will the rowers make ready the ships, and Hacon shall sail with us southwards to the land of Bergen, and there another Thing shall be summoned, and we and the bodyguard that dwells there will declare him king. Now choose."

Then Skuli saw that there were many against him, and he let a high seat be built close to the church of St. Nicholas, and Onund, standard-bearer of the Birchlegs, stood up and said that the Croziermen were gathered in the bay which lies south of Christiania and were ruled by a king. But when tidings reached them that the men of Norway were but a headless host the Croziermen would agree with the bishops and strife would be in the land. A great shout arose when Onund had finished speaking, and twelve men of the king's guard were sent to fetch Hacon, who was at the school over against Christ Church. The boy was sitting on a bench, his eyes bent on a priest who was reading out from a Latin roll the tale of the burning of Dido, and when he had done it was his custom to make each boy in turn tell him what he had heard. Suddenly, with a clatter, the door flew open and the twelve messengers entered.

"God greet you, king's son," spake the oldest of them. "The Birchlegs and the yeomen who meet in the courtyard of the palace have sent us to fetch you."

Hacon looked first at the priest and then at the Birchleg, and held out his hand, and went with them down to the church of St. Nicholas. Then Skuli the earl said that many were present who did not hold that the boy was Sverrir's grandson, and that until he had proved his right to sit on the high seat he must be content with a low one.

"Ingi and Hacon the earl knew well he was the king's son," cried a voice from out the crowd; but Skuli pretended not to hear, and declared that by the counsel of his friends, Inga, Hacon's mother, must be tried by the ordeal of hot iron.

In those days it was a common thing that anyone accused of a great crime should prove his innocence in three ways, and he might choose which of them pleased him best. Either he might walk over red-hot ploughshares, or hold in his hand a piece of red-hot iron, and if his hands or feet were marked with no scar he was held to be accused falsely. Or he could, if so he willed, be tried by the ordeal of water and, having his hands and feet bound, be cast into a river. If, after being in the water a certain time or floating a certain distance, he remained alive and unhurt, he also was let go free. In Norway the ordeal of iron alone was used, and gladly did the king's mother offer to submit to it. Straight from the meeting she went to the church of St. Peter, and fasted three days and three nights and spoke to no one. On the third day she came forth, her face shining, but the iron bar, which should have been lying in a chest in the church, was nowhere to be found. For in truth the canons and priests, who were Skuli's men, had misdoubted their cause, and had hidden it away, lest the ordeal should prove their own undoing. But the captain of the Birchlegs understood well what had befallen, and sent messengers over the land to summon a Thing, to be held in a month's time. And daily they set Hacon in the high seat beside the earl, and Skuli dared not gainsay them.

So the Thing was held in the meadow, and trumpets were blown, but the canons forbade the holy shrine to be brought out from the church of St. Olaf, as was the custom at the choosing of a king. In this they acted unwisely, for the hearts of many of their own men grew hot at this base device, and turned against them, and Hacon was proclaimed king, and oaths were sworn to him. After that Hacon the king and Skuli the earl sailed together to Bergen, in a ship of twenty benches. At the mouth of the fiord a messenger brought him word that the canons and priests of Bergen, moved by their fellows at Drontheim, did not mean to pay him kingly honours. To this Hacon made answer that, as their king, he expected the homage they had paid his fathers, or they would have to bear the penalty, and his words bore fruit, for he rowed up the fiord with all the church bells ringing and the people shouting. Then a Thing was held, and he was chosen king by the people of Bergen also. But, better than ruling over assemblies, Hacon loved to watch the strange games of boys and men. King though he was, many troubled years were in store for Hacon. Skuli was not minded to sit down quietly as Hacon's liegeman, and at once began to lay plots with the Croziermen and with John Earl of Orkney. He had taken for himself all the money which Sverrir, Hacon his son, and Ingi had stored up, and all the gold that Hacon possessed was a brooch and a ring. Thus it became plain even to the Birchlegs that Hacon could not fight both the earl and the Croziermen, and so it was agreed that Skuli should be lord over a third part of Norway and that peace should be made.

Hardly was this done when there arose in the east a band of poor men, under the lead of Benedict the priest, whom folk called Benny. From their torn garments they were known as the Ragged Regiment, and at first they did nothing but steal from farmyards and rob houses. But afterwards, when rich and strong men who would not obey the laws joined them, they grew bolder and attacked Tunsberg, the chief city near the Bay, and though they were driven back and many were killed, yet for long they harried the lands of Hacon, and with another band of rebels, called the Ribbalds, laid waste the country. Till they were conquered, which took Hacon ten years, little rest had he, and always Skuli was there to trouble him.

It was when Hacon was fourteen years old that the archbishop and earl Skuli sent messengers to Bergen to ask that Inga, his mother, might once more go through the ordeal of iron to satisfy all men of his right to the throne. In answer Hacon summoned the bishops and archbishops and Skuli, together with some of his liegemen, to assemble in the vestry of the church, and spoke to them in this wise:

"It would seem hard to many a king to undergo the ordeal when his rule was established. Before, when my mother offered herself to suffer it, I had not been chosen king, and you all know how it happened that when she came forth the iron was hidden. You know, too, that when we first entered Norway she declared herself ready to undergo the ordeal, but Ingi the king and Hacon the earl answered that none misdoubted, neither was there any need for it. Yet now I will do as you will for three causes. First, that no man may say I have claimed what is not mine by right; second, that I would that my subjects should learn that in all things I strive to content them; and third, that the Judge into whose hands I put myself will fail none whose cause is true. And therefore I go gladly to this judgment.

Then Inga went into the church to fast for three days and three nights, and some men fasted with her, and, twelve watched on the outside as before. But on the Wednesday before the trial was to take place Sigar, one of Skuli's men, skilled in learning, came secretly to good man Dagfinn, Hacon's liegeman, and said thus: "I know your heart is vexed and sore because of this ordeal, but I can promise to make all things right so that the king's mother shall not suffer."

"How mean you?" asked Dagfinn who was not minded to talk with the man, not liking his face.

"It is in this wise," answered Sigar with a cunning look; "I have only to rub this herb over the hand of Inga and the iron will not harm her, however hot it be."

"I thank you," said Dagfinn; "but tell me what name has this herb, and where I may find it."

"It grows on every house in Bergen," replied Sigar, who knew well full that there was no virtue in the herb at all, but thought that Dagfinn was with him in the matter, and that together they might proclaim that Inga had sought the aid of leechcraft, and so discredit her in the eyes of all men. But Dagfinn made as though he would spring on him, and bade him begone while he kept his hands off him. After that Dagfinn told the tale to Inga, and warned her lest she should fall into any snares.

Next morning Hacon the king, and Skuli, and the archbishop, and John Earl of Orkney, and many other notable men, went into the church where the priest said the office. Then the piece of holy iron was taken from the great chest and heated in a brazier under the eyes of all, and when it glowed white, so that none could look on it, the priest drew it forth with long pincers and placed it in Inga's hand. As she took it, Hacon shivered, as if the pain had been his. He alone turned his head away; but the rest never lifted their gaze from the face of Inga, which was calm and peaceful as ever.

"It is enough," said the priest at last, and Hacon sprang forward as if to go to his mother, when the priest stopped him. "All is not yet finished; back to your place," and, standing in front of Inga so that no man could behold her hand, he wound a white cloth many times round it. "Now you may come," said the priest, and Hacon went with his mother to her house.

For many days they waited, and then the priest sent word to Hacon the king, and Skuli the earl, and the archbishop and the bishops and the nobles, that the following evening they should meet in Christ Church, and he would unbind the hand of Inga. Not one of them was missing, and in the presence and sight of all the priest unwound the linen and stretched out the hand of Inga, and behold! the skin of that hand was whiter and fairer to see than the skin of the other. And the archbishop proclaimed a Thing to be held the next Sunday in the space in front of the church, and there he gave out how that the king's mother had won through the ordeal, and that any who from that day misdoubted Hacon's right to the crown should be laid under the ban of the Church. Also, he said that Hacon the king and Skuli the earl had made a new compact of friendship.

But compacts did not count for much with Skuli, not even when, a year later, Hacon, then fifteen, was betrothed to his daughter Margaret. In this matter the king followed the counsel of his friends, though he himself knew Skuli too well to expect that the earl would suffer a marriage or anything else to bind him. "It will all come to the same thing, I fear," he said to his mother, as he set out at Michaelmas for the ceremony at Drontheim. For some reason we do not know the marriage was delayed for six years, and it was not until 1225, when Hacon was twenty-one, that it actually took place. Then, after Easter, Hacon took ship at Tunsberg on the Bay, and sailed for five days till he reached Bergen. As soon as he arrived the preparations for the wedding began, and on Trinity Sunday, when the sun remains in the sky all night long in the far north, Hacon and Margaret were married in Christ Church. Afterwards great feasts were held for nearly a week in the palace. Hacon sat at the high table at the head of the men in the Yule Hall, and Margaret gathered round her the women in the Summer Hall, and the monks and abbots held a banquet in another place.

All the days that Hacon lived Margaret was a good wife to him, and wept sore for the trouble that Skuli, her father, brought on the land. For Hacon the king had been right in his prophecy, and for fifteen years Skuli never ceased from scheming against him, and murdering those that stood in his way, till even his own men grew ashamed and tired of him. Nothing was there which he held sacred, and this brought him more dishonour than all his other crimes. Once Hacon sent Ivar and Gunnar to him with letters. Warm was their welcome from Skuli, and splendid were the presents which he gave them when they left. But secretly he bade men ride after them and slay them where they could find them. Fast rode Skuli's men, but Ivar and Gunnar rode faster, for Hacon had need of them. At length they rested for the night in a farm belonging to the king, and Skuli's men, with Gaut Wolfskin and Sigurd Saltseed at their head, came unawares to the house also. As they entered they beheld Gunnar leaning against the lattice of the window, and they threw open the door and slew him where he stood, but not before many of their band lay dead upon the ground. When Ivar saw that his help could be of no avail he sprung into the loft close by, and, squeezing himself through a narrow opening, leaped to the ground and sought to take refuge in the church, but it was locked. Then he seized a ladder which was standing by and ran up it to the roof, throwing the ladder down when he reached the top. In the dark no man troubled him; but it was November, and the wind was keen, and no clothes had he upon him save a shirt and his breeches. When the sun rose he found that Skuli's men were gathered below, watching that he should not escape; but, indeed, his hands were so frozen with cold that he could have taken hold of nothing. He prayed them to grant him his life; but they laughed him to scorn, and Sigurd Saltseed seized the ladder and set it up against the church, and climbed upon it, and thrust Ivar through with a spear so that he fell dead to the ground.

Now these things displeased the people of Norway, and one by one his liegemen departed from Skuli and took service with Hacon, till at length so few followers had the earl that he was forced to fly. The Birchlegs sought him everywhere, and one day news was brought to them that he was lying hidden in a monastery, and some of his men also. So the Birchlegs came up to the monastery to attack it, but the archbishop went forth to meet them and begged that Skuli might be let pass in peace to see the king. Some listened to the archbishop, but others, whose hearts were harder, crept away and set fire to the monastery, and the fire spread. Then Skuli saw that the time for fighting was past, and, lifting up his shield, he stood in the doorway crying, "Strike me not in the face, for not so is it done to princes"; therefore they thrust him through in the body, and he died.

But all this happened fifteen years after the marriage of Hacon, and it is no longer the concern of this tale, which treats only of his youth. At sixty years old he died, having worn the crown of Norway forty-seven years. In spite of his enemies at home, he did many things for his people, and ruled them well. The poor were mercifully dealt with, and his soldiers were forbidden to steal from either friends or foes. Churches and hospitals and great halls he built in plenty, rivers he widened and numbers of ships he had, swift sailing and water-tight, for he was overlord of lands far away over the sea. Iceland and Greenland paid their dues to him. The Isle of Man, which owned a king, did him homage, and so did the south isles of Scotland—the "Sudar" Isles as they were called, Jura, and Islay, and Bute, and the rest—and their bishop was known as the Bishop of Sodor and Man, as he is to this day. Besides this, the friendship of Hacon was sought by many foreign princes: by the Emperor Frederick the Second, "the Wonder of the World"; by the Grand Prince of Russia; by the Pope Innocent IV, who sent a legate to crown him king. Hacon also sent his daughter to Spain with a great dowry, to marry whichever of the king's four sons pleased her best. Still, in spite of his fame, his voyages were few, and it seems strange that he should have been seized with mortal illness at the bishop's house in Kirk wall. At first they read him Latin books, but his head grew tired, and he bade them take the scrolls away and tell him instead the tales of the Norse kings his forefathers. And so he died, and when the ice was melted and the sea set free, his body was carried to Bergen and buried in Christ Church, where he had been married and where he had been crowned.

THIS IS THE TALE OF Hacon the King.

V

MI REINA! MI REINA!

When Marie Louise d'Orléans, daughter of Madame, and niece of Louis XIV, was born, on March 27, 1662, both her grandmothers as well as her mother were terribly disappointed that she was not a boy. "Throw her into the river," exclaimed Madame, in fun, of course; but the queen-mother of England, the widow of Charles I, whose sorrows had crushed all jokes out of her, answered gravely that after all, perhaps, things were not quite so bad as they seemed, for by-and-by she might marry her cousin the dauphin who was only a few months older.

Quite unconscious of her cold welcome, the baby grew and thrived, and was so pretty and had such charming little ways, that they soon forgave her for being only a girl, especially as when she was two years old she had a little brother. The Duc de Valois, as he was called, was a beautiful child, strong and healthy, whereas the dauphin was always ill, and Louis XIV had no other sons to inherit his crown. So great rejoicings were held at the Duc de Valois' birth in the château of Fontainebleau; bonfires were lighted and banquets were given, and, more than that, an allowance of money was settled on him by the king. His other uncle, Charles II, was his godfather, and the baby was given his name, with that of his father Philippe. The children lived mostly at St. Cloud, where there were splendid gardens to run about in and merry little streams to play with. When their mother drove to Paris or St. Germain to attend great balls or fêtes at Court, Madame de St. Chaumont took care of them, and saw that they did not fall into any mischief. For some time they never had an ache or a pain, but when the Duc de Valois was about two years old he was very ill, from the difficulty of cutting his teeth. Madame de St. Chaumont stayed with him and nursed him night and day till his mother could reach him; however, he soon improved, and Madame was able to go back to St. Germain, knowing that his governess would take as much care of him as she could herself. After he grew better, the great coach and six horses were got ready, and he was driven to the Palais Royal in Paris, and placed in the charge of the fashionable doctor of the day, Maître Gui Patin. But unhappily, in spite of all their precautions, the boy managed to catch cold; convulsions followed, and Monsieur insisted on preparations being made for the christening, instead of only having, as was usual, a hasty ceremony, while the public rite was commonly put off till the royal child had passed its twelfth birthday. It was on December 7, 1667, that little Philippe Charles was baptized, and the following day he had a fresh attack, and died of exhaustion, to the despair of his mother, who adored him. All the honours customary to be paid to one so near the throne were bestowed on the dead child. For three days he lay in state, and the princes of the blood, headed by the king himself, passed before him and sprinkled water on his bier. Then the people were let in, and many a woman's eyes grew wet at the sight of that beautiful baby. Three days later he was put to rest in the royal burying-place at St. Denis, near Paris.

The next few years passed peacefully away. Marie Louise was a clever little girl, and not only was fond of books, like her mother, but had sharp eyes, and noticed everything that went on round her. On wet days she danced in the rooms of St. Cloud or the Palais Royal, as Madame had danced twenty years ago at the Louvre; and when she was seven there was a small sister, Anne Marie, for her to play with and to nurse. "She can move her fingers and toes, and squeaks without being squeezed. She is more amusing than any doll," said Marie Louise.

But the quiet of the child's life was soon to be disturbed, and Mademoiselle was to learn her first sorrow. One morning, at the end of 1669, a messenger in the royal livery arrived from the king, bearing a letter for Madame, who burst into sobs while reading it. Dismissing the messenger with a wave of her hand—for she was unable to speak—she sank back on the sofa, and for some minutes wept bitterly. Then, gathering up her strength, she passed into the adjoining room, where Madame de St. Chaumont was sitting over her embroidery.

"Read this, my friend," said Madame, and walked to the window. The letter, which Madame de St. Chaumont read silently to the end, was from the king. It was very short, and merely informed Madame that his Majesty had reason to think that her children's governess had been concerned in an intrigue whereby the bishop of Valence had incurred his displeasure, and he begged, therefore, that she might be at once dismissed from her post. Grieved though she was at parting from a woman who for nearly eight years had shared both her cares and her troubles, Madame had no choice but to obey, and Madame de St. Chaumont knew it. So they parted, and during the winter and spring that followed Madame missed her friend daily more and more. Then, with the bright June weather, came Madame's sudden seizure and death, and Monsieur, poor foolish, womanish man, was left with two little girls to look after.

How could he do it? Well, he began very characteristically by dressing up Mademoiselle, now eight years old, in a violet velvet mantle which trailed on the ground, and announcing that she would receive visits of condolence. Of course members of the Court and the great officials flocked in crowds, and when they had paid their respects to Mademoiselle, they were, much to their surprise, shown into the nursery where little Anne Marie, Mademoiselle de Valois, at this time hardly past her first birthday, was awaiting them. The baby was too young to be hurt by her father's follies, and as long as she had good nurses to look after her could safely be left to their care; but with Marie Louise it was different, and, luckily for her, the kind queen, Marie Thérèse, had pity on her, and took her to Court to be brought up with the dauphin. Together they danced and played, and no doubt quarrelled, but in all their games, the lively, sharp-witted little girl took the lead of the slow and rather dull boy. In a year's time Monsieur married again, and his choice fell on his dead wife's cousin, Charlotte Elizabeth, daughter of the Elector Palatine, only ten years older than Marie Louise herself. The new Madame, ugly, awkward, ill-dressed, plain-spoken, but kind-hearted and full of sense, was a great contrast to her predecessor, Henriette, but she was very good to the two little girls, and never made any difference between them and her own children. We may be sure that Marie Louise, who was gentle and sweet-tempered, as well as pretty and clever, was quick to notice all her good qualities and to be grateful for her stepmother's care and affection, though at first it was a trial to leave the court and her friend the dauphin and go and live in the Palais Royal. But then, how amusing Madame was, and what stories she could tell of "when I was a little girl," which was not so long ago, either!

"I longed to be a boy, and was always playing boys' games; but as I grew bigger I was not allowed so much liberty, and had to make up my mind to be a girl, and do stupid things at home, and dress up, which I hated. I was also obliged to drink tea or chocolate, which I thought very nasty. My only pleasure was hunting, and I was never so happy—I never *am* so happy now—as when I got up at dawn and rode away to hunt with my dogs yapping round me. How all your French ladies are so lazy I can't imagine; I can't bear to stay in bed when I am awake."

No doubt Madame made a very strange figure in the splendid Court of Louis XIV; and she on her part looked down with scorn from the superiority of a stout riding habit and a man's wig on the beautiful, ladies with their elegant dresses and plumed hats! But the king himself was not more particular about forms and ceremonies than she was, and though her manners and free remarks often made him shudder, yet he had a real respect for her good sense, and was grateful to her for making the best of his silly brother.

So the years slipped by, and one day Marie Louise was seventeen, graceful and charming like her mother, with "feet that danced of themselves," as Madame de Sévigné said to her daughter. The dauphin was seventeen too, and in those days young men, especially princes, married early. Would the prophecy uttered over her cradle by her grandmother, Henrietta Maria, come true, and the beautiful, quick-witted girl be queen of France? The Parisians would have liked nothing better, and even the princes of the blood would have been content; she had been like a daughter to the queen, and was sure of a welcome from her; but the king—why did the king stand aloof and say nothing? Marie Louise guessed what was being whispered, and waited and wondered too, till she grew pale and thin, and Madame watched her and said angrily to Monsieur: "Did I not warn you not to let her go to Court so much, if you did not want to make her miserable? Now she will never be happy anywhere else."

At length the king's silence was explained. Marie Louise would never be queen of France—a German princess must be the wife of the dauphin; but she should be queen of Spain, and her husband was to be Charles II, the brother of Marie Thérèse. True, the King of Spain was ill-educated and ugly, and so stupid that some doubted if he had all his wits. He was very delicate too, and at four years old could scarcely walk or talk, and never stood without leaning on somebody. But he was lord over vast possessions, though, perhaps, he had not much real power out of Spain, and there the country was in such poverty that there was but little money passing from hand to hand. His mother, Marie Anne of Austria, had held the reins of government, but at length, aided by his half-brother, Don John, Charles suddenly banished her to Toledo, and announced that he meant to be king in fact as well as in name. His first step was to break off negotiations with the emperor, whose daughter the queen-mother had chosen for his wife. This was done under the influence of Don John, and it was he who first suggested that King Charles might look for a bride in France. The king was slow to take in new ideas, and as backward in parting with them. Don John let him alone, and did not hurry him, but he threw in his way a portrait of the princess, and contrived that he should overhear the conversation of some Spanish gentlemen who had lately returned from Paris, and were loud in praises of the lovely and fascinating Mademoiselle. Charles looked at the miniature oftener and oftener; soon he refused to part with it at all, and by-and-by began even to talk to it. Then he told Don John he would never marry any woman but this.

Soon an envoy was sent to the King of France to ask the hand of his niece, which, after the usual official delays, lasting fully nine months, was joyfully granted to him. Tales of Charles II, who was, after all, Marie Thérèse's brother, had not failed to cross the Pyrenees, and Mademoiselle's heart sank as she thought of what awaited her. Once she summoned up all her courage and threw herself at the king's feet, imploring him to let her stay in France, even though she were to remain unmarried.

"I am making you queen of Spain," he answered; "what more could I have done for my daughter?"

"Ah, Sire! you could have done more for your niece," she said, turning away, for she saw it was hopeless.

ALTHOUGH THE FORMAL CONSENT OF Louis XIV was not given till July 1679, King Charles had nominated the persons who were to form the household of the young queen ever since January. He had Don John continually with him, asking his advice about this and that, though he never even took the trouble to tell his mother of his marriage, and left her to learn it from common rumour. At length all was ready; the king was informed of the day that the princess would reach the frontier, and Don John was about to start for the Pyrenees, when he was seized by a severe attack of fever, and in ten days was dead. According to etiquette he lay in state for the people to visit, in the splendid dress which had been made for him to wear when he met the new queen.

It was on a little island in the middle of the river Bidassoa that Marie Louise said good-bye to France. She had thought she could not feel more pain when she had bidden farewell to the friends of her childhood—to the king and queen, to her father and stepmother, to her young sister, now ten years old, whose daughter would one day be queen of Spain too; worse than all, to the dauphin himself. Yet as long as she remained on French soil she was not wholly parted from them, and now and then a wild hope rushed through her heart that something, she did not know what, would happen, and that she might see one or other of them again. But as she entered the pavilion on the island where her Spanish attendants awaited her she knew that the links that bound her to the old life were broken, and she must make the best of that which lay before. It was a very strange Spain over which she was to reign, and she may often have dreamed that she was living in a fairy tale, and that some day her ugly king would throw off his enchanted mask and become the handsomest and most charming of princes. Spain itself really began in the old French town of Bayonne, where ladies paid visits with fat little sucking pigs under their arms, instead of being followed by long-eared spaniels, as in France. The pigs had ribbons round their necks to match their mistresses' dresses, and at balls were placed, after their entrance, in a room by themselves, while their owners danced with a grace no other nation could equal the *branle*, the *canaris*, or the *sarabande*. At certain times the gentlemen threw their canes into the air, and caught them cleverly as they came down, and they leapt high, and cut capers, all to the sound of a fife and a tambourine—a wooden instrument like a ship's trumpet, which was struck by a stick. As to the clothes in which the young queen was dressed by her *Camarera Mayor*, or chief lady of the bedchamber, on her arrival at Vittoria, Marie Louise did not know whether to laugh or to cry when she caught sight of herself in a mirror. Her hair was parted on one side, and hung down in five plaits, each tied with a bow of ribbon and a string of jewels. In winter, twelve petticoats were always worn, and though the upper one was of lace or fine embroidered muslin, one at any rate of the other eleven was of thick velvet or satin, worked in gold, while, to support the weight, which was tremendous, a huge stiff hoop was fastened on underneath them all. The dress itself was made very long, so as to conceal the feet, shod in flat, black morocco slippers. The bodice, high in front and low behind, which gave a very odd effect, was made of rich cloth of gold, and glittered with diamonds. "But I can never move in these clothes," said the queen, turning to the Duchess of Terranova, who knew no French and waited till the Princess d'Harcourt interpreted for her.

"In summer her Majesty the Queen of Spain will wear only seven petticoats," replied the duchess, dropping a low curtesy; and Marie Louise gave a little laugh.

Odd as her own dress seemed, that of the old Camarera Mayor and the mistress of the maids of honour was odder still. They were both widows, and wore loose, shapeless black garments, with every scrap of hair hidden away. When they went out of doors large hats concealed their faces, and in this guise they rode on mules after their mistress, who was mounted on a beautiful Andalusian mare; As she travelled to Burgos, near which the king was to meet her, Marie Louise noticed with surprise that all the carriages were drawn by six mules, but they were so big and strong that they could gallop as fast as any horse. The reins were usually of silk or rope, and each pair was harnessed at a great distance from the next, the coachman riding on one of the first two. When she inquired why he did not sit on the box, as in France, and have postillions in front, she was told that since a coachman had overheard some state secrets discussed between Olivares and his master, Philip IV, no one had ever been allowed to come within earshot of his Majesty.

On November 20, at a small village called Quintanapalla, near Burgos, she was met by the king. Her journey had not been a pleasant one, for the Duchess of Terranova appeared to think that her position as Camarera Mayor enabled her to treat the queen as she chose, and she behaved not only with great severity, but with positive rudeness. Besides this, a dispute arose between the Duke of Osuna and the Marquis of Astorga as to who should ride nearest the queen, and, to put an end to it, Marie Louise was obliged to quit her horse and enter a carriage, surrounded, as the custom was, by curtains of shiny green cloth, which were kept drawn. Right glad was she to think that she would soon be free of this tyranny, and be with someone who wanted her—and Charles did want her to the end of her life.

It was at ten o'clock in the morning that the news was brought to her that the king had arrived. Dressed in her Spanish costume, in which she still felt awkward, she hurried to greet him, but before she reached the antechamber he was in the room. The queen tried to kneel in order to kiss his hand; but he saluted her in the Spanish manner by taking hold of her arms, looking admiringly at her, and murmuring "My Queen! my Queen! mi reina! mi reina!" She answered in French, assuring him of her love and obedience; and he replied in Spanish, for neither knew a word of the other's language, which seems the more strange when we remember how long the marriage negotiations had lasted, and that the Queen of France, with whom Marie Louise had passed so much of her life, was herself a Spaniard. Under these circumstances, conversation is apt to come to a standstill; but, luckily, the French ambassador, the Marquis de Villars, was present as well as a number of Spanish grandees, and he was able to interpret—or perhaps to invent—everything that was suitable to the occasion. It was decided that the marriage should take place at once in the queen's antechamber, and as the archbishop of Burgos was ill, the benediction should be given by the Patriarch of the Indies, who was also grand almoner. As the king and queen knelt side by side a white ribbon was knotted round them, and a piece of white gauze fringed with silver was laid on the head of the queen and on the shoulders of the king.

After seeing a bull fight and some races at Burgos, the king and queen entered their carriage, and, with the shiny green cloth curtains drawn back, they began their drive to Madrid. It must have felt terribly long to both of them, as neither could speak to the other; but then Charles was accustomed to be silent, and Marie Louise was *not*. How thankful she must have been when the evening came, and she could exchange a few words with her nurse or her French maids! But she could not chatter as she would have *liked* to do, or the Camarera Mayor would drop the low curtesy which Marie Louise was fast growing to hate, and say, "Her Majesty the Queen of Spain is not aware that it is past nine o'clock, and time she was in bed." Marie Louise was not clever at languages, and had as yet picked up no Spanish; but she knew quite well that whenever her lady-in-waiting began "Her majesty the Queen of Spain," she must stop whatever she was doing at the moment and make ready to do something else. Her maids of honour happily soon became fond of their new mistress, and did all they could to make her like her adopted country, and some of them who knew a little French would try and explain any custom that puzzled her. The rest looked their sympathy when the old duchess had done something specially rude or disagreeable, as when, for instance, she would put her finger into her mouth and attempt to dab down the queen's curly hair into the smooth locks admired by the Spaniards!

It was from the maids of honour that Marie Louise learned to know many things about Spanish life, for she was naturally curious about what went on around her, and had little to distract her thoughts. From them she heard that no great noblemen would ever think of dismissing his servants, but, on the contrary, when any members of his family died he added all their retainers to his own. As to actual wages, the servants were paid very little; why, even the gentlemen who formed part of the household only received fifteen crowns a month, and out of that they were expected to feed themselves, and to dress in black velvet in winter and in silk in summer. But, as her Majesty would soon notice, they lived mostly on vegetables and fruit, which were cheap, and they took their meals at the public eating-houses at the corners of the streets. Her Majesty was surprised to see all the carriages drawn by mules? But in Madrid horses were coming into fashion, which were much better. The late king had been frequently painted on his horse by one Velasquez, and it had a beautiful tail, which nearly swept the ground, and a long mane decorated with ribbons. Then, if the dreaded Camarera Mayor did not happen to be present, they would begin to talk about the fashions.

Yes, Spanish ladies had quantities of splendid jewels, but they were not cut and set like those the queen wore. Many of the devout ones had belts made entirely of relics, and if their husbands were away it was customary for every wife to dress herself during his absence in grey or white. Indeed, as a rule it was only young girls or brides who were permitted by etiquette to put on coloured skirts; the elder ladies were generally in black silk. "Rouge their shoulders? Why, of course! Did they not do so in France?" But at this the queen burst into such fits of laughter that the old duchess came hurrying in and sternly ordered them all to be silent.

The palace of Madrid was not yet ready, so the king and queen had to go to Buen-Retiro, a charming house, with a beautiful park, on the outskirts of the city, just above the river Manzanares. The garden was laid out in terraces, and ornamented with female statues, all of them with rouge on their cheeks and shoulders like the ladies. Marie Louise was surprised to see only two or three guards standing in front of the palace, and exclaimed that in Paris they would have half a regiment.

"Ah! Madame," replied the French ambassador, the Marquis de Villars, "that was a remark made lately by Madame la Comtesse d'Aulnoy to a Spanish gentleman, and she received for answer, 'Are we not all the king's guards?'"

The first days at Buen-Retiro passed pleasantly enough. The young king gave himself a holiday from his state duties, and was pleased with the interest the queen showed in his country. He took all his meals in her company, and they would even help—or hinder—the maids of honour in laying the table for dinner. In the evenings they sometimes went to the theatre, but this was not much amusement for the queen, as the plays were very long and she could not understand them. When the king was not with her—and before long he was forced to spend several hours a day with his ministers—the Duchess of Terranova never left her alone. If she unfastened the lattice in order to see what was happening in the park or gardens, the Camarera Mayor would rise from her seat and drop a low curtesy, and say: "Her Majesty the Queen of Spain never looks out of the window"; or if she tried to teach the tiny little pages or maids of honour, six or seven years old, the games she had played with her own little sister, she was stopped at once by hearing that "Her Majesty the Queen of Spain never condescends to notice children!" If she was eating her supper beyond the hour which custom had fixed for her to go to bed, at the command of the lady in waiting her ladies would begin to undress her at table, and she would find herself lying on her fourteen mattresses before she realised that she had moved from her seat. In fact, the only human beings with whom she had perfect freedom were the dwarfs, who were allowed to do and say what they liked. There were quantities of them at Court, and one of them, called Luisillo, or "little Luis," was a special favourite of the king's. He was a tiny creature, who had been brought from Flanders, and he might have been Oberon, king of the Fairies, he was so handsome and well made and so full of wisdom. He rode a pony which was an exact copy of his master's horse, and was generally to be seen with him in public and in processions.

It seems strange that, considering how greatly Marie Louise feared and disliked her Camarera Mayor, she should have listened to her abuse of the king's mother, and allowed it to influence her conduct. The queen-dowager had quite forgotten her disappointment at her son's choice of a wife, and had given Marie Louise a hearty welcome, even trying to prevail on the king to alter some of the strictest rules, and allow Marie Louise a little more amusement and freedom. She did her best, too, to win her daughter-in-law's confidence, and in spite of the distrust implanted in her by the old duchess, the queen could not help enjoying her company, and the story of her experiences when she herself, a bride younger than Marie Louise, arrived in Spain from Vienna. One of the places at which she stopped was a town famous for its undergarments, and a quantity of beautiful petticoats, stockings, and other things were sent up to the house where she lodged as a wedding present. When they were unpacked, the major-domo indignantly caught up the parcel of stockings and flung them back at the astonished citizens. "Know, then, that the Queen of Spain has no legs!" he cried, meaning that so sacred a personage would never need to touch the ground with her feet; but the archduchess understood the words literally, and shed many secret tears in her room over a letter to her brother the emperor, saying that if she had known they were going to cut off her feet she would never, never have come to this country!

December was now nearly at an end, and the young queen's state entry into Madrid was fixed for January 13. Notwithstanding the poverty that was so severely felt, the city was splendidly decorated, and along the street of the goldsmiths great silver angels were placed, and golden shields, blazing with jewels. After the trumpeters, the city officers, the knights of the military orders, the grandees of Spain, and many more, came the royal procession, headed by the young queen on a grey Andalusian horse, dressed in a habit that glittered with gold, wearing round her neck a huge pearl called La Peregrina, or the pilgrim, and followed by her attendants. Marie Louise loved riding, and was thoroughly happy on her prancing steed, and felt secretly amused when she thought of the discomfort of the two noble old widows who rode behind her in their hideous black clothes, trying, on the one hand, to keep near the queen, and on the other to prevent their mules from going faster than they liked—which was very slowly indeed. The naughty young maids of honour, all splendidly mounted, looked at each other and smiled at the evident terror of the old ladies, for whom they had no love, and as they passed along they talked rapidly to each other on the fingers of one hand, an accomplishment which all Spanish ladies possessed. They belonged to the noblest families in Spain, and were very pretty and covered with magnificent jewels; but the prettiest and most gorgeous of all, the Duke of Alba's daughter, wore an ornament which does not generally form part of the dress of a young lady. This was a pistol, slung by a ribbon from her side, and plainly intended for use. Under the balcony of the Countess of Ognate, where the king and his mother were stationed, the queen drew rein and looked up. The gilded lattice of the balcony opened about a hand's breadth, and the face of the king could be partly seen. He touched with his handkerchief his mouth, his eyes, and his heart, which was the warmest sign of devotion a Spaniard could give, and after he had repeated this several times the queen bowed low over her saddle and continued her way.

Thanks to the queen-mother, and very much to the wrath of the Camarera Mayor, Marie Louise was sometimes permitted to see the

Marquise de Villars, the French ambassadress, and together they would practise the language of the fan, which no one but a native-born Spanish woman can speak properly. Marie Louise would gaze with admiration, too, at the walk of her maids of honour, so different from that of even the great ladies of France. Yes, in spite of the hideous clothes they wore, and the stupid customs which made her life a burden, there was plenty worthy of praise in her new home, and if only she could get rid of that terrible old lady-in-waiting, and have a few of her friends about her, she would soon be perfectly happy. And it was a great thing that she could go out with the king on the hunting expeditions which he loved! No queen of Spain had ever done *that* before, and she owed it to the queen-mother. To be sure it was rather tiresome to have to drive to the meet in one of the coaches with shiny green curtains, and, standing on the step, spring by yourself into the saddle, because it was death to any man to touch the queen; but by-and-by that might be altered, and meantime she must have patience. By-and-by it was altered, and she was allowed to mount at the door. One day a hunt had been arranged, and the queen grew tired of waiting for the king, who was talking to his minister on the balcony, and ordered her horse to be brought for her to mount. The courtyard was full of people, and something must have frightened the animal, for before the queen had seated herself firmly in the saddle it reared and threw her on the ground, her foot still in the stirrup. The horse plunged wildly, and it seemed as if she must be kicked to death or dashed to pieces. What was to be done? Everyone looked on in horror, but no one dared stir. Each movement of the horse might mean death to her, but a finger laid on her body would certainly mean it to them. Yet it was not a sight that a Spanish gentleman could bear calmly, and with one impulse Don Luis de Las Torres and Don Jaime de Soto Major sprang out from the crowd and rushed towards the horse. One seized it by its bridle and checked its rearing, though it nearly knocked him down; the other caught the queen's foot and freed it from the stirrup. Then, the danger to her being over, they turned and fled to the stables, prepared to ride to the frontier before the penalty could be enforced. The queen, strange to say, was unhurt, except for bruises, and had not lost her senses. Unaided she scrambled to her feet, when the young conde de Peñaranda knelt before her, and implored her to obtain the pardon of his friends from the king. His Majesty, who by this time had run down from the balcony, and in great agitation had reached the queen's side, overheard the count's words, and ordered the two gentlemen to be summoned before him that he might give them his own thanks and that of the queen for rescuing a life so dear to him at the peril of their own. But all this was later, and in 1680 the Queen of Spain had to mount as best she could from her coach.

On the evenings on which they did not go to the theatre she and the king played at ombre together; but the Spanish cards were almost as thin as paper, and were painted quite differently from the French, and she had to learn them all over again. On the days that they did not hunt the king used often to take her to visit some of the convents, which were numerous in Spain; but this she disliked more than anything. The nuns were so stiff and so silent, and she grew so weary of putting questions to them, to which they only answered "Yes" or "No." Luckily the king always took two of his dwarfs with him, and *they* chattered without fear of anybody; but, even so, the queen was thankful when she was told that lunch was ready. A roast chicken was always provided for her, and the king felt rather vexed with her for eating so much and not being content with the light cakes and fruit that satisfied him. Poor Marie Louise! as time went on, and the king's health grew weaker and her pleasures fewer, she became fonder and fonder of sweet things— "dulces" as they were called—and was always sucking lozenges of some sort while she played with her dogs, till at length she ended by losing her figure, though she never lost her beauty. However, now she was only just married, and did not know the ten weary years that stretched in front of her before she died, for although the king adored her, he very seldom allowed her to influence his will or to change any of the iron rules of custom. She was, indeed, permitted to have an occasional interview with Madame d'Aulnoy, who was at that time living in Madrid, and has left a most interesting account of all she saw there. On the first visit she paid she found Marie Louise in a room covered with mirrors, seated, in a beautiful dress of pink velvet and silver, close to the window, which was covered by a gilded lattice and blue silk curtains, so that for anything she could see outside there might just as well have been no window at all. The queen jumped up with delight at the sight of her visitor, to whom she could talk freely about all the gossip from Paris, of which she only heard in letters from the kind Madame her stepmother. Of course she knew quite well that the Camarera Mayor hated her to speak French, which *she* could not understand, and would be crosser than ever that evening; but the queen did not care, and when she said good-bye to her visitor implored her to come again very soon and to bring all her letters with her. As it happened, the very next day Madame d'Aulnoy received some particularly interesting ones about the marriage of the queen's cousin, the Prince de Conti, and wrote to ask if the queen would like to see it; but the Duchess of Terranova answered that "Her Majesty the Queen of Spain never received the same visitor at such short intervals," so Madame d'Aulnoy was forced to copy out the description of the wedding ceremonies, and beg humbly that the lady-in-waiting would give it to her mistress.

As time wore on the duchess became more and more tyrannical, and the queen more and more impatient. From her childhood she had always loved pets of all kinds, and had brought two talking parrots and several silky-eared spaniels with her to Spain. Her favourite dog always slept in her room, on a cushion of blue silk, close to the queen's bed; but one night, instead of sleeping soundly, as it generally did, it got up and moved restlessly about. The queen heard it, and fearing it might wake the king, she crept out of bed to bring it back to its place. Now, in those times, when there were no matches, it was very difficult to get a light, and unfortunately it was the custom that the Queen of Spain should sleep in total darkness, except for the fire, which had gone out. In groping about the huge room after her spaniel the queen upset a chair, which woke the king, who likewise got up to see if anything was the matter. At the first step he took he fell over his wife, and struck his foot against a table, which made him very cross, as she perceived by the tone of his voice when he asked her what she was doing.

"I was looking for my dog," she said; "it was so restless I was afraid it would wake you."

"What!" he cried angrily, "are the king and queen of Spain to leave their beds because of a miserable little dog!" And as at this moment the wandering spaniel lurched up against his leg, he gave it a kick which made it howl violently. Marie Louise stooped down and patted it, and consoled it, and laid it on its cushion again, while she returned to bed. Meantime the king, afraid to move lest he should hurt himself more than he had done already, stood still where he was, and shouted for the queen's ladies to bring a torch and light the candles, which they did as fast as possible, and all grew quiet again. But when the queen awoke in the morning the dog was not on its cushion, neither was anything more known of it, in spite of the bitter tears the queen shed over its fate. Soon after this her Majesty was out driving in the afternoon, when the Camarera Mayor, who had been in a very bad temper for many days, suddenly ordered the two parrots to be brought to her. The French maids who had charge of them felt very uncomfortable, but dared not disobey, and when the birds arrived she wrung their necks with her own hands. Shortly after the queen came in, and bade her dogs and parrots to be fetched to amuse her, as she often did when the king was not in the room, for he did not like animals. The two maids looked at each other, but did not move.

"Don't you hear me? What is the matter?" asked the queen.

"Oh! Madame!" faltered the maid; and then, bursting into tears, stammered out the story. The queen's face grew white, but she said nothing, and sat where she was, thinking. By-and-by the Camarera Mayor entered, and, as required by etiquette, stooped down to kiss the queen's hand; but, when she bent over, a stinging pain ran through her, as her Majesty dealt her a violent slap on each cheek. The duchess staggered back from surprise as much as from the blow, but her furious words were checked on her tongue at the sight of the still, pale girl whose face was so new to her. Leaving the room, she summoned all her relations, and, choking with anger, she informed them of the insult she had received; then, accompanied by no less than four hundred kinsfolk, all belonging to noble families, she went to complain to the king.

Now Charles had passed all his life with people who did everything according to rule, and it took some time for his slow mind to grasp that a queen of Spain could have so far lost command of herself as to have administered punishment with her own hands, whatever might have been the provocation. He rose from his seat with an expression of sternness, which filled the heart of the cruel and revengeful old woman with triumph, and made his way to the queen's apartments. But his wrath, great through it was, melted like snow before the caressing ways of his wife, and when the duchess entered, certain of victory, she found only defeat. However, furious though she might be, the Camarera Mayor saw that she had gone too far, and that unless she wished to drive the queen to confide in her mother-in-law, she must give her more liberty, and treat her with greater respect. She really tried to be gentler and more agreeable, and gave permission to the French ambassadress to visit the queen oftener; but her prejudices were so strong, and her temper so bad, that she usually broke her good resolutions. Foreigners she particularly hated, the French more than any others—and this the queen resented bitterly; so matters grew worse and worse.

AFTER EASTER, CHARLES WENT, AS regulated by custom, to pass a few days at the palace of the Escorial, which had been built by Philip II to commemorate the battle of St. Quentin. Marie Louise found it very dull when he was away. She could not hunt, or drive, except with the curtains of the coach closely drawn, the duchess was crosser than ever, and time hung heavy on her hands. She wrote to her husband daily, and told him how much she missed him, and asked when he was coming back to Madrid. The king was always delighted to get her letters, though the effort to answer them was beyond him. Once, however, when the queen had expressed herself even more kindly and affectionately than usual, he seized a pen, and slowly and painfully wrote these words:

"Señora, it is very windy, and I have killed six wolves."

This he enclosed in a beautiful box of gold and enamel, and sent off by a messenger.

It was not only the queen who suffered from the tyranny of the Camarera Mayor; her French maids fared even worse, and at length they could bear it no longer, and begged the queen to let them go back to France. This was a great blow to her, but she did not blame them, though how to get the necessary money she did not know, for the country grew daily poorer, and the queen herself never had a penny to spend. Still, she felt she must raise it somehow, and at length, to her bitter humiliation, had to borrow it, probably from the French ambassador, though this we are not told. When her French maids had departed for the "charmant pays de France," which she herself was never again to see, she had no society but that of the king and the Camarera Mayor, for the maids of honour were forbidden to speak to her. Her naturally good temper became irritable, and her high spirits began to settle down into melancholy. The king, unobservant though he was, noticed this, and it troubled him, though he was too much used to royal etiquette to guess the cause. It was a trivial thing which, as generally happens, caused the smouldering quarrel to break forth into a flame. The queen found the duchess spying on some of her letters, in the hope that she might steal one or two from France which it would be worth while to get interpreted. The queen was quite aware of these practices—she had found her more than once listening at the door when the king was talking over state affairs; but the duchess had been more than usually rude that day, and Marie Louise could bear it no longer. Standing perfectly still at the door till the lady-in-waiting should turn round and see her, she waited in silence. The duchess *did* turn round,

ANDREW LANG AND LEONORA BLANCHE LANG

and, starting violently, began to stammer out excuses. The queen took no notice; she did not even look at her, but slowly left the room and walked straight to the king's apartments. Once there her self-control gave way, and, her eyes blazing with anger, she told the king that she would submit to the Camarera Mayor's insolence no longer, and that she insisted on her dismissal at once.

"I don't understand," answered Charles, in a puzzled way; "what is it you say? Dismiss the Camarera Mayor? But it is impossible! Such a thing was never heard of!"

"It will have to be heard of now," said the queen sternly. Then, throwing her arms round his neck, she cried: "Oh! Señor, don't you see how unhappy she makes me? Surely you do not wish me to be sorry I came to Spain? I thought you loved me, and yet you suffer me—me, the queen—to be insulted and made miserable all the day long."

Charles did not reply; but his face changed and softened, and he pressed his hands upon her arms. "My queen, my queen," he murmured gently, "I do love you; and if the duchess makes you miserable, as you say, I will dismiss her, and you shall choose a Camarera Mayor to take her place. Only be careful, because next time it must be for ever."

"Oh, thank you! thank you! how good you are," exclaimed the queen. And she returned to her own apartments, with her head held high, and an expression which boded little good to the duchess, who was watching behind a curtain. But weeks went on, and as no new lady-in-waiting was appointed, the duchess began to hope that she would remain after all, and as her spirits rose, one by one she tried to resume all her little tyrannies. But, to her surprise, the queen no longer obeyed as she had done before. She did not argue or scold—she simply took no notice, and behaved as if the duchess was not there. And this angered the old lady far more deeply than any other treatment could have done. The truth was Marie Louise had laid to heart the king's warning, and was very careful in making her choice. It was not easy, for she had her husband and his mother to please as well as herself, and two or three ladies, to whom she offered the post, returned humble thanks for the honour, but either were too old or could not leave their children. The position of gaoler to the queen was not one envied by everyone. At length, to the joy of them all, the place was accepted by the Marquesa de Aytona, a lady of great good sense and a charming companion. The Duchess of Terranova shook with rage, and gave orders that her trunks should be packed. But before she could leave the palace, or the marquesa enter it, the new Camarera Mayor was seized with illness, and in a few days was dead. The duchess was triumphant. "The luck is all on my side," she said to herself, and desired her maids to put her clothes back in the great wardrobes.

So the whole weary business had to be gone through again. But after much talk the queen agreed to accept the Duchess of Albuquerque, a clever, well-read woman, who could enjoy conversation with learned people and knew what was being thought and done outside the bounds of Spain. The king, who was greatly pleased at her appointment, sent for the duchess to his own apartments, and told her that he was well satisfied at the queen's choice, but that he desired the new Camarera Mayor to understand that her Majesty was to have more liberty and more amusement than before; she was to drive out when she wished, and was to ride, and go late to bed, as had been her strange custom when in France. For himself, *he* could never sit up after eight; but under the Duchess of Albuquerque's rule he found so much to amuse him, that, by-and-by, he did not say good-night till it was fully ten.

The nomination of the Duchess of Albuquerque had taken place so secretly that the old lady-in-waiting was in ignorance of it, and had by this time persuaded herself that the king could not do without her. Her numerous relations also took this view, and by their advice she determined on a master-stroke of policy to render her position securer than ever. One day, while the king and queen, surrounded by the court officials, were waiting for dinner to be announced, the duchess came forward as the king rose to pass into the dining-room, and, dropping a low curtesy, asked leave to retire from her post about the queen's person. She imagined—and so did the courtiers who watched breathlessly for the result—that his Majesty would bid her continue in her charge; while the queen's heart stood still, fearing that the king's courage might fail before the woman who held the chains of custom in her hands; that his promise to her would be broken, and her last chance of happiness and freedom thrown to the winds. But "it is always the unexpected that happens," so says the proverb.

"Go as soon as you like, Señora," answered the king; "you have my permission to retire immediately, as you wish it." The duchess was struck dumb for an instant with surprise, then, recovering herself, began to stammer out some excuses; but the king did not wait to hear what they were, and walked on to his dinner.

Whatever the duchess's wrath might be, she went all through that evening (which must have seemed endless) without showing her feelings.

She knew she was hated by every creature in the palace, and would not give them the satisfaction of noting her humiliation. The night was passed in feverishly walking up and down, and in giving directions to her maids to pack her boxes afresh. Quite early she entered the queen's room to take farewell of her mistress, and when Marie Louise, who felt some pity for her mortification, tried to say a few good-natured words, the duchess only answered haughtily that she hoped her successor might please her Majesty better, and left. When she returned to her own apartments she found them filled with ladies, who condoled with her on the ingratitude of the queen and the weakness of the king.

"I have no need at all of your compassion," replied the duchess, who probably did not believe in their lamentations. "I am thankful to quit this place, where I shall never more set foot, and to be going to Sicily, where I can enjoy the rest and peace which Madrid could never give me." But as she spoke she picked up a beautiful fan that was lying on a table, and breaking it in two, threw the pieces on the floor and stamped on them.

The winter of 1680 was very cold, and the poor people suffered dreadfully. The queen did all she could to help them, but it was not much, for money was scarce, and though great galleons still sailed into Cadiz laden with nuggets of gold and silver, as in the palmy days of the Emperor Charles V (Charles I of Spain), most of them belonged to the merchants, and only a small part reached the king. The days passed heavily for the queen, who had in great measure lost the love of books which had marked her childhood, and had been an inheritance from her Stuart mother. She did read sometimes, but she loved far better to be in the open air, riding or hunting, and now this was impossible. So she welcomed joyfully the news that some Flemish ladies and gentlemen were skating on a lake near Buen-Retiro, and instantly ordered her coach, to go and watch them from the windows of the palace. *They* did not look cold, as they swept round in curves, with shining eyes and glowing cheeks; and how Marie Louise longed to be skimming about with them! But this would not have been permitted even in France, and after a while she remembered that it was growing late, and returned to Madrid. That evening a message was brought to her, through the Duchess of Albuquerque, that some Spanish ladies had come to request her Majesty's leave to skate in masks the following day. They did not wish their names to be known, they said, but they were quite sure they could prove themselves as much at home on the ice as any of the

Flemings. The queen not only granted permission to wear the masks, but sent word that she would come and watch them and judge of their skill. It was certainly very surprising, and the fact that Spanish ladies could at that time skate at all was still more so. They all wore short skirts, which showed their beautiful feet, and had black velvet masks under their plumed hats. They danced the *branle*, and the *sarabande*, their castanets sounding merrily through the air, till Marie Louise gulped down a sob of envy as she recollected sadly that "a queen of Spain has no legs." Suddenly, in the dance, the most graceful skater of them all backed on to a piece of thin ice; it gave way under her, and she fell in, screaming. The gentlemen at once came to her aid, but the ice broke beneath their weight, and soon several of them were struggling in the water together. At last the poor lady was brought dripping to the bank, and as she had lost her mask the queen could see that she was about sixty, and very ugly. "Ah, she did well to wear a mask," said Marie Louise, with a laugh, to her Camarera Mayor.

If the queen could not skate she could by this time dance the Spanish dances as well as anybody, and especially she delighted in the *canaris* and the *sarabande*. One evening Don Pedro of Aragon gave a ball for her, and she proved herself so graceful and so spirited in all the steps and figures, that the king came up when it was over and, taking her by the arms, he repeated more than once: "My queen! my queen! you are the most perfect creature in the whole world."

And so he thought, not only till her death, but after it. As long as she lived her brightness and enjoyment of everything that she was allowed to enjoy seemed to kindle some answering sparks in him; but when she died, at the age of twenty-seven, he ceased to make any efforts, and sunk more and more into a state of semi-idiocy. They had no children, and the dogs which the queen petted and spoilt did not make up for them. It was not the custom in those days for royal people to travel about from one country to the other, and in spite of her real affection for her husband and his mother, Marie Louise was very much alone. She had no one to laugh with, no one to whom she could talk freely, no one who cared for the things she cared for. She was young, yet life was one long effort, and perhaps she was not sorry when the end came.

VI

Henriette the Siege Baby

On a hot June day in the year 1644 a baby lay by her mother's side in Bedford House in Exeter. The house itself is gone now, but its name still remains behind in "Bedford Circus," which lies between quiet, old-fashioned Southernhay and the busy High Street. It seems a strange far-off birthplace for a daughter of a king of England, but the Civil War was then at its height, and Charles I had bidden the queen leave Oxford, where she had taken refuge, and seek for safety in the loyal West. So on a bright spring morning, just before the battle of Newbury, Henrietta Maria set out on her journey, saying farewell to her husband for the last time, though this she did not know. The baby, a tiny delicate creature, had for its lady-in-waiting a niece of the famous duke of Buckingham, who had been stabbed sixteen years before. She had been married as soon as she grew up to lord Dalkeith, the son of the earl of Morton, but had left her own children at the prayer of the queen, who felt that the baby would be safer anywhere than with its mother. Indeed, not a fortnight after the birth of the little girl a messenger rode in hot haste into Exeter, saying that an army under Essex was marching upon the town. To remain in the city was only to attract danger to her child, so, weak and ill as she was, the queen laid her plans for a speedy flight. There is a letter from her to Charles, dated June 28, telling him that it is for his sake she is seeking shelter in France, as well she knows he would come to her help, which would only place him in the more peril. Then she kissed her baby, and, with three faithful attendants, started for Falmouth.

It was mid-summer, yet when we read of all that the queen suffered it seems wonderful that she ever lived to reach the town. Hardly had the party got out of sight of the Cathedral towers of Exeter when they saw a troop of men in glittering armour riding towards them. Luckily in a wooded hollow near by was a small hut, half in ruins, and here they hid themselves, scarcely able to breathe from fear, as the loud voices of the soldiers broke the stillness, jesting over the queen's fate. But they passed in a cloud of dust, never guessing that only a few feet of grass had lain between them and their prey, and when darkness fell the fugitives crept out and were soon making their way over Dartmoor. Here they were joined by lord Jermyn, who till her death loyally followed the queen's fortunes, and by the little dwarf Sir Geoffrey Hudson, who in happier days had been made a knight by Charles I. This terrible journey had lasted for a fortnight before the queen found herself on board a small Dutch ship bound for France. Half-way across the Channel the ship was spied by an English vessel on the lookout for French cruisers, which immediately gave chase. At one time escape appeared impossible, and all the fighting blood of Henri IV beat high in the veins of his daughter. "If capture is sure, blow up the vessel," she said to the captain, who stood at the prow, keeping an anxious watch. "As for death, I fear it not at all, but alive they shall never have me." Fortunately a crowd of French boats now appeared in the offing, and the English ship altered her course and steered for the coast of Devon. Then a gale sprang up and again they were all in peril. When morning broke the friendly fleet had been scattered far and wide, and the Dutch captain placed the fugitives in a small boat, which was rowed to shore. Oh how thankful Henrietta Maria was to hear her native language once again and to feel herself in France! She had only a peasant's hut to sleep in and peasant's food to eat, but for the first time during many months she was able both to sleep and eat without a dread, of being roused up to fly. By and bye all her terrors would awake on behalf of those whom she had left behind her, but at present she was too exhausted to be able to think at all. And so she rested till the news of her arrival reached Paris, and the king of France's mother, Anne of Austria, sent carriages and an escort to bring her unfortunate sister-in-law home to the Louvre.

Now the queen had been quite right when she said that when the king heard of her plight he would march with all speed to her deliverance; but the messenger to whom she had entrusted her letter was forced to go warily for fear of being captured, and the royal army was already far on the road to Exeter before Charles learned that Henrietta Maria was safe in France. It was then too late to turn back, and, besides, was there not the child to think of? So onward he marched, Charles, prince of Wales, then fourteen, riding beside him. Right glad was lady Dalkeith to see the royal standard floating from the walls of Exeter Castle, for the Parliamentary forces had long since gone elsewhere. The king was delighted with his baby daughter, who had been christened a few days before his arrival by her mother's name; for the child was so delicate that it was doubted whether each fresh attack of convulsions would not be her last. He made what arrangements he could for her comfort and safety, and then bade good-bye to her for the last time. "You are safer here than you would be with me," he said as he bent over her cradle; then he mounted his horse and galloped away, for the tide of battle had rolled east.

A YEAR LATER EXETER HAD to suffer a real siege, which lasted all through the winter. It was in vain that lady Dalkeith formed plans for escaping with the baby into Cornwall; Essex and Waller laid their schemes better than that, and she soon found that it was quite impossible to get through the lines. By April all the supplies were exhausted, and Sir John Berkeley, governor of the city, as well as guardian of the princess, was obliged to surrender. Faithful to the end, he had obtained leave from the Parliamentary generals to carry away all the goods that belonged to his charge, and then accompanied her and lady Dalkeith to Salisbury. The Parliament, however, had other uses for their money than the payment of Henriette's pension, which had likewise been agreed on, and if lady Dalkeith had not taken her and her attendants to her own house on the Thames the poor child might have fared badly. When, however, the rulers of the nation had time to think about the matter, they desired that the princess should be taken away from her governess and placed with her brother and sister, Henry and Elizabeth, in St. James's Palace. But this was more than lady Dalkeith could bear. Finding that all her letters were unnoticed and unanswered, she made up her mind what to do, and one July morning she rose early and put on a suit of ragged old clothes that lay ready for her and fastened a hump on her shoulder. Then, waking the little princess, she quickly dressed her in a set of boy's garments as dirty and ragged as her own.

"Now you are my little boy Pierre," said she; but Henriette cried and declared she wouldn't wear such ugly things, and that she was not Pierre but a princess. Happily she was only between two and three and could not speak plain, for she never failed to repeat this to every kind soul who stopped to give them a groat or a piece of bread. With the child on her back lady Dalkeith walked the whole way to Dover, stopping every now and then to rest under the green hedges, and seeking at night the shelter of a barn. The farmers' wives were very good-natured, and praised the baby's beauty and curling hair, and gave her warm milk to drink and soft sweet-smelling hay to lie on.

"Dear heart! What bright eyes he has," they would say, "and what might his name be?"

"Pierre! he is a French boy," answered lady Dalkeith in broken English; and then the child would frown and say something about "Pierre" and "ugly clothes," which nobody could make out.

"Hearken to him, then," they would murmur with admiration, "don't he speak pretty?" But the governess, fearful lest someone quicker witted than the rest might understand his prattle, hastened to thank them heartily and to go on her way. Weary and worn was she when the walls of Dover hove in view, but the sight gave her fresh courage, and she went straight to the harbour, where a French ship lay at anchor. Here she was joined by Sir John Berkeley, who had never lost sight of her all through her journey, and now came forward and placed her under the charge of the captain, whose vessel was ready for sea. The wind was fair, and in a few hours lady Dalkeith and the child were standing on the French shore, safe at last.

"Now you are not 'Pierre' any more but princess Henriette," said lady Dalkeith as the vessel cast anchor, and she drew out a beautiful blue satin dress and lace cap from a small bundle which Sir John Berkeley had handed to her. Henriette's face brightened into smiles as she looked, and she stood quite still while they were put upon her. A messenger was hastily sent off to Paris to inform the queen-regent, Anne of Austria, of the escape of her niece, and as soon as possible carriages were again to be seen taking the road to the sea-coast. Great, heavy, lumbering vehicles they were, needing six or even eight horses to drag them through mud or out of ditches, but they seemed like the softest of beds to poor lady Dalkeith, after all she had undergone. When they reached the palace of St. Germain, where Henrietta Maria was awaiting them, she fell seriously ill.

The gratitude of both Charles and Henrietta knew no bounds, and poets made songs about the wonderful escape. At the urgent wish of the poor queen, lady Dalkeith, or lady Morton as she had now become, went with them to Paris, and found there that she was almost as much a heroine as Henrietta Maria. But, indeed, misfortune only appeared to have doubled their friends, and everyone at court tried to see how much kindness they could show them. Queen Anne, her two sons, Louis XIV, then about eight years old, and his brother Philippe, duke of Anjou, drove to the gate of Paris to meet them, and, assisting the royal exiles to mount the state coach which was in readiness, they escorted them through the crowded, shouting streets to the Louvre. This was to be their home, when they were not at St. Germain, and a large sum of money was given them for a pension. For a little while Henrietta felt that she was a queen again. English poets and nobles, and English royalists waiting for brighter days, flocked around her, and played with the little princess. At home she had as many servants and attendants as of old, and when she took an airing soldiers and running footmen escorted her carriage. But later things began to change. Affairs in England grew worse and worse. The king needed more money than ever, and who should send it—as long as she had it—but his wife? Besides this, the civil war, called the Fronde, soon broke out in France. The pension allowed the English queen was paid more and more irregularly, and by and bye ceased altogether. Her own plate had been melted down, her jewels sold for her husband's cause; at last a little golden cup, which she used daily, was the only piece of gold she had left. The queen-mother and the king were no better off than she. "I have not a farthing with which to procure a dinner or buy a dress," says Anne of Austria, while at St. Germain the beds were bare and without hangings.

The winter that followed was bitter for all—for Henrietta and the little princess no less than for the poor of Paris. Three weeks before the execution of Charles I the cardinal de Retz went to pay a call on the exiled queen at the Louvre. It was snowing fast, and his carriage wheels frequently stuck in the drifts, yet when he entered the room there was no fire, and the air struck chill in his bones. The child was lying in bed and her mother was sitting by, telling her stories. The queen received the cardinal cheerfully, but he was almost too shocked and distressed to speak at first, then bit by bit he found out that they were not only frozen but almost starved. They could not pay for food, and the tradespeople would not trust them. Instantly taking leave, the cardinal hastened home, and loaded a cart with all that they could possibly want, while as soon as possible he induced the Parliament of Paris to vote the exiles a sum of money large enough to keep them till better times came. Meanwhile it was well indeed for little Henriette that lady Morton was with them. Her mother's heart grew heavier and heavier as the days passed on without news from England. She would sit by the fire for hours together, staring straight before her, seeming neither to hear nor to see. Even the child's voice failed to rouse her. At length, towards the end of February, the blow fell. Charles was dead—had been dead three weeks—and not a whisper had ever reached her. Silent as before, she rose up, and leaving the princess in the hands of lady Morton and her confessor, father

Cyprian, she fled for solitude and prayer to a Carmelite convent. When the queen returned, dressed in the deep mourning of those times—even the walls were hung with black—her little daughter felt that a change had come over her, though she could not have told exactly what it was. But lady Morton knew. It was that all hope had died out of her face, and to the end she would be, as she often signed herself, "the unhappy queen, La Reine Malheureuse."

Between Paris and St. Germain little Henriette passed the first seven years of her life, and if the clash of arms and the roar of cannon were as familiar to her as nursery songs are to more fortunate children, the echo of the same sounds came to her across the water from England, where her brother Charles was fighting for his crown. One day when she entered the room, she found the queen sitting with her head on her hands, weeping bitterly. The child stood for a moment at the door wondering what to do, and then went up softly and laid her cheek silently against her mother's. "One by one they are going," cried the poor woman; "your sister Elizabeth"—and Henriette wept too for the death of the sister whom she had never seen. A few weeks later arrived the news that the queen's son-in-law, William of Orange, had died of small-pox at The Hague, and in him the family had lost another friend, and a sure refuge in all their troubles. Henrietta Maria's heart ached for her eldest daughter, gay, charming, yet melancholy like all the Stuarts, left a widow at nineteen, with only a baby son to comfort her. Henriette was very much grieved for her mother's distress, but as her sisters were merely names to her, she was soon ready to attend to her lessons again, given to her daily by lady Morton and the good father Cyprian. She would leave the side of her sad mother and seek her governess, and, sitting at one of the windows of the Louvre that overlooked the Seine, would sing some of the songs composed by the loyal Cavaliers who had fought for her father. And the passers-by beneath would look up at the sound of the guitar, as the little singer would pour out with all her heart "My own and only love I pray," by the great Marquis of Montrose; or "When love with unconfined wings hovers within the gate," or "Bid me to live, and I will live, Thy Protestant to be." Only she never sang this in the queen's presence, for Her Majesty did not love Protestants, as Henriette well knew! But the guitar was not the only instrument the princess was taught to play. She played too on the harpsichord, which she did not love as well as the guitar, for one reason because it was a lumbering thing and she could not carry it about with her. She also learnt to dance, and when the mob besieged the gates of Paris, or poured shouting through the streets, in one small room on the top of the old palace a little girl might have been seen practising the steps of the coranto, the pavane, the branle, and other dances in fashion at court. And when she was tired of dancing, lady Morton would read to her tales out of the old chronicles of Froissart or de Comines, or stories from Malory of Lancelot and Arthur, or repeat to her some of the poems of days gone by.

So the months slipped by, when one evening a messenger arrived at the Louvre and asked to see lady Morton, who was at that moment telling Henriette about the Crusades, in which her ancestors, both French and English, had borne so great a part. The man was admitted, and bowing low first to the princess and then to her governess, he held out a letter bound with a black ribbon and sealed with black wax. Lady Morton turned pale as she took it, and as she read grew paler still. Her husband was dead; and there was no one to look after her children; she was therefore prayed to return at once. That was all. Signing to the messenger to retire, she hastened to the queen and laid the letter before her. "Your Majesty will see that I have no choice," she said in a quiet voice which spoke of the pain of the present and that which was to come. Henrietta stooped and kissed her faithful servant, and answered, "No, none; but we shall miss you sorely. Every day and every hour." And so they did; and when, three years later, the news of her death was brought to them, it was the greatest grief that Henriette was to feel until she lost her little son.

Look which way she would the poor queen could see nothing but disaster. Charles II's expedition proved an absolute failure, and once more he took refuge in France. But no misfortunes could damp his spirits, and, as always, his visit was a joy to Henriette. How he made her laugh by describing his ride on the pillion in woman's clothes, after the battle of Worcester, and the hours he spent seated in the oak, while his enemies passed and re-passed beneath him. And about the time he hid in a cottage, with his hair cropped close like a serving-man, till he could make his way to London and get on board a vessel bound for France; and fifty other hairbreadth escapes, which interested even his cousin, the "Great Mademoiselle," who usually cared about nothing that did not concern herself. Soon after this the Fronde ended, and things began to look a little brighter for France, and also for Henrietta. When Anne of Austria came into power again, she thought of her unhappy sister-in-law and her niece, and resolved to do what she could to make them more comfortable. She begged Henrietta Maria to leave the Louvre, where she had suffered so much, and come and live with her in the Palais Royal; and the English queen felt it would be ungracious to refuse such kindness, though she would have preferred staying where she was. After that a larger pension was given her, and with this Henrietta was able to buy a house outside Paris built nearly a hundred years before by Catherine de Medici, and, after putting aside a few rooms for herself, she invited some nuns from the convent of Sainte Marie to take up their abode in the other part, with mademoiselle de la Fayette as their abbess.

Here the queen passed many months of every year, bringing with her the little princess. How pleased the nuns were to have the child, and how they petted and spoilt her! Many of them were women of high birth, and had lived at court before they determined to leave it for good, and the elder ones could tell Henriette thrilling tales of the War of the Three Henries, in which *their* fathers and *her* grandfather had fought. By and bye the road which led from Paris would be covered with coaches and noisy with the tramp of horses, and Henriette would strain her neck out of the top windows to see which of the great ladies was coming to pay them a visit and to pray in the chapel. Ah! those were the royal uniforms surrounding the big carriage drawn by six white horses. It was her aunt, queen Anne, who was always so good to her! and Henriette ran joyfully down to tell her mother. These excitements took place very often, and, in spite of the many services she had to attend, and the lack of other children to play with, the princess had hardly time to be dull. Besides, at the end of this same year, 1652, her two brothers, Charles and James, came to Paris, and of course the English queen and her daughter had to hurry back to the Palais Royal to receive them. Charles had been all his life very fond of his little sister, fourteen years younger than himself, with eyes that flashed with fun at his when La Grande Mademoiselle gave herself more airs than usual, or allowed herself to be impertinent to her poor relations, who never seemed to be aware of their position. Of course outwardly they behaved beautifully and paid her the compliments that she loved, and as it never entered into her head that any one could make fun of *her*, Mademoiselle, the Centre of the Universe, no harm was done. But this time a quarrel broke out between the good-natured, easy-going young king Charles and his mother. She had fallen under the influence of Walter Montagu, abbot of Pontoise, and he had persuaded her to put a stop to the services of the English

ANDREW LANG AND LEONORA BLANCHE LANG

Church, which had been held, for the benefit of the many fugitives from their native country, in a hall of the Louvre, and anyone wishing to use the form to which he was accustomed had to go to the house of the ambassador appointed by Charles himself. Very unwillingly the king was forced to attend this chapel, and his brother James also. Now the queen's three elder children were very much troubled at little Henriette being brought up a Roman Catholic, and had several times entreated vainly that she might be allowed to follow the faith of her father. This made Henrietta Maria very angry, and although her confessor, father Phillips, who was a sensible man, contrived for some years to keep the peace, when he was dead she suffered herself to be led entirely by the evil counsels of Montagu. Matters were made still worse a few months later, when her youngest son, Henry, duke of Gloucester, then about thirteen, arrived to join his family, and in his daily walks to and from his dancing and riding lessons always stopped at the ambassador's house to hear morning prayers. Henry's open affection for the English Church was more than his mother could bear. With the help of the abbé Montagu she began to persecute the poor boy to change his religion, which he steadily refused to do. Charles had gone to Cologne, and only James, duke of York, was left to guard his young brother, whom Montagu was doing his best to force into a Jesuits' college.

"They cannot send you there without your own consent, and that you must never give," said James. "You are an English subject, and bound to obey the king"; and then he sat down and wrote letters to the princess of Orange, to their aunt, the queen of Bohemia, and to Charles, who replied by upbraiding his mother with more anger than he had ever shown about anything in his life. But the fact that her children thought her in the wrong only increased Henrietta's obstinacy. She refused even to admit Henry to her apartments, and sent a message to him by Montagu that she would never see him again unless he would do as she wished. The duke of York tried to soften her heart and bring her to reason, but fared no better, and when Henry fell on his knees before her as she was getting into her coach to go to Chaillot, she only waved him out of her path and bade the coachman drive on. The boy rose up, and turned, his eyes blazing with anger, to Montagu, who stood watching.

"I owe this to you," he said, "and I will repeat to you the queen's message to me. Take heed that I see your face no more," and, sorely distressed, he went straight to the chapel at the Embassy for comfort. When he returned to the Palais Royal he found that his bed had been stripped of its sheets, and that by the queen's orders no dinner had been cooked for him. Not knowing what to do, he went to the house of lord Hatton, where he was warmly welcomed, and bidden to stay as long as he liked. But by the advice of the duke of York it was settled that he should quit Paris at once and put himself under Charles's protection at Cologne. This counsel seemed good, but where was the money to be got for the journey? No one had any, for the queen held the purse. Then the marquis of Ormonde stepped forward and pointed to the George, which hung from the blue ribbon of the Garter on his breast. "I will get the money," he said. It was the last thing he had to sell, and he sold it.

That evening, in the early dusk, Henry crept into the Palais Royal to say good-bye to his sister.

"But where are you going?" asked she, clinging to him, "and when will you come back?"

"Never, I think," he answered bitterly. "My mother has bidden me see her face no more, and I must begone before she returns from vespers."

"Oh me! my mother! my brother!" cried Henriette, clasping him more tightly to her, and sobbing wildly as she spoke, "What shall I do? what shall I do? I am undone for ever."

Thus Henry disappeared from her life, and though she did not forget him, many other things happened to occupy her thoughts. First there were her lessons, which she loved, and then the regent Anne, who pitied her loneliness, often gave parties at the Louvre, at which Henriette was present. Her mother thought her too young for these gaieties, as indeed she was according to our notions; but queen Anne would listen to nothing, and of course the princess herself enjoyed it all heartily. At the Louvre there were masques and balls and fancy dances, at which Henriette's future husband, the duke of Anjou, appeared dressed like a girl; but the most brilliant festivity of all was given in 1653 by Cardinal Mazarin, when his niece Anne-Marie Martinozzi married the king's cousin, Armand, prince de Conti. Henriette, who was only nine, and small for her age, was escorted by her brothers James and Henry, and her beautiful dancing won her the praise of all. Three months later a court ballet, or what we should call now a musical comedy, was performed in a theatre, the music being written by the famous Lulli himself. The young king, who was then about fifteen, played several different characters, but appeared at the end as Apollo, with the Nine Muses grouped around him. While the little theatre rang with applause there stepped from their ranks, the princess Henriette as

Erato, the muse of poetry, crowned with myrtle and roses. Holding a lyre to her breast, she recited some verses written expressly for her by the court poet Benserade and the pathos of the words and the beauty of the child drew tears from the eyes of the spectators.

During the next two years queen Anne's beautiful rooms in the Louvre were the scene of many small dances, and none was thought complete without Henriette. With practice her dancing became more and more graceful, and fortunate indeed was the young man who was allowed to be her partner in the coranto or the branle. All but king Louis; for it was noticed that he alone never asked his cousin to dance. This was, of course, observed by his mother, who was much grieved at his rudeness, though for a long while she said nothing, fearing lest he should take a dislike to the child, whom in her secret heart she might have been glad to welcome as a daughter-in-law. But one evening in the year 1655 the slight was so marked that the queen-regent could contain herself no longer. One of the usual small dances was to take place in the Louvre, and queen Anne begged her widowed sister-in-law for once to come out of her solitude and to see the king perform some new steps. Henrietta, touched both by the queen's kindness and the entreaties of her daughter, consented, especially as the ball was to be very private, and queen Anne, who had been ill, announced that she herself did not intend to wear full dress, and that no one else need do so. When the little company had assembled the signal was given, and the branle was struck up by the violins. At the first note Louis XIV, who by this time was about seventeen years old and very handsome, advanced to the side of madame de Mercoeur, one of the cardinal's nieces. "The queen," says an eye witness of the scene, "astonished at his want of manners, rose quickly from her seat, drew away madame de Mercoeur, and told her son he must take the English princess for his partner. Queen Henrietta, who saw that queen Anne was really angry, went up to her hastily, and in a whisper begged her to say nothing to the king, for her daughter had hurt her foot, and was unable to dance."

"Very well," replied queen Anne, "if the princess cannot dance, the king shall not dance either." Upon this the queen of England gave way, and allowed her daughter to dance, in order not to make a fuss, though she felt very much annoyed with the king for his behaviour. After the ball was over, queen Anne spoke to him very seriously about his behaviour, but he only answered sulkily.

"I do not like little girls." Henriette did not, however, trouble herself about the king's lack of attention and respect to her position as his cousin and a princess, but "took her pleasures wherever she found them," according to the counsel of the wise French proverb. The court was never dull in Louis XIV's early years, and he was always planning something new, in which he could play the important part, for nobody in the world could ever be so great as Le Grand Monarque thought himself to be! When he got tired of balls, he arranged a band of nobles for the old sport of Tilting at the Ring. He divided them into parties of eight, and himself headed the troop, dressed in white and scarlet liveries embroidered in silver. The duke of Guise was the chief of the second set in blue and white and silver, and the duke of Candale of the third, whose colours were green and white. They wore small helmets with plumes to match, and their horses were decorated with fluttering ribbons. The three bands assembled in the gardens of the Palais Royal, and every window was filled with ladies, each waving to her special knight. We are not told where the tilting actually took place, nor who won the prize, though we may feel pretty sure that it was arranged that the king should be the victor. Unluckily madame de Motteville who describes it all, cared more for the fine sight than for the game itself.

Now that there was once more a court in Paris, it was visited by all kinds of distinguished people, and on these occasions Henriette was always present. But of all the guests that came to the Louvre, none was so strange as Christina, queen of Sweden, daughter of the great Gustavus Adolphus. Christina was very clever, and could read Greek, Latin and Hebrew, as well as several other languages, but she dressed as much like a man as she was able, and hated ceremonies and rules of courts. She was received by the duke of Guise when she entered France, and very much surprised was he at the curious sight she presented. "The queen wore," he writes, "a man's wig, very high in the front and full at the sides, but the back of her head was dressed with some resemblance to a woman." Her bodice was always laced crooked, and her skirt hung to one side, and was half open, showing her underclothes. "She uses a great deal of pomade and powder; never puts on gloves, and her shoes exactly resemble those of a man." Yet the queen, who had recently abdicated her throne in favour of her cousin and her liberty, was only now a little past thirty and not bad looking. But her untidiness seems to have struck everybody, for a little later madame de Motteville speaks of a visit she paid the king and his mother at Compiègne, when she arrived with her wig uncurled and blown about by the wind, looking for all the world like a crazy gipsy. In spite of her odd appearance and ways, however, she was very popular with the French people; but we are not told what King Louis thought about her, and no doubt Henriette's sharp eyes saw many a funny scene, when the royal politeness of both Louis and Christina was severely taxed. Happily for her during that year the widowed princess of Orange was paying her mother a long visit, so that the girl had someone to laugh with. Everybody was charmed with the princess royal, and she on her part was enchanted to get away from her stiff Dutch court, and enjoy herself with the young sister whom she had never seen. Balls were given in her honour, to all of which she took Henriette; and very unwillingly she herself was obliged to play the part of a spectator, as her aunt, queen Anne, had forbidden all widows to dance in public. However, there were plenty of private fêtes, and here she could dance as much as she liked—and that was a great deal! Then plays were given at the Louvre for her amusement, and the young king wrote and acted a ballet on Cupid and Psyche, which everyone said was "wonderful," though perhaps nobody thought it quite so "wonderful" as the king himself. "I have scarcely time to snatch a piece of bread," the princess of Orange exclaims happily, and even Mademoiselle has a good word for her cousin and for the jewels which she wore. It was a great holiday for princess Mary, but she did not suffer all the pleasure and admiration to spoil her or turn her head. We find her still thinking of how she can help her brothers, and making time to mourn her husband and to keep the day of his death sacred, though it was several years since his death. On Sundays she never missed going to the service at the English ambassador's, though her mother would fain have had her company in her visits to the convent of the Carmelites. Thus the year passed away till the illness of the little prince of Orange, afterwards William III, obliged her to return to the Hague.

Henriette spent a dull time during the next two years, and her life seemed more dismal after the gay time of her sister's visit. Her mother grew more and more ill, and lived chiefly at Colombes or Chaillot. Every now and then, however, queen Anne begged leave for Henriette to come to a ball at the Louvre, or to a specially brilliant fête such as that given by Séguier, where Mademoiselle, with her accustomed rudeness, tried to take precedence of Henriette, which the queen of France would by no means allow. During the spring of 1658 cardinal

Mazarin invited the royal families of France and England, Monsieur, the king's uncle, and his daughter Mademoiselle to be present at a supper and small dance held in his private apartments. As it was Lent, of course nothing but fish was eaten, but never had so many sorts of fish been seen before, cooked in so many different ways. After supper, and while the remainder of the guests were dancing, the two queens, Henriette and Mademoiselle, were conducted into a long gallery, filled with all kinds of beautiful things—jewels, china, furniture, rich stuffs of gold and silver, plate, gloves, fans, scent-bottles and a thousand other objects—for the cardinal's collection was famous throughout Europe.

"Here, Madame," said Mazarin, bowing low before the queen, "are the prizes for a lottery in which no one will draw blanks." Mademoiselle drew a big diamond, but the first prize of all was a diamond bigger still, worth four thousand crowns, and this was won by a lieutenant in the King's Guards, called La Salle.

It was towards the close of 1659 that the marriage of the king with his cousin Marie Thérèse, daughter of the king of Spain, was decided upon. In the country house of Colombes on the Seine tales of the preparations floated to the ears of Henriette, who would have enjoyed nothing so much as being in Paris in the midst of all the talk. In her secret heart she longed to go south with the royal cavalcade; and gladly would her aunt have taken her, but queen Henrietta was ill and out of spirits, and greatly agitated by the news from England, where, Cromwell being dead, parties were divided as to the prospects of the accession of Charles II. She needed her daughter, and Henriette, though she loved amusement, was very tender-hearted and did not let her mother guess how great was her disappointment. The princess was now passed fifteen, and was looked on by the French people as their adopted child. She was taller than anyone had expected her to become, and had the long face of the Stuarts. Her hair was a bright brown, her skin was fair, and her eyes, unlike her mother's, were blue, while her hands and arms were famous for their beauty. Many women were more beautiful than she, but none had her charm, or could, like her, point a jest which left no sting behind it. Her aunt saw with pleasure that the eyes of her younger son frequently rested on her niece, whom a short time before he had been tempted to despise, following in this the example of the king. If this marriage could be, as well as the other—ah, how happy it would make her! To Anne of Austria it mattered little that the princess was an exile and entirely dependent on France for the bread she ate and the clothes she wore. Such trifles might be of consequence to the duke of Savoy and the grand duke of Tuscany, both of whom had hastily rejected the timid proposals put forth by the English queen, but the duke of Anjou (soon, by the death of his uncle, to become "Monsieur" and duke of Orléans) was rich enough and distinguished enough to take a bride without a dowry. So the queen-mother set forth on the journey southwards which was to end in that other wedding, and before that was celebrated Charles II had been called to his father's throne and his sister was a match for any king.

"MY HEAD IS STUNNED WITH the acclamations of the people," writes Charles from Canterbury on May 26 to his "deare, deare sister," and amidst all the "vast amount of business" attending the Restoration he found time to remember her love of riding, and to send her a saddle of green velvet, with trimmings of gold and silver lace. Even queen Henrietta forgot his illness and her troubles for a moment. She was no longer La Reine Malheureuse, but the mother of a reigning king, and when Monsieur came galloping up to Colombes immediately after the royal couple had returned to Fontainebleau, Henrietta received him with open arms as her future son. Queen Anne was no less delighted than her sister-in-law, and herself came to Colombes in state to carry both mother and daughter to Fontainebleau in one of those old painted and gilded glass coaches that contained nine or ten people. Here they paid their respects to the bridal pair, who received them with great kindness. The young queen was a good-natured girl, with pretty fair hair and pink and white face, but stupid and ignorant, and never likely to be a rival to Henriette. Still they soon made friends, and then the princess drove home with her mother, both of them much pleased with their visit. After a ball given by Monsieur at his palace of St. Cloud, and other fêtes at which Henriette was almost as much stared at as Marie Thérèse, came the state entry of the king and queen into Paris, and the queen-mother (as Anne of Austria was now called) invited Henrietta Maria and her daughter to her balcony near a wonderful triumphal arch in the Rue Saint Antoine. It was August 26 and a beautiful day, and the narrow streets, as well as the windows and even roofs of the houses, were thronged to overflowing. The young queen sat alone in her glass coach, wearing a black dress heavily embroidered in gold and silver and covered with precious stones, which suited her fair complexion and pale golden hair. The king, also in gold and silver and mounted on a magnificent black horse, rode on the right of the coach, followed by his cousins, the Princess of the Blood, and the highest nobles in France, while on the left was Monsieur, gay and gallant on a white charger, diamonds blazing on his coat and on his plumed hat.

Monsieur and the queen-mother wished that his marriage should take place at once, but Henrietta Maria would not hear of this, and insisted that it should be put off till she and her daughter had paid a visit to England, where, after sixteen years of exile, the family were at last to meet. But no sooner had they started than the news arrived that the young duke of Gloucester had died of smallpox after a few days' illness, and all their joy was damped. Henriette, indeed, amidst all the excitements around her, was more quickly consoled than either her mother or the princess royal, and the feelings of the queen were tinged with remorse, as she remembered her last parting with the boy. The short period of mourning over, the court festivities began, and Charles was besieged by envoys asking for the hand of his sister, for her engagement to Monsieur had not yet been publicly announced. Among the petitioners was the emperor Leopold I, whom Mademoiselle intended for herself, and great was her wrath when the fact came to her ears. Charles, however, was quite satisfied with the marriage that had been arranged, and contented himself with prevailing on Parliament to settle a handsome sum on Henriette; which it was quite willing to do, as she had managed to charm both the Lords and the Commons, as well as everybody else. Great preparations were made for keeping Christmas in the good old fashion, which had been set aside for so many years. Everything was to be done according to the old rules, and a branch of the flowering thorn at Glastonbury was brought up by relays of horsemen for presentation to the king on Christmas Eve. But once again death stepped in, and turned their joy into grief, for the princess royal fell ill of small-pox, and died in a few days, at the age of twenty-nine. The queen, in an agony of terror for her one remaining daughter, removed Henriette from Whitehall to St. James's, where she received a letter from Monsieur, imploring them to set out at once for France. This they did, but Henriette was seized on board ship with an attack of measles, and the vessel was forced to put back into Portsmouth. Much anxiety was felt throughout both kingdoms as to the recovery of the princess, but at the end of a fortnight the doctors declared her well enough to travel. The risk was great, for it was January, and the slightest cold might have gone to her lungs; however, mercifully she took no harm, and her mother gave a sigh of relief when they landed on French soil at Havre. Once in France it seemed as if no one could show them enough kindness. The king and queen, accompanied by Monsieur, came out from Paris to greet them, and on their entry next day the air was filled with the shouts of welcome given by the people. Everybody wished that the marriage should take place at once, but as Lent was close at hand the Pope's consent had to be obtained. This was always a long affair, and in the meantime cardinal Mazarin died, and, by order of the king, court mourning was worn for a fortnight, so that it was March 30 before the ceremony of betrothal was performed in the Palais Royal, by the grand almoner, monseigneur Daniel de Cosnac, bishop of Valence. Though the guests were few, consisting only of the nearest relations of the king of France, with the English ambassadors, they were beautifully dressed, and wore all their jewels. Next morning, at twelve o'clock the bishop read the marriage service in the queen of England's private chapel, in the presence of Louis XIV, Anne of Austria, and Henrietta Maria.

PERHAPS IT MAY SEEM THAT childhood ends with marriage, and that on her wedding-day we should say good-bye to Madame, as Henriette was now called. But, after all, she was not yet seventeen, and had a great deal of the child about her, and it may be interesting to hear how she spent the earliest months of her married life. Just at first she was as happy as even her mother could have wished. She and Monsieur lived at the Tuileries, and as Marie Thérèse was ill her part in the Easter ceremonies fell to Madame. It was she who washed the feet of the poor on Maundy Thursday, a duty always performed by the queen, and she did it with all the grace and kindliness natural to her. When Easter was over balls and masques began. Poets made songs for her, everybody praised her, and when the king and queen left for Fontainebleau, Monsieur and Madame remained behind at the Tuileries for some weeks longer. Yet, much as she loved amusement and flattery, Madame was far too clever to be content with the diversions which satisfied most of the people about her. The friends whom she gathered round her in the gardens of the Tuileries or in the shady avenues of the Cours de la Reine were women who were remarkable for their talents or their learning, and among them was Madame's lifelong companion, madame de la Fayette, the friend of madame de Sévigné, and the duke de la Rochefoucauld, who understood Greek and Latin, and wrote novels which are still read. There was also mademoiselle de Tonnay-Charente, afterwards famous as madame de Montespan, who kept them all laughing with her merry jests; and for a listener there was madame's favourite maid-of-honour, the lovely, gentle Louise de la Vallière, always a little apart from the rest. As the spring evenings drew in they would all go and sup with Monsieur, and afterwards there would be music, or cards, or *bouts rimes*, which is sometimes played now, or better, much better than all, they would pay a visit to the Théâtre du Palais Royal and see Molière and his company act *Les Precieuses-Ridicules* and *Les Femmes Savantes*. Then the courtiers found out that Molière was like nobody in the world, and would pay any sum that was asked to sit in one of the chairs, which, after the strange fashion of the time, were placed upon the stage itself. We are not told how Monsieur enjoyed this kind of life. His good looks were perhaps the best part of him; he had been taught nothing from books, and was not, like his brother, quick enough to pick things up from other people. He was very jealous too, and could not bear his wife to speak to any other man, so most probably he was delighted to leave Paris in the end of May for his palace of St. Cloud, with its yew hedges clipped in all sorts of odd shapes, its grassy terraces, clear brooks, and its wide view over the Seine valley. But soon there came a letter from the king, and then the great coach and its eight horses drove up to the door, and Monsieur and Madame were on the road to Fontainebleau.

Well whatever Monsieur might do, there was no doubt which Madame loved best! What a fascination there was in the beautiful old palace, with its histories, some gay, some grim; and Henriette remembered as she walked down the gallery that it was only four years since the queen of Sweden's secretary had been done to death—righteously, as some said, in that very place. Still, one need not be always going down that gallery, and how graceful was the carving of the great front, and how attractive were the old trees of the forest, with tales of the Gros Veneur and his yapping dogs, which at nightfall haunted its glades. However, these things were forgotten in the morning when the sun shone bright and the coaches were ready to carry Madame and her ladies down to the river, where they played like children in the water, riding home on horseback as the sun grew lower, only to go out upon the lake after supper and listen to the music that came softly to them from a distant boat. It was a summer always to be remembered in Madame's life—indeed, it was the only one worth remembering. She had many troubles, partly, no doubt, of her own making. Her quarrels with her husband became more and more frequent, and the queen-mother, Anne of Austria, who had always loved her, was deeply grieved at her passion for pleasure and her refusal to take heed to the counsels given her. Perhaps they were all rather hard upon her, for she was still very young, only twenty-six, when one hot day at the end of June, she caught a sudden chill and in a few hours she lay dead. Unlike her brother Charles II she was not "an unconscionable time dying."

VII

The Red Rose

"From the time I was five years old I was either a fugitive or held a captive in prison."

Most likely we should guess for a long while before we hit upon the person who said those words. Was it Richard, duke of Normandy, we might ask, carried out of Laon in a bundle of hay? Was it prince Arthur, escaping from the clutches of his uncle John? Was it Charles I's little daughter Henriette, who owed her life, as a baby, to the courage of one of her mother's ladies? No; it was none of these children whose adventures have thrilled us with sorrow and excitement; it was a man who has seemed to us all about as dull as a king could be. It was Henry VII. His birthday was on June 26, 1456, exactly 453 years ago, and as soon as he was old enough to be christened he was named Henry, after the king, his uncle. The Wars of the Roses were raging fiercely over England, but it was easy to forget them in any place so far out of the world as Pembroke castle, and the baby Henry must have felt like a doll to his mother, Margaret Beaufort, countess of Richmond, who was only thirteen years older than himself. However, in a little while, the doll ceased to be merely a plaything, and became a person of real importance, for the death of his father, when he was five months old, made him the head of the great Lancastrian house of Somerset. Perhaps, before we go any further in the story of Henry's childhood, it might be as well to say that at that time England was split up into two parties, each of which claimed the throne. Both were descended from Edward III, and in these days probably no one would hesitate as to which of the two had the better right. But then men's minds were divided, and some supported Richard, duke of York, father of the future Edward IV, and others, Henry VI, the reigning king. The old story tells how a band of young men were one morning disputing in the Temple gardens, on the banks of the Thames, as to which side could best claim their allegiance. Words ran high, and threatened to turn to blows, when a young knight passionately plucked a white rose from a bush and stuck it in his hat, commanding all who swore fealty to the duke of York to do likewise, while the youth who had heretofore been his friend and comrade sprang forward and tore a red rose from its stalk and, waving it above his head, called on those who did homage to Henry of Lancaster to take as their badge the red rose. And thus the strife which laid waste England for so many years became known as the Wars of the Roses.

Now the countess of Richmond knew very well that, in spite of the danger of bringing the boy forward, and, indeed, in spite of the perils which beset travellers when bands of armed and lawless men were roaming over the country, it would be very unwise to keep him hidden in Wales till his existence was forgotten by everyone. So, when he was about three years old, and strong enough to bear the bad food and the jolting over rough roads and rougher hills, she set out with a few ladies, and a troop of trusty guards, to the place where Henry VI was holding his court. The king was pleased to welcome his sister-in-law and his nephew. Friendly faces were not always plentiful, and the fierce energy of his wife, queen Margaret, had often hindered rather than helped his cause. With the countess of Richmond he had many tastes in common; both loved books, and would spend many hours poring over the pictured scrolls of the monks, and although she had been married so young, and was even now but seventeen, Margaret had the name of being the most learned as well as the best lady in the whole of England. So the travellers were given hearty welcome, and wine and a great pasty were set before the little boy and his mother, instead of the milk, and bread and jam that he would have had in these days. That night he was so sleepy that he quite forgot he was hungry, and he was soon carried off by his nurses to be laid in a carved wooden cradle by the side of the wide hearth; but the next morning he was dressed in a crimson velvet robe, his hair combed till it shone like silk, and with his little cap in his hand he was led by his mother into the presence of the king. Henry sank on his knees on entering the room, as he had been bidden, but the king smiled and held out his hand, and the child got up at once and trotted across the floor, and leaned against his uncle's knee.

"A pretty boy, a pretty boy," said the king, softly stroking his hair; "may his life be a wise and good one, and happy withal!" And then he added, with a sigh, "In peace will he wear the garland for which we so sinfully contend."

Margaret Beaufort started in surprise as she heard the words. Edward, prince of Wales, was only three years older than the little earl of Richmond, and surely the "garland" could belong to him and to no other? But before she had time to speak, even if she had the courage to do so, an audience was solicited by one of the king's officers, and, bowing low, she led away her son. This moment of pleasure soon came to an end. Attempts were made by the Yorkists to get the young earl into their power, and with many tears his mother was forced to part from him, and to send him back to the castle of Pembroke, under the care of his uncle, Jasper Tudor, who shortly after was summoned to his post in the royal army, and fled to hide himself after the disastrous defeat of Mortimer's Cross. Instantly a body of troops, under command of the Yorkist, William Herbert, marched to Pembroke, and after much hard fighting took the castle by assault. When Herbert entered to take possession he found the little boy, not yet five, in a room of the keep guarded by his attendant, Philip ap Hoel, who stood before him with his sword drawn.

"Fear naught," said Herbert, "I am no slayer of children! the boy is safe with me."

Henry did not understand the words, for during these long months he had spoken nothing save Welsh to the men who attended on him; but he could even then read faces, and he came boldly out from behind his defender. "I will take you to my lady," said Herbert; "she is well-skilled in babes." And swinging the child on his shoulder, he carried him to the tent where his wife awaited the news of the combat. "A new nursling for thee," he said, with a smile, setting the boy on her knee; and Henry stayed there, well content to have a mother again.

FOR NINE YEARS HENRY, THOUGH still a prisoner, if he had had time to remember it, was as happy as a child could be. He had many of his own playfellows amongst lady Herbert's children, and on fine days they might all have been seen on the green of Pembroke castle throwing small quoits, or *martiaux*, as they were then called, or trying who could win at closheys, or ivory ninepins. If it was wet, as very often happened, then any courtier or man-at-arms whose business took him up the narrow winding staircase ascended at his peril, for out of some dark corner there was certain to spring upon him one of the boys and girls moving stealthily about in a game of hide and seek. When they were quite tired with running about, they would seek lady Herbert's own room, and beg her to help them at some new game with picture cards, or to show them how to move one spillikin without shaking the rest. Those were pleasant times, and Henry never forgot them; nor did he forget the best loved of all the children there, lady Maud, who

ANDREW LANG AND LEONORA BLANCHE LANG

afterwards became the wife of the earl of Northumberland, and lady Katherine, to whom, many years later, he proposed marriage himself.

But when the earl of Richmond had reached the age of fourteen this happy state of things came to an end. One day the children, rushing hastily into lady Herbert's bower, found her in tears, with a letter, tied by a piece of silken cord, lying beside her. They all crowded round her, stroking her hands, patting her cheeks, asking twenty questions, and all talking at once, till at length she found voice to tell them that their father, now earl of Pembroke, had been taken prisoner with his brother, after the battle of Banbury, and had been treacherously beheaded. "You are all I have left," she cried; and the boys and girls looked at each other, grief-stricken, but not knowing how to speak words of comfort. During a short time Henry remained at Pembroke with the Herberts, but soon after the king obtained an important victory, and Jasper Tudor, uncle of the boy, returned to Pembroke. Then lady Herbert refused to stay longer within the walls of the castle, and departed with her children to rejoin her own friends. Blinded with tears, which he was too proud to show, Henry watched their departure from the battlements of the castle, and when they were out of sight turned sadly to take counsel with his uncle Jasper as to what had best be done to repair the defences, and how to put the castle in a condition to bear a state of siege.

"We cannot tell who may gain the upper hand from one moment to another," said Jasper; and Henry, nephew though he was to the king, hardly knew on which side his sympathies lay. The siege, which had been foreseen by Jasper Tudor, began; but, thanks to the preparations that had been made, every assault was repelled successfully. At last, one night information was brought secretly to Jasper that a plot had been contrived by one Roger Vaughan to seize or to kill both uncle and nephew. Luckily it was not too late to act. With the help of some of his own soldiers Jasper contrived to capture Roger Vaughan, instantly beheaded him, and then, by help of the besieging general, who refused to see or hear what was going on, he and his nephew stole out at midnight through a postern door and hastened to Tenby. From this place they found a ship which undertook to convey them and their few followers to France, where they were kindly received by Francis II, duke of Brittany.

JUST AT FIRST EDWARD, DUKE of York, now known as Edward IV, was too busy with affairs at home to interfere much with them. But when he considered that his throne was secure, he sent messengers to Brittany laden with promises of rewards of all sorts, provided that Henry and his uncle were delivered up to him. However, by this the duke perceived, what he had hardly realised before, that his captives were too valuable to be lightly parted with, and declined to accept Edward's proposals, though he promised that, instead of the freedom they had hitherto enjoyed, his prisoners should now be confined apart, and a strict watch set on them. With this answer Edward at first seemed satisfied. The claws of the young lion were for the moment cut, and the king had more pressing business to attend to. So five years slipped by, and Henry spent many of the hours that hung heavily on his hands in studying Latin, and most likely in reading some of the old romances of Arthur and his knights, which have their root in Brittany. English he never heard spoken, and not often real French; but he loved the Breton tongue, which bore so strong a resemblance to his native Welsh, and could talk it easily to the end of his life.

In this way Henry reached his twentieth year before any further attempt was made by Edward to get him into his power. Then the bishop of Bath, Stillington, who shrunk from no employment where money was to be made, arrived at St. Malo, and sent a message to the duke, saying that the king desired all strife between the Houses of York and Lancaster to cease, and to this end he was prepared to give his daughter Elizabeth in marriage to the young earl of Richmond, and to restore to Jasper Tudor the earldom of Pembroke. Fair words; but the ambassadors had secret orders to buy the consent of Francis II at his own price, the money only to be paid on the delivery of the captives. The duke agreed to everything; he had, so he told the envoys, "no scruple or doubt in the matter"; but, all the same, after the gold was safe in his hands he contrived to convey a warning to Henry not to trust himself on board the ship. Unluckily for the Yorkists, the wind blew from a contrary quarter, and delayed their departure, and a severe attack of low fever and ague confined Henry to his bed. His uncle, however, guessed the danger he ran, as indeed did Henry himself, though he felt almost too ill to care what happened to him. Things were in this state when, by some means or other, the story of the bargain made by the duke reached the ears of Jean Chevlet, a great Breton noble. Knowing that any moment a change of wind might cost the lives of Henry and his uncle, he bade his swiftest horses to be saddled, and rode at full speed to the court. Without stopping to ask for an audience he strode into the presence of Francis, and pausing before him looked silently and steadily into his eyes. The duke reddened, and moved uneasily in his great carved chair, and at last inquired if anything had happened that the lord Chevlet should come to him in this wise.

"If anything has happened yet, I know not," answered Chevlet sternly; "but happen it will, and that speedily, unless it is hindered by those with more truth and honour in their souls than the lord duke. Rather would I have died in battle than see my sovereign a traitor."

Again there was silence. Francis would gladly have sprung to his feet and struck him dead for his insolence, but something held him back; Chevlet's words were true, and his conscience bore witness to it. At length he plucked up a little courage, and stammered out that all would be well, as Henry was to wed the king's daughter and heiress of England.

"Else would I not have parted from him," added he. But Chevlet did not deign to even notice his excuses.

"Let him leave Brittany by a foot, and no mortal creature can save him from death," was all he said. "You have thrown him into the jaws of the lion, and you must deliver him from them."

"But how?" asked the duke, who, now that his treachery was so plainly set before him, felt both shame and repentance. "Counsel me what to do, and I will do it."

Then Chevlet's voice softened a little, though the light of contempt still remained in his eyes, and he bade the duke send Pierre Landois, his treasurer, in all haste to St. Malo, to bring back the Englishmen at all hazards: by fair means if he could, by force if need be. Right gladly did Landois undertake the task.

"He did not slug nor dream his business," says the chronicler, but on his arrival at St. Malo sought at once an interview with the bishop, and by some pretext which he had invented managed again to hinder the sailing of the vessel, as the wind showed signs of veering to a favourable quarter. That night, while the treasurer was deeply engaged in conferring with the envoys, a little procession stole through the narrow streets of the towns. It consisted of a litter with a sick youth in it, carried on the shoulders of four stout men, with a tall grey-haired man walking at their head. Noiselessly they passed along, creeping ever in the shadow, stopping every now and then in some doorway darker than the rest to make certain that no one was following them. At last they reached their goal, the Sanctuary of St. Malo; and here not even the emperor himself had power to touch Henry. He was safe under the protection of the Church. Early next morning the captain of the vessel sent a sailor to inform the bishop that the ship could put to sea in an hour's time, and at the same moment arrived a messenger wearing the livery of the duke of Brittany.

"My master, Pierre Landois, the grand treasurer, bade me tell you that your bird has flown," said he; "and he wishes you a safe voyage," he added, tinning to the door, where his horse awaited him.

The bishop did not ask questions; perhaps he thought the less time wasted the better. "We will come on board at once, so that the wind may not shift again," he answered the sailor somewhat hastily; and by noon even the white sails had vanished from sight.

HENRY REMAINED IN THE SANCTUARY till the fever left him, when he returned to the castle of Elvin, which he very seldom left. In a few months events happened which greatly changed his position. Edward IV died, his sons were murdered in the Tower, and the murderer sat on the throne as Richard III. But fierce indignation and horror seized on the people of the southern part of England, and numerous plots were hatched to dispossess the usurper and to crown Henry king, with Elizabeth of York for his wife. For Edward, prince of Wales, the son of Henry VI, had been long dead, having been stabbed on the field of Tewkesbury by the duke of Clarence. One of these plots, concocted by Henry's mother and the duke of Buckingham, seemed so promising that the duke of Brittany agreed to furnish the earl of Richmond with money and ships; but when they put to sea a gale came on, which dispersed the whole fleet. Next morning Henry found himself, with only two vessels, before Poole in Dorset, and noticed with dismay that the shore was strongly guarded by men-of-war.

"Can the conspiracy have been discovered?" thought he. And, alas! the conspiracy *had* been discovered, or, rather, betrayed to Richard, and the duke of Buckingham was lying dead. But though Henry had no means of knowing the truth, experience had taught him caution, and he despatched a small boat, with orders to find out whether the ships were friends or foes. "Friends," was the answer; but Henry still misdoubted, and as soon as it was dark he put about his helm and returned to Brittany.

Feeling quite sure that Richard would never cease from striving to get him into his power, Henry took leave of duke Francis, and sought refuge with Charles VIII, then king of France. In Paris he found many Englishmen, who had either fled from England during the troubles, or "to learn and study good literature and virtuous doctrine," as the chronicler tells us. So, for the first time in his life, Henry was surrounded by his own countrymen, and they did homage to him and swore to sail with him to England in the ships that the regent, Charles's sister, had promised him; while the earl on his side took an oath to do all that in him lay for the peace of the kingdom by marrying Elizabeth of York.

It was on August 1 that Henry and his uncle sailed from Harfleur, and some days later they reached Milford Haven. But somehow or other the news of their coming had flown before them, and a large crowd had assembled to greet them, and the air rang with shouts of joy.

"Thou hast taken good care of *thy* nephew," they said grimly to Jasper, in the familiar Welsh tongue; for it was only the people of the North who still clave to Richard the murderer. But Henry did not linger amongst them, and gathering more men as he went, marched, by way of Shrewsbury and Tamworth, to Leicester. The weather was fine, and they made swift progress, and on the 20th of August, Henry left his camp secretly, and went to meet lord Stanley, his mother's husband, on Atherstone Moor. Their talk lasted long, and, much to Henry's disappointment, Stanley declared that until the battle which was pending was actually in progress, he would be unable to throw in his lot with the Lancastrians, as his son remained as a hostage in the hands of Richard. Henry spent a long while in trying to convince him how necessary was his support; but it was quite useless, and at last he gave it up, and, taking leave of each other, they set out for their own camps. By this time it was quite dark, and as the country was unknown to Henry he soon found himself at a standstill. Richard's scouts lay all about him, and he dared not even ask his way, lest his French accent should betray him. For hours he wandered, looking anxiously for some sign that he was on the right road. At length, driven desperate by fatigue and hunger, he knocked at the door of a small hut, against which he had stumbled by accident. It was opened by an old shepherd, who, without waiting to ask questions, drew him to a bench and set food before him. When he was able to speak, Henry briefly said that he was a stranger who had lost himself on the moor, and begged to be guided back to the Lancastrian camp.

"If I live, I will reward you for it some day," he said; and the old man answered, "I need no reward for such a small service."

When at last the camp was reached the earl was received with joy by his men, who had given up hope, and felt certain that he must have been taken prisoner; but little rest did he get, as preparations for the coming battle had to be made. It was on August 21 that the armies met on the field of Bosworth, and though Henry's force numbered far fewer men than Richard's, the desertion of the Stanleys and their followers won him the day. Among all the Yorkists none fought harder than Richard himself; but in a desperate charge to reach the standard by which Henry stood he was borne down and slain. When the fight was over, and his body sought for, it was found stripped of all its armour, while the crown, which he had worn all day, had been hastily hidden in a hawthorn tree hard by.

"Wear nobly what you have earned fairly," said Stanley, placing the golden circlet on Henry's head, and then bent his knees to do him homage. And on the battlefield itself the army drew up in line and sang a Te Deum.

VIII

The White Rose

In a corner of Westminster, adjoining both the Abbey and the house and garden belonging to the Abbot, there stood in the fifteenth century a fortress founded four hundred years before by Edward the Confessor. It was immensely strong, and could, if needed, withstand the assaults of an army, for it was intended as a harbour of refuge for runaways, and was known by the name of the sanctuary. Once there, a man was safe whatever his crime, for the Church protected him: the sanctuary was a Holy Place. But for a long while the townspeople of London had suffered much from the right of sanctuary thus given to all without distinction. The fortress had become the home of thieves and murderers, who would break into their neighbour's house and steal his goods, or knock a man on the head for the sake of an old grudge or a well-filled purse, sure that, if he were only nimble enough, no one could touch him. "Men's wives run thither with their husbands' plate," writes the duke of Buckingham, "and say they dare not abide with their husbands for beating. These bring thither their stolen goods, and there live thereon. There they devise new robberies; nightly they steal out, they rob and kill, and come in again as though those places gave them not only a safeguard for the harm they have done, but a license also to do more." Most true; yet the sanctuary was sometimes put to other uses, and to those intended by the Church when the great fortress was built. It was a refuge for innocent people who were suspected wrongfully of crimes which they had never committed, and kept them safe from hasty vengeance, till the matter could be tried in a court of law.

Late one evening, however, in the autumn of 1470 the gates of the sanctuary opened to admit a party of fugitives of a very different kind from those who generally sought its shelter. It consisted of a lady nearly forty years of age, her mother, her three little girls, and a gentlewoman, and their faces bore the look of hurry and fear common to all who entered there. When asked their names by the officer whose duty it was to keep a list of those who claimed the sanctuary, the younger lady hesitated for a moment, and then threw back her hood and looked straight at him.

"The queen!" cried he; and the lady answered hurriedly:

"Yes, the queen, and her mother and her children. The Tower was no longer safe, so we have come here."

The officer gazed at her in dismay. Owing to the late disturbances in the city, and the flight of Edward IV to France, things had come to such a pass that no man dared trust his fellow, and when the king's brother was seeking to obtain possession of the king's wife, who could tell if the sanctuary itself would be held sacred? And even if the enemies of the king—and they were many and powerful—dared not bring down on their heads the wrath of the Church by openly forcing their way into the refuge she had granted—well, there were other means of getting the fugitives into their hands, and none could prevent them posting soldiers outside and hindering any food from passing in. Such were the thoughts that flashed through the man's mind as the queen spoke; but he only bowed low, and begged that they would follow him. Taking down a torch from the wall he lit it at the fire, and went before them down a gloomy passage, at the end of which he unlocked the door of a good-sized room, almost bare of furniture, and lighted only by one or two narrow windows, through which a ray of moonlight fell on the floor.

"This is all I can do for to-night, madam," he said; "but to-morrow—" And the queen broke in hastily: "Oh, yes, yes, we are safe at last. Never mind to-morrow."

When the officer had left them, lady Scrope came forward.

"Madam, rest you here, I pray you, and get some sleep, or you will be ill," she whispered softly. "See, I will put these cloaks in this corner, and wrap you in them, and the children shall lie beside you and keep you warm." And with tender hands she forced her mistress to lay herself down, while the old duchess of Bedford held little princess Cicely in her arms. The two elder children stood by her side watching gravely, as well as their sleepy eyes would allow.

THE PRINCESS ELIZABETH WAS AT this time about four and a half, and her sister Mary a year younger. Elizabeth had long yellow hair like her mother, and the beautiful white skin for which the queen was famous, while she had her father's quick wit and high courage. Of all his children she was the one he loved the best, and already she had made her appearance on many public occasions, bearing herself seriously, as a little girl should whose velvet frock has a long train, and who wears on her head a high sloping head-dress shaped like an extinguisher, with a transparent white veil floating from it. Still, children will play, however long their frocks may be, and in the lovely gardens of the palace of Shene, where Elizabeth and her sisters had lived till only a few weeks before, they ran and tumbled about and rolled in the grass as freely and happily as if their dresses had stopped at the knee. But there was little play for them during that dreary winter that they passed in the sanctuary. As the officer had feared, the duke of Clarence, their uncle, and the great earl of Warwick, his father-in-law, surrounded the place, hoping to starve the prisoners into surrender. Once in their power, the two conspirators believed that the king would be forced to accept whatever terms they might choose to dictate. But, luckily for the queen, a friendly butcher took pity on her sad plight, and every week contrived by a secret way to carry "half a beef and two muttons," into the sanctuary, and on this food, and the water from a spring in the vaults, the royal captives lived, sharing their scanty supply with the men who were always in charge of the place.

It was in this dismal fortress that Edward V was born on November 1, 1470. He was small and thin, but his little sisters were delighted to have him, and would kneel by Lady Scrope's side, and play with his hands, and watch his tiny toes closing and unclosing. Sometimes, when he was asleep in his mother's arms, lady Scrope would tell them stories of babies with fairy godmothers, and of the gifts they brought; and then Elizabeth would guess what the fairies might have in store for little Edward. And what excitement there was at his christening in the Abbey, which, as it formed part of the sanctuary, was sacred ground, even though his only godfather was the lord abbot, and his godmothers the duchess of Bedford and lady Scrope. The ceremony was hurried over because, in sanctuary though they were, there was no knowing what might happen; but Elizabeth looked with awe at the high arches and the tombs of the kings, never thinking that she herself would be married before the altar, or be buried in a chapel there that was still unbuilt.

One fine morning, early in March 1471, the children came in from a short walk in the abbot's garden, under the care of lady Scrope. They found their mother pacing impatiently down the dark corridor, smiling at them as she used to do in the happy days before they were hurried away from Shene.

"Your father is back again," she cried; "the men of the North have flocked round him, and now all will be well."

"Then we shall soon be able to leave the sanctuary and go on the river once more!" said little Elizabeth, who had kept her fifth birthday on February 11.

"Yes, yes; and how proud he will be of his son!" exclaimed the queen. And the day was spent in joyful plans for the future.

Some weeks, however, passed by before they either saw king Edward or were able to quit their gloomy dwelling. At last the city of London, which had hitherto hung back, openly declared itself on his side, and yielded up the Tower in which king Henry VI was a prisoner. Then Edward hastened to Westminster Abbey, and after giving thanks for his victory before the altar dedicated to Edward the Confessor, he crossed over to the sanctuary, where, "to his heart's singular comfort and gladness," he at last beheld his wife and children.

"You are the first king who has ever entered sanctuary," said Elizabeth, as she sat on her father's knee. And Edward laughed, and answered that he hoped it was the last time he might ever see it, though it had proved a good friend to them during all the past winter.

AFTER A FEW HARD-FOUGHT BATTLES, England accepted Edward as its king, and until his death, thirteen years after, the royal children had no more hardships to suffer. They lived in rooms of their own in the palace of Westminster, and had carpets on the floors, and tapestry on the walls and beds of down to lie on. For Edward loved everything rich and beautiful, and thought nothing too good for his children. He did not forget John Gould, the butcher, who had saved them from starvation, but rewarded him handsomely for the many "half beeves and muttons" they had eaten in those dreary six months.

Elizabeth's wish had come to pass, and a splendid barge, with eight men to row it, all gaily dressed in fine scarlet cloth, was moored at the foot of the steps at Westminster. Here, when the tide was high, the princesses and lady Scrope used to go on board, and be rowed down to Richmond, which they loved. Or on wet days, when the mist hung thickly about the river, they would gather round lady Scrope, in the queen's withdrawing-room, while she showed them how to play "closheys," a kind of ninepins, or scatter spillikins on a table for the elder children with serious, intent faces, to remove one by one without shaking the rest.

"Elizabeth, Elizabeth! where are you?" cried princess Mary one afternoon, when the rain was pouring down so heavily that you could not see that there was a river at all. "My lady Scrope has some new toys, and will teach us a fresh game. It is called *maritaux*, and the boys play it, and I want to learn it. Be quick, be quick! where *are* you?"

But no Elizabeth came running eagerly to throw the little quoits. Unperceived by her nurse, she had stolen away to that part of the palace where she knew she would find her father, and, creeping softly to the table in front of which he was sitting, she knelt down beside him to ask for his blessing, as the queen had always bidden her. He lifted her on to his knee, and she saw that the open book before him contained strange figures and circles, and that the paper beside it which the king had written was covered with more of these odd marks.

"What does it mean? and why do you look like that?" she asked, half frightened. King Edward did not answer, but, catching up the paper, carried her to a high window, where he set her down in the seat formed by the thickness of the wall. Glancing round, to make sure that none of the men-at-arms who guarded the door could hear him, he bade her hide the paper carefully and keep it always, for it was a map of her destiny which he had cast from the stars, and that they had told him that it was she who would one day wear the English crown. "But my brother—but the prince of Wales?"—asked Elizabeth, who had heard much talk of the baby being heir to the throne.

"I know not," he answered sadly; "but so it is written. Now go back to the queen, and mind, say nought of this, or it will grieve her sorely."

So Elizabeth returned slowly to her own rooms, feeling half afraid and half important with the burden of the secret entrusted to her. She put the paper away in a little box, whose bottom would lift out, given her by her father on her fourth birthday—quite a long time ago! Here she kept all her treasures: a saint's figure, which was a most holy relic, though she could not have told you much about the saint; a lock of hair of her spaniel, which had died at Shene more than a year ago, and the first cap worn by her little brother in the sanctuary, which she had begged from lady Scrope as a remembrance. Then she climbed on to the settle by the fire to place the box on the high mantelshelf, and went to see what her sister was doing. In five minutes she had quite forgotten all that had happened in the absorbing adventures of Beauty and the Beast.

NOT LONG AFTER THIS THE court removed, in litters and on horseback and in strange, long vehicles that looked rather like railway carriages, down to Windsor, in order to give a splendid welcome to the lord of Grauthuse, Louis of Bruges, governor of Holland, in place of his master the duke of Burgundy. And a great reception was no more than his due, in return for his kindness to Edward when he had entered Holland as a fugitive two years before, having sold his long fur-lined coat to pay his passage. Grauthuse has himself left a record of his visit and the gorgeous decorations that everywhere charmed his eye at Windsor, and the beauty of the cloth-of-gold hangings, and the counterpane, edged with ermine, on his bed, while his sheets had come from Rennes, in Brittany, and his curtains were of white silk. He seems to have been given supper as soon as he arrived, in his own apartments, and when he had finished he was escorted by Edward to the queen's withdrawing-room, where she and her ladies were playing games of one kind and another—some at closheys of ivory, some at *martiaux*, some again at cards. They all stopped at the entrance of the king and his guest, and made deep curtseys; but very soon Edward proposed they should go into the ball-room, where a ball was to be held. It was opened by Edward and princess Elizabeth, who danced as solemnly as it was possible for a maiden of six to do. She was allowed one more partner, her uncle the duke of Buckingham, who had married her mother's sister. Then, making her obeisance to her father and mother, to the guest and to the ladies, she went off to bed.

The following morning the prince of Wales, who was a year and a half old, was lifted up by the lord chamberlain, Sir Richard Vaughan, to play his part of welcome to his father's friend; then followed a great dinner, and later a banquet, at which the whole court was present. At nine o'clock the lord of Grauthuse went, attended by lord Hastings, to one of the rooms prepared for him by the queen, in which were two baths, with a tent of white cloth erected over each. When they came out they ate a light supper of green ginger, and sweet dishes, washed down by a sort of ale called hippocras, and after that they went to bed. Grauthuse seems to have stayed some time in England, for he returned with the king and queen to Westminster, and was created earl of Winchester at a splendid ceremony held in the presence of both Lords and Commons. Here the Speaker, William Alington by name, publicly thanked him for "the great kindness and humanity shown to the king in Holland," and praised "the womanly behaviour and constancy of the queen," while her husband was beyond the sea.

Then, highly pleased with his visit, Grauthuse took his leave, bearing with him as a gift from the king a beautiful golden cup inlaid with pearls, having a huge sapphire set in the lid.

FOR THE NEXT THREE YEARS we hear nothing special about the life of the little princesses. Another brother was born to them, and given the name and title of his grandfather Richard duke of York, and there was also a fourth daughter, princess Anne, eight years younger than Elizabeth. The following year, peace being restored at home, Edward IV grew restless at having no fighting to do, and crossed over to France to try to see if there was any chance of regaining some of the former possessions held by the English. But before quitting the country he made a will leaving his two eldest girls 10,000 marks each, which, however, they were to lose if they married without the consent of their mother. Edward IV was a clever man, especially in anything that concerned the trade of the nation; but in Louis XI, then king of France, he met more than his match. It did not suit Louis to have a war with England just then, for he was already fighting his powerful neighbour, Charles the Bold, duke of Burgundy, so he amused Edward by offering to do homage to him for the immense provinces to which the English king laid claim, and to pay tribute for them. Besides, he agreed to betrothe his son Charles to the princess Elizabeth, and likewise consented that part of the tribute money should be set aside for her.

Although she was only now nine years old, this was the fourth time at least that Elizabeth had been offered in marriage. She was scarcely three when Edward, then a prisoner in the hands of the earl of Warwick, proposed an alliance between her and George Neville, Warwick's nephew. The scheme was eagerly accepted by the earl and his two rich and powerful brothers; but Edward contrived to make his escape, and, to the, great wrath of all the Nevilles, nothing further was said on the subject. Indeed, a few months after, a still greater insult was offered to the family by the reckless Edward, for he tried to break off the marriage between Edward prince of Wales, son of Henry VI, and Warwick's young daughter, Lady Anne, by proposing that Elizabeth should take the bride's place. But Margaret of Anjou, the bridegroom's mother, though hating Warwick almost as much as she did her husband's enemy Edward, at length gave her consent to the betrothal, and the wedding was celebrated in the castle of Amboise in the presence of the king of France. And in 1472 we find that, for the first of many times, Elizabeth's hand was offered to Henry of Richmond.

All these things had happened some years before, and now this same king of France was begging for this same Elizabeth as a wife for his son! From the moment that the treaty was signed the young princess was always addressed as "Madame la dauphine." In addition to the lessons in reading and writing given to her and her sisters during these years by "the very best scrivener in the city," Elizabeth was taught to speak and write both French and Spanish. By and bye the dower began to be talked of, and then came the important question of the trousseau. French dresses were ordered for her, all of the latest fashion, and many yards of lace were worked for her stomachers and hanging veils, while the goldsmiths of London vied with each other in drawing designs for jewelled girdles. Suddenly there came from over the sea a rumour that Louis XI had broken his word and the articles of betrothal, and that the bride of the little dauphin was not to be the princess Elizabeth, but the heiress of Burgundy and Flanders, Mary, daughter of Charles the Bold. This news struck Edward dumb with wrath; as for Elizabeth, she only felt happy at being left in England with her brothers and sisters, and did not in the least mind when everyone ceased calling her "Madame la dauphine," and began to treat her as a little girl instead of as a grown-up woman. She continued to be the companion of her father and mother, and went on with her lessons as before, though it was now certain that she would never be queen of France. After a while there was talk of another wedding in the family, and this time the bridegroom was the duke of York, little Richard, who was not yet five years old, while the bride, Anne Mowbray, heiress of Norfolk, was but three. Of course such marriages were common enough, as Elizabeth could have told you; but, even then, such a very young bridegroom was seldom seen, and his sisters made merry over it.

"Fancy Richard a married man!" they would say, dancing in front of him. "Oh, how wise he will be; we shall all have to ask counsel of him." And Richard, half pleased with his importance and half ashamed, though why he did not know, bade them "Begone," or burst into tears of anger. His brother Edward, who was more than six, felt a little bewildered. He was a quiet, gentle child, but from his birth he had been brought forward, yet now no one thought of anything but Richard, and Edward was not quite sure how he ought to behave. However, by the time the wedding-day came, a bright frosty morning in January 1477, he had grown used to this strange state of things, and was as excited as the rest.

A large crowd was assembled before the palace door, for then, as now, the people loved to see a royal wedding, and the citizens of London liked well Edward and his family. Loud cheers greeted the king and his children as they rode across the open space on beautiful long-tailed horses with splendid velvet saddles. Louder still were the cheers that greeted the queen as she came forth, with the bridegroom on a pony of bright bay with light blue velvet trappings, ambling by her side. Loudest of all was the greeting given to the bride as she appeared, seated on the smallest white creature that ever was seen, led by Lord Rivers, the queen's brother.

"It is a fair sight indeed," murmured the women, and these words came back to them six years later.

THE MARRIAGE WAS CELEBRATED IN St. Stephen's chapel, and as no one ever thought in those days of heating churches, the stone walls were covered with hangings of cloth of gold, which made it a little warmer. The king arrived first, with the prince of Wales, clad in a blue velvet tunic bordered with ermine, on his right hand, and princess Elizabeth, in a long dress of silver tissue, on his left. Mary and Cicely walked behind, and they were followed by the great officers of state and the ladies of the court. After they had taken their places the heralds sounded their trumpets, and in came the queen, wearing a tight-fitting gown of white velvet, with an ermine mantle, her golden hair hanging to her feet, from under the high head-dress with its floating veil. She led by the hand the noble bridegroom, who looked shy and frightened, and stared straight before him, as he walked up the aisle, his face nearly as white as his heavy mantle which glittered with diamonds. The bride, on the contrary, who was conducted by lord Rivers, seemed quite composed and looked about her, taking care not to trip over the skirt of her trailing white satin dress, whose hem shone with diamonds and pearls. The princesses in their seats watched her with approval.

"She could not have borne herself better had her father been a king," they whispered one to another. "I would that Richard had carried himself as well," added Elizabeth, who, being six years older, felt something of a mother to him. Then the bishops and priests took their places, and the service began.

Shouts of "Long live the bride and bridegroom!" "Health and happiness to the duke and duchess of York!" rent the air as the procession left the chapel to attend the banquet laid out in the Painted Chamber. Great pasties were there for those that liked them, cranes, curlews, and bitterns—which would have seemed very odd food to us, and all very difficult to eat without forks, of which they had none. At the top and bottom were peacocks with their tails spread, beautiful to behold. But what pleased the children best were the "subleties," as they were then called—sweet things built up into towers, and ships, and other strange shapes. And the largest and finest of all, a castle with a moat and drawbridge, and surrounded by battlements defended by tiny men-at-arms, was placed in front of the bride and bridegroom.

FOR THE NEXT FIVE YEARS the lives of the princesses went on quietly enough. Two more daughters were born, Katherine, in 1479, and Bridget, who afterwards became a nun, in 1480. But troubles of many sorts were hard at hand. In 1482 Elizabeth lost her sister Mary, who had been her companion and playfellow all through their eventful childhood, and before she had recovered from this bitter grief the state of the king's health caused much alarm. Though a brave soldier and a good general, and capable in time of war of enduring hardships as well as the poorest churl who fought for him, Edward loved soft lying and good eating, which ended in his ruin. He grew indolent and fat, and his temper, which had never recovered the slight put upon him by Louis XI in the breaking off of the dauphin's marriage, became more and more moody. At length a low fever came upon him, and he had no strength to rally. Knowing that death was at hand he sent for his old friends Stanley and Hastings, and implored them to make peace with the queen and to protect his children from their enemies. The vows he asked were taken, but ill were they kept. Then the king died, acknowledging the many sins and crimes of which he had been guilty, and praying for pardon.

During nine hours on that same day (April 9, 1483) the king's body, clad in purple velvet and ermine, was exposed to view, and the citizens of London, headed by the lord mayor, came sadly to look upon it, so as to bear witness, if need be, that it was Edward and none other that lay there dead. When the procession of people was finished bishops and priests took their places, and repeated the Psalms from beginning to end, while all through the hours of darkness knights clad in black watched and prayed. As soon as the preparations were completed, the dead king was put on board a barge draped in black, and rowed down to Windsor, as, for reasons that we do not know, he was buried in St. George's chapel, instead of at Westminster. It is curious that his son Edward, now thirteen, was not allowed to come up from Ludlow Castle, where he had been living for some time with lord Rivers, neither is there any mention of Richard attending his father's funeral. His stepsons were there, but not his sons, and the chief mourner was his nephew the earl of Lincoln. Never were people more helpless than the queen and her children. The poor queen knew not whom to trust, and indeed a few weeks taught her that she could trust nobody. Gloucester, her brother-in-law, who at first gained her faith with a few kind words, soon tore off the mask, seized the young king, and arrested his uncle lord Rivers.

"Edward is a prisoner, and I cannot deliver him! And what will become of us?" cried the queen, turning to her eldest daughter; and Elizabeth, whom these last few months had made a woman older than her seventeen years, answered briefly: "There is still the sanctuary where we are safe."

That evening, after dark, the queen, her five daughters, and Richard, duke of York, stole out of the palace of Westminster into the shelter of the abbot's house, which fortunately lay within the sanctuary precincts. All night long the dwelling, usually so quiet, was a scene of bustle and confusion, for every moment servants were arriving from the palace at Westminster bearing with them great chests full of jewels, clothes, hangings, and carpets. The princesses, who were for the most part young children, were running about, excitedly ordering the arrangement of their own possessions, while Richard the "married man," had quietly fallen asleep in a corner on a heap of wall-hangings that happened to have been set down there. So it was that the archbishop and lord chancellor, who arrived long after midnight to deliver up the Great Seal to the queen, in trust for Edward V, found her alone, seated on a heap of rushes in the old stone hall, "desolate and dismayed," as the chronicler tells us. The archbishop tried to cheer her with kind words and promises of a fair future, but the queen had suffered too much in the past to pay much heed to him. "Desolate" she was indeed, and "dismayed" she well might be, and in his heart the archbishop knew it, and he sighed as he looked at her hopeless face set in the tight widow's bands, while her hair, still long and golden in spite of her fifty years, made patches of brightness over her sombre black clothes. Yet he could not leave her without making one more effort to rouse her from her sad state, so again he spoke, though the poor woman scarcely seemed to know that he was in the room at all.

"Madam, be of good comfort. If they crown any other king than your eldest son whom they have with them, we will, on the morrow, crown his brother whom you have with you here. And here is the Great Seal, which in like wise as your noble husband gave it to me, so I deliver it to you for the use of your son." Having done his mission, the archbishop departed to his own house close to the Abbey. The May dawn was already breaking, and as he looked on the river he saw the shore thronged with boats full of Gloucester's men, ready to pounce on the queen did she but leave the sanctuary by a foot. "Poor thing! poor thing!" murmured the archbishop, as he gazed, "it is an ill life she has before her. I doubt what will come of it."

Still, unhappy though they were, the royal family were at first far better off in the abbot's house than they had been thirteen years before in the fortress itself. The rooms were more numerous and better furnished, and it was summer, and the flowers in the garden were springing up, and the air began to be sweet with early roses. Up and down the green paths paced Elizabeth and her sister Cicely, talking over the events of the last month, and of all that had happened since the death of their father.

"If only Edward were here," said princess Cicely, "I for one should dread nothing. But to think of him in my uncle Gloucester's power—ah! the world may well ask which is king and which is prince!"

"Yes, since Gloucester broke his promise to the council to have him crowned on the fourth of May my heart is ever fearful," answered Elizabeth; "of little avail was it to bring him clothed in purple and ermine through the city when he was surrounded by none but followers of the Boar"—for such was the duke's device. "I misdoubt me that he will not long be left in the palace of the good bishop of Ely." Then both sisters fell silent for a long time.

Elizabeth had reason for what she said, for the next day came the tidings that Gloucester had carried his nephew to the Tower, there to await his coronation. The queen turned white and cold when the message was brought to her, but worse was yet to come. At a council held in the Star Chamber, presided over by Gloucester, it was decided that as children could commit no crime they could need no sanctuary, and that therefore the duke of Gloucester, as acting regent, might withdraw his nephew Richard from his mother's care whenever he chose. A deputation

ANDREW LANG AND LEONORA BLANCHE LANG

of peers, headed by the cardinal archbishop of Canterbury waited on the queen to try to prevail on her to give up her boy, saying the king was wishful of a playfellow, but it was long before she would give her consent. She had no reason to love the lord protector, she said, who had ever shown himself ungrateful for all the late king had done for him; but at length she began to yield to the solemn assurances of the cardinal that the boy's life was safe.

"Pray His Highness the duke of York to come to the Jerusalem Chamber"—the words, though spoken by the queen, seemed to be uttered in a different voice from hers, and there was silence for some minutes till the white-faced, sickly boy, clothed in black velvet, walked up to his mother. "Here is this gentleman," said she, presenting him to the cardinal. "I doubt not he would be kept safely by me if I were permitted. The desire of a kingdom knoweth no kindred; brothers have been brothers' bane, and may the nephews be sure of the uncle? Notwithstanding, I here deliver him, and his brother with him, into your hands, and of you I shall ask them before God and the world. Faithful ye be, I wot well, and power ye have if ye list, to keep them safe, but if ye think I fear too much, beware ye fear not too little." So Richard bade her farewell—a farewell that was to be eternal. He was taken straight away to the Star Chamber, where Gloucester awaited him, and embraced him before them all. That night they lay at the bishop's palace close to St. Paul's, and the next day he rode by his uncle's side through the city to the Tower.

Sore were the hearts of the poor prisoners in the sanctuary, and little heed did they take of the preparations in the Abbey for Edward's coronation. In vain the kindly persons about them sought to reassure the queen and her daughters by dwelling on the orders given for the food at the royal banquet, and on the number of oxen to be roasted whole in the space before the palace.

"Banquet there may be, and coronation there may be," was all the queen would answer; "but Richard will never eat of that food, and Edward will never wear that crown."

Blow after blow fell thick and fast. Everything that Gloucester could invent to throw discredit on the queen and her family was heaped upon her, and as Clarence had not feared to blot his mother's fair fame, so Gloucester did not hesitate to cast mud on that of his brother Edward's wife. Then, one day, the abbot sought an audience of the princess Elizabeth.

"Madame, I dare not tell the queen," said he, staring at the ground as he spoke. "But—but—the king has been deposed, and the lord protector declared king in his stead!"

Elizabeth bowed her head in silence—it was no more than she had expected, and she awaited in the strength of despair what was to follow. It was not long in coming. Ten days later Richard III was crowned in the Abbey with great splendour, and her brothers removed to the Portcullis Tower and deprived of their attendants. Edward at least knew full well what all this meant. "I would mine uncle would let me have my life though I lose my kingdom," he said to the gentleman who came to inform him of the duke of Gloucester's coronation; but from that moment he gave up all hope, and "with that young babe his brother lingered in thought and heaviness."

Who can describe the grief and horror of the fugitives in the sanctuary when all that they had feared had actually come to pass? The queen was like one mad, and though her elder daughters did all they could to tend and soothe her, their own sorrow was deep, and the dread was ever present with them that, as children had been declared unfit persons to inhabit the sanctuary, there was nothing to hinder the usurper from seizing on them if he thought fit. And to whom could they turn for counsel or comfort? Only three months had passed since the death of king Edward, yet his sons, his step-son, and his brother-in-law, had all been slain by the same hand. The queen's other son by her first husband, the marquis of Dorset, was in Yorkshire, trying to induce the people to rebel against the tyrant, but few joined his standard; the insurrection planned by her brother-in-law, the duke of Buckingham, in the West came to nothing, while the leader was betrayed and executed. They had no money, and it is quite possible that Richard contrived that the abbot should have none to give them. The trials and privations of the winter of 1469 were light in comparison to those they suffered in that of 1483, for now they were increased by agony of mind and every device that could be invented by cruelty. What wonder, then, that, not knowing where to look for help, the queen should at last have consented to make terms with her enemy?

So, in March, 1484, she lent an unwilling ear to Richard's messenger, but refused absolutely to quit the sanctuary till the king had sworn, in the presence of his council, of the lord mayor and of the aldermen of the city of London, that the lives of herself and her children should be spared. Even Richard dared not break that oath, for there were signs that the people were growing weary of so much blood, and, in London especially, the memory of Edward was still dear to the citizens. Therefore he had to content himself with depriving the queen of the title which she had borne for twenty years, and of hinting at a previous marriage of Edward IV. She was, besides, put under charge of one of Richard's officers, who spent as he thought fit the allowance of 700*l.* a year voted for her by Parliament. It is not very certain where she lived, but most likely in some small upper rooms of the palace of Westminster, where she had once dwelt in splendour and reigned as queen. During the first few months she seems to have had her four elder daughters with her—Bridget was probably in the convent of Dartford, where she later became a nun; but after the death of his son, Edward, Richard sent for them to court. Their cousin, Anne of Warwick, the queen, received them with great kindness, and together they all wept over the sorrows that had befallen them. Richard himself took but little notice of them, except to invent projects of marriage between Elizabeth and more than one private gentleman—rather for the sake of wounding her pride than because he meant seriously to carry them through. At Christmas, however, it was necessary to hold some state festivals, and both Anne and the princesses put off their mourning and attended the state banquets and balls which the king had ordered to be held in Westminster Hall. It was Anne's last appearance before her death, three months later, and it was remarked by all present that the queen had caused Elizabeth to be dressed like herself, in gold brocade, which marvellously became the princess, and with her bright hair and lovely complexion she must have made a strong contrast to the dying queen.

While at court Elizabeth met and made friends with the lord high steward, Stanley, the second husband of the countess of Richmond. This lady, who had desired for years to see her son Henry married to princess Elizabeth, had been exiled from court owing to her numerous plots to this end; but Richard thought that the best means of keeping Stanley loyal was to retain him about his person, as he was too useful to be put to death. One night, however, a fresh thought darted into the king's brain. Henry of Richmond was his enemy; the Lancastrian party in England was growing daily, owing as Richard told himself quite frankly, to the number of people he had felt obliged to execute. If Henry married Elizabeth he would gain over to his side a large number of Yorkists, and together they might prove too strong for him. But suppose *he*, the king, was to marry the "heiress of England," as her father loved to call her, would not *that* upset all the fine plans that were for ever being hatched? True, he was her uncle; but a dispensation from the Church was easily bought, and in Spain these things were done every day. So Richard went to bed delighted with his own cleverness.

Great was Elizabeth's horror when the rumour reached her ears, told her by one of queen Anne's ladies. "Never, never will I consent to such wickedness," cried she, and sent off a trusty messenger to Stanley to tell him of this fresh plot by her brothers' murderer, and to entreat his help. This Stanley agreed to give, though insisting that the utmost caution and secrecy were necessary, for any imprudence would cost them all their lives. He next induced Elizabeth to write herself to his powerful brothers, and to others of his kinsmen, and despatched these letters by the hand of one of his servants. The Stanleys all agreed to join the conspiracy against Richard, provided that the princess should marry Henry, earl of Richmond, thus uniting the two Roses, and to discuss this a meeting was arranged in London. That night, when all was still, Elizabeth noiselessly left her room in Westminster Palace, and stole down a narrow stone staircase to a door which was opened for her by the sentry, who had served under her father. At a little distance off one of Stanley's men was awaiting her with a horse, and together they rode through byways till they reached an old inn on the outskirts of the city, towards the north. They stopped at a door with an eagle's claw chalked on it, and on entering she found herself in a room with about a dozen gentlemen, who bowed low at the sight of her.

"Let us do our business in all haste," said Stanley, "as time presses." And he began shortly to state his scheme for sending Humphrey Brereton over to France bearing a ring of Elizabeth's as a token of his truth, and likewise a letter, which she was to write, telling of the proposal that the Houses of York and Lancaster should be united in marriage, and that Henry should be king. But here Elizabeth held up her hand, and, looking at the men standing round her, she said steadily:

"Will you swear, my lords, by Holy Church that you mean no ill to the noble earl, but that you bid him come hither in all truth and honour?"

"Ah, verily, Madam, we swear it," answered they, "for our own sakes as well as for his."

"Then the letter and the ring shall be ready to-morrow night," replied Elizabeth, "and shall be delivered to you by lord Stanley. And now, my lords, I will bid you farewell." And, attended as before by a solitary horseman, with a beating heart she made her way back to the palace.

Only when safe in her own room did she breathe freely; and well might she fear, for had Richard guessed her absence, short would have been her shrift.

As it was the conspirators were just in time. Somehow or other the news of the king's intended marriage with his niece leaked out, and so deep was the disgust of the people that Richard saw that his crown would not be safe for a single day if he were to persist. So, in order to appease his subjects, as well as to avenge himself on Elizabeth for her ill-concealed hatred of him, he dismissed her from court, and despatched her under a strong guard to the castle of Sheriff Hutton in Yorkshire, where the owner, her cousin, the young earl of Warwick, was then living. Oh! how thankful Elizabeth was to escape from London, and to know that hundreds of miles lay between her and her persecutor. To be sure, her mother and sisters were still there; but it was she, and not they, whose life was in danger, for had it not been foretold that the crown of England should rest on her head? What peace it was to roam in the castle gardens, or to sit by the window of her little room embroidering strange devices, or looking out on the broad moorland where the larks and thrushes sang all day long! Only one thing spoiled her content, and that was anxiety as to how the messenger had sped who had gone over the seas to the earl of Richmond.

That tale has been told in another place, and how king Henry sent an escort, after the battle of Bosworth, to bring his future queen to London. As she rode along, under summer skies, the nobles and people thronged to meet her and do homage, and at length the happy day came when openly and fearlessly she could join her mother in Westminster Palace. It was no light task to settle things in England after a strife which had lasted for thirty years; and besides, a terrible plague, known as the Sweating Sickness, was raging in London, so it was not till January 18, 1486, a month before Elizabeth's twentieth birthday, that the much-talked-of marriage took place. The papal legate, a cousin of Elizabeth's, performed the ceremony in the Abbey, and London, which had so long looked forward to the event, celebrated it with banquets and bonfires—rather dangerous in a city whose houses were mostly of wood. "By which marriage," says the chronicler, "peace was thought to descend out of heaven into England."

And there we leave Elizabeth, her childhood being over.

IX

RICHARD THE FEARLESS

Nearly a thousand years ago a little boy was living in a castle which stood on the edge of a lake in the midst of a very large forest. We should have to go a long way nowadays before we could find any so big; but then there were fewer people in Europe than at present, and so for the most part the wild animals were left undisturbed. In the forest that surrounded the lake, which from the stillness of its waters was called Morte-mer, or the Dead Sea, there were plenty of bears, besides boars and deer. Of course, from time to time the lord of the castle, William Longsword, whose father Rollo had come from over the seas to settle in Normandy, called his friends and his men round him, and had a great hunt, which lasted two or three days. Then everyone in the castle would be busy, some in taking off the skins of the animals and hanging them out to dry, before turning them into coverings for the beds or floors, or coats to wear in the long cold winter; while others cut up the meat and salted it, so that they might never lack food. In summer the skins were rolled up and put away, and instead rushes were cut from the neighbouring swamps—for around the Morte-mer not even rushes would grow—and silk hangings were hung from the walls or the ceilings, instead of deer skins, and occasionally a rough box planted with wild roses or honeysuckle might be seen standing in a corner of the great hall.

But when little Richard was not much more than a year old a dreadful thing happened to him. As often occurred in those days, duke William sent away his wife, Richard's mother, who was poor and low-born, in order to marry a noble lady called Liutgarda, whose father, the rich and powerful count of Vermandois, might be of use in the wars which William was always carrying on with somebody. Although Liutgarda had no children of her own, she hated Richard, and never rested till she had prevailed on her husband to send him away to the palace of Fécamp, where he was born. William, though fickle and even treacherous to his friends, was fond of his little boy, and for a long while he refused to listen to anything Liutgarda said; but when he was leaving home he suddenly bethought him that the child might be safer if he were removed from the hands of the duchess, so he pretended to agree to her proposal. Summoning before him the three men in whom he had most faith, Botho, count of Bayeux, Oslac, and Bernard the Dane, he placed Richard in their care, and bade them to take heed to the child and teach him what it was fitting he should learn.

We know little of Richard's early childhood, but it was probably passed in just the same manner as that of other young princes of his day. We may be sure that his guardians, all mighty men of valour, saw that he could sit a kicking horse and shoot straight at a mark. Besides these sports, Botho, who loved books himself, had him taught to read, and even to write—rare accomplishments in those times—and on the whole Richard was very happy, and never troubled himself about the future.

After eight years of this peaceful life a change came. Long before his guardians had been obliged to leave him, and others, chosen by William with equal care, had taken their place. One morning the boy came in from spending an hour at shooting at a mark, and ran up proudly to tell his old tutor, who was sitting in the hall, that he had eight times hit the very centre of the target, and that his hand shook so from pulling his bow that he was sure he could not guide his reed pen that day.

"Say you so?" answered the old man, smiling, for he knew the heart of a boy, "well, there is something else for you to do. Your father, Richard," he continued, his face growing grave, "is very ill, and has sent to fetch you to him."

"My father!" said Richard, his face flushing with excitement at the prospect of a journey, "where is he? Where am I to go? And who will take me? Is he at Rouen?"

"No, at Chévilly, and we start in an hour, after we have dined, and I will take you myself," was the answer; and Richard hastened away, full of importance, to make his preparations. He was not at all a hard-hearted little boy, but he had not seen his father for four years, and remembered little about him.

William Longsword was lying in his bed when Richard entered the small dark room, only lighted by two blazing torches, and by a patch of moonlight which fell on the rush-strewn stone floor. In the shadow stood three men, and as the boy glanced at them he made a spring towards one and held out his hands.

"Ah, he loves you better than me, Botho," gasped William in a hoarse voice, between the stabs of pain that darted through his lungs. "Take off his clothes, and let us see if his body is straight and strong as that of a duke of Normandy should be." Yes, he was tall and straight-limbed enough, there was no doubt of that! His skin was fair, as became one of the Viking race, and his eyes were blue and his hair shone like gold. His father looked at him with pride, but all he said was:

"Listen to me, boy! My life is nearly done, but I am so weary that I cannot even wait till it is over before giving up my ducal crown to you. I have done many ill deeds, but my people have loved me, for I have defended the poor and given justice to all. I can say no more now; take his hands in yours and swear!" Then the three men clad in armour knelt before the boy, and one by one, taking his hands in theirs, they swore the oath of obedience. The duke watched eagerly, and when the ceremony was over he motioned them all to leave him, murmuring in a low voice, "To-morrow."

The following day William was a little better. He had taken the first step towards Richard's inauguration as duke of Normandy, and his mind was more at ease. The ceremony itself was to take place on Whit-Sunday, May 29, 942, and was to be held at Bayeux, where the boy was to live. For the duke wished his son to be brought up in the full knowledge of the Danish language and customs, and Bayeux was the one city in the whole of Normandy where the old tongue was spoken and the pagan religion prevailed. At the same time he was to learn the best French of the day, that of the court of the king Louis d'Outre Mer—Louis from Beyond the Seas—and to be properly educated in the Christian faith. To this end no man was so suitable as Richard's former tutor, Botho, count of Bayeux, a man of renown both as a scholar and a warrior, and who, though a Dane by birth, had become a Christian and had adopted French ways.

By slow stages William made the journey to Bayeux, his son riding by the side of his tutor, chattering merrily all the way. In obedience to his summons, all the nobles and chieftains from Normandy and Brittany were assembled there, and met him on the day appointed in the great hall of the castle. In spite of his illness, from which he had by no means recovered, William was a splendid figure as he sat on a carved chair placed on the dais, with the ducal crown upon his head, and looked down on the stalwart men gathered before him. By his side stood Richard in a green tunic, a small copy of his father, and he faced them with a smile in his eyes, till their hearts went out to him. Amidst a dead silence, William rose to his feet.

"I cannot speak much," he said, "for I have been sick unto death, but I have brought here my young son, to bid you accept him as your duke in my stead, and to tell you the plans I have made for his guidance, while he is still a boy. He will live here at Bayeux, and will learn the lore of his forefathers, and three good men and true, Botho, Oslac, and Bernard the Dane, have the care of him, as before in his early years. Besides them, seven other nobles will give counsel. This is my wish. Will you swear to abide by it, and to take the oath of fealty to your new duke?"

"We swear," they cried with one voice, and then each man in turn took Richard's hand in his, and did homage. Then father and son bid each other farewell, for William must needs go on other business.

After this wonderful scene, in which he had played so important a part, life felt for a while somewhat tame to Richard, and at first he was rather inclined to give himself airs of authority and to refuse obedience to Botho. The count of Bayeux was not, however, a person to put up with behaviour of this sort, and in a short time Richard was learning his lessons and shooting and fishing as diligently as before. But this state of things did not last long. One evening a man-at-arms rode up on a tired horse and demanded speech of Bernard the Dane. It was a sad story he had to tell; duke William had been bidden, as all men already knew, on a certain day to meet king Louis at Attigny, in order to answer some charges of murder which had been made against him. It was the custom to allow three days of grace on account of the accidents that were apt to befall travellers in those rough times, but the appointed hour was past when William rode up to the castle, and found the door closed against him. Furious at being shut out, he ordered his men to force an entrance, and, striding up to the dais, dragged his enemy Otho of Germany from the throne by the side of the king, and beat him soundly. Of course, such an insult to the ally of the king of France could not be passed over, but instead of punishing it openly, William was entrapped into going to an island in the middle of the river, and there murdered.

At this news all Normandy was in an uproar, for, as has been said, William's subjects loved him well and grieved for him deeply; and by none was he more sorely mourned than by his cast-off wife Espriota, who had for these few past months been living near her son, and had seen him occasionally. But this was now at an end, for Richard was at once removed by his guardians to the palace of Rouen, there to attend his father's burial and his own coronation, which was in its way as important an event as that of the king of France, who had but little territory or power in comparison with some of his great nobles.

When the young duke reached Rouen he found that his father's body had been removed from the palace whither it had been taken after his murder, and was lying in state in the cathedral of Notre Dame, with the famous long sword, from which he had gained his nickname, on his breast. The grave had been dug close by, opposite to his father Rollo's, the first duke and conqueror of Normandy, and beside it was an empty place, where Richard guessed that he would some day rest. The cathedral was crowded that morning, and many thoughts of love and pity were given, not only to the dead man, but to the fair-haired boy of nine who stood by the bier, not overcome with grief for the father whom he had scarcely seen, but awed and a little bewildered at what would be expected of him. All through the long service Richard stood still, now and then gazing wonderingly at the multitude which filled the body of the cathedral. Then, after the coffin had been lowered into the grave, the great doors were thrown open, and he was led forward by Bernard and presented to his subjects, Normans, Bretons, and Danes, who welcomed him with a shout. The priest next came slowly down the chancel, and Richard, kneeling before him, received his blessing, and swore as far as in him lay to preserve peace to the Church and to the people, to put down tyranny, and to rule justly. Rising to his feet, the ring of sovereignty was put on his finger and the sword of government buckled to his side; then, taking his stand before the sacred shrine, the book of the Gospels being held by a priest on his left hand, and the Holy Rood or Cross by another on his right, he waited for the chiefs and nobles to take the oath of loyalty to him.

Now it was plain to all men that troubles were nigh at hand for the duchy. "Woe to the land whose king is a child" it is written in Scripture, and Richard's wise councillors knew full well what they might expect from king Louis. They met together the night after the funeral, when the little duke, worn out by all he had gone through, was fast asleep, and consulted together how they could get the better of king Louis, and at last they decided that they would escort Richard without delay to Compiègne, where the king then was, and induce Louis to invest him at once with the duchy. No time was lost in putting this plan into execution; but even Norman cleverness was no match for the wiliness of the king. Blinded by their kind reception and by flattering words, they awoke one day to find that they had taken the oath of fealty to Louis as their immediate overlord, and thus it was he, and not Richard, whom they were bound to obey. Deeply ashamed of themselves, they returned with their charge to Rouen; but during their short absence the Danish party, headed by Thermod, had obtained the upper hand, and soon got possession of Richard himself, even persuading the boy to renounce Christianity and declare himself a pagan. This of course gave the chance for which Louis had been hoping. It was, he said, a duty he owed both to the Church and to Richard to put a stop to such backsliding, and forthwith he marched straight to the capital. After several skirmishes, in one of which Thermod the Dane was killed, Louis entered Rouen as a conqueror, and under pretext of protection took Richard into his own custody, and proceeded to administer the laws.

Perhaps if Louis from Beyond the Seas had been brought up in France he would have known better the sort of people he had to deal with; but when he was a little child his mother had been forced to fly with him to the court of his grandfather Athelstan, where he had grown up, learning many things, but not much of his subjects, several of whom were far more powerful than he. To these Normans, or Northmen of Danish blood, and to the Bretons, who were akin to the Welsh, the king of France, though nominally their sovereign, was really as much a foreigner as Otho of Germany. *He* was not going to rule them, and that he would soon find out! So one day they appeared before the palace and demanded their duke, and as he was not given up to them they broke into open revolt, and not only gained possession of Richard, but made Louis himself prisoner. In this manner the tables were turned: Richard was once more duke in his own duchy, and Louis was kept in strict confinement till he swore to Bernard the Dane to restore to Normandy the rights which had been forfeited at Compiègne. But even so the boy's guardians had not learned wisdom, for in spite of what had happened before they were persuaded by Louis on some slight pretext to allow him to carry Richard back to the royal town of Laon, and once there he was instantly placed, with Osmond a Norman noble, under arrest in the tower.

By this time, 944, Richard was eleven years old, and the strange life he had led since his father died had ripened him early. On many occasions when his life had been in peril he had shown not only great courage but self-control beyond his age. Danger he delighted in, it only excited him; but in the tower of Laon time hung heavy on his hands, for he was forbidden to go outside the walls, and he was growing weak and languid from want of exercise. Great, therefore, was his delight when one morning at the hour that Louis sat in judgment on the cases brought by his people, his guardian Osmond came to tell him that he had two horses standing at a small gate at the back of the courtyard, and would take him out for a day's hawking.

"How delicious!" cried Richard, springing up out of the deep seat of the window, from which he had been looking longingly over the country. "Has the king given leave, then, or shall we go without it?"

"Without it," answered Osmond with rather an odd smile. "It may not reach his ears, or if it does he can hardly slay us for it."

"Oh, never mind!" said Richard again, "what matters it? I would give twenty lives for a good gallop once more," and following Osmond down the winding staircase, they reached the postern door unseen. The autumn evening was fast closing in when they returned, Richard full of excitement and pleasure over his day's sport. Osmond, however, was not quite so light-hearted. He knew that he had done wrong in tempting the boy out, and he feared the consequences. Well he might! The wrath of Louis was fearful at finding that his birds had flown, and messengers had been sent in all directions to capture them. In his anger he threatened to kill them both, and his rash words were carried far and wide; but, as Osmond knew, he dared not for his own sake carry out his threat, though he could and did make their captivity even more irksome than before, and much they needed the constant prayers offered up for them in Rouen. Things would have been still worse than they were had not Osmond, fortunately, been a man of some learning, and for some hours every day he taught the young duke all he knew. By and bye the severity of the rule was slightly relaxed, and Richard was bidden to perform the duties of a page, and wait at dinner on Louis and his queen Gerberga. This on the whole pleased Richard, though he felt that he ought to consider it an outrage to his dignity; but at any rate it was a change, and it showed him something of the life of courts, though, as matters were, it did not seem very likely that he would ever govern one!

The weather was very wet, and the rain stood in great pools about the courtyard and in the country outside the castle. The damp told upon Richard's health, which had already been weakened by his long captivity, and at last he was too ill to rise from his bed. Osmond nursed him carefully, and by the king's order better food was given him, so that he

ANDREW LANG AND LEONORA BLANCHE LANG

soon began to show signs of mending; but his guardian was careful that he should not get well too soon, for he had made a plan of escape, and the more the boy was believed incapable of moving the less he would be watched, and the easier it would be to carry out. So when the seneschal of the castle or the king's steward came to make inquiries for the noble prisoner, Richard would turn his head slowly and languidly, and answer the questions put to him in a soft, tired voice.

"The young duke looks in ill case," the man would report, "and I misdoubt me"—and then he would stop and shake his head, while the king nodded in answer. Such was the state of affairs when one day it was announced that a huge banquet would be held in the castle of Laon, at which the queen would be present. Great preparations were made in the courtyard, and cooks and scullions and serving-men kept running to and fro. Richard spent all his time at the window, watching the excitement, but on the morning of the feast, when the seneschal paid his daily visit, he was lying on the bed, hardly able to answer, as it seemed, the questions put to him.

"To-night is our time," said Osmond when they were once more alone.

"Time for what?" asked Richard, who had obeyed, without knowing why, the orders of his guardian to appear more ill than ever.

"Our time to escape from this den of thieves," replied Osmond. "I would not tell you before, for the eyes of Raoul the seneschal are sharp, and I feared lest yours should be brighter than need be. But eat well of what is set before you, for you will want all your strength."

"But how shall we pass the sentries?" asked Richard again.

"Ah, how?" said Osmond, laughing. "Never puzzle your brain, but what has been done once can be done twice"; and that was all he would tell him.

Hours were earlier then than now, and by seven o'clock there was not a creature to be seen in the passages or before the gates, for all who had not been bidden to the banquet were amusing themselves in the guard-room, quite safe from any detection by their masters. Then Osmond, wrapped in a thick cloak, beckoned to Richard, and they crept across the courtyard, most of which lay in shadow, till they reached the barn where the hay was kept. There Osmond took down a large truss, and tying it securely round Richard hoisted the bundle on to his back.

"Whatever happens, make no noise," he whispered hurriedly, and stepped out into the moonlight that lay between the barn and the stables.

Here was the only danger, for he might be spied by one of the men in the guardroom, and even be stopped if he or his bundle looked suspicious. A voice from behind gave him such a start that he almost dropped his hay; but the man was too drunk to see clearly, and a timely jest satisfied him that Osmond was an old comrade, and was only doing the work of a friend who was too busy feeding himself to have leisure to think of his horses. His heart still beating high, Osmond reached the stable, and, choosing a lean black horse, he put on it both saddle and bridle, and led it out by a side door, which opened out on a dark muddy street. Rapidly he cut with his hunting knife the rope which had bound the hay, and flung it into a corner.

"You must sit in front of me," he said, lifting Richard on to the saddle. Then, jumping up behind him, he wrapt his big cloak round the boy, till nothing could be seen of him. Carefully they went till the town was passed, when Osmond shook the reins, and the horse bounded away in the night.

"Where are we going?" asked Richard at last, after they had ridden for several miles.

"To Couci," answered Osmond, "and there I will leave you in safety with a friend of your father's, while I will get a fresh horse and ride on to your great uncle count Bernard at Senlis."

Fierce was the wrath of the king when the seneschal awoke him early next morning with the news that Richard's room in the tower was empty, and that both Osmond and the horse Fierbras were gone.

"But how—how did he do it?" asked the king, when he had somewhat recovered the power of speech. "For none could reach the stable without passing first under the windows of the guardroom, and besides the moon was at the full, and a man and a boy would be noted by all the sentries?"

"Yes, my lord, doubtless," replied the trembling seneschal; "and truly a man was seen and challenged by one of the soldiers, but no boy was with him. He was going to feed the horses, and he had on his back a truss of hay."

"*Ah!*" exclaimed the king, starting to his feet, and fell to silence, for through the years there came to him the remembrance of how his mother Ogiva had borne him out of reach of his enemies in a truss of hay. Truly, what had been done once could be done twice, as Osmond the Norman had said!

Now, as has been told, there were several nobles in France much more powerful than the king, and of these the greatest was Hugh le

Grand, father of the celebrated Hugh Capet from whom all the French kings traced their descent. Him Bernard count of Senlis sought, and implored his aid on behalf of Richard, which Hugh readily promised; but the compact did not last long, for when Louis offered him half of Normandy as a bribe, Hugh abandoned Richard's cause, and made ready for the invasion of the duchy. Bernard turned white with rage when he learnt what had happened, but he did not waste words, and after going to Rouen in order to consult with Bernard the Dane, a swift little ship sailed down the Seine and steered for the coast of Denmark. At the same time a messenger was secretly sent to Paris, where Richard was in hiding, and by night he was brought down the Seine and into Rouen. Three weeks later a fleet with Viking prows, commanded by the famous warrior Harold Blue-tooth, appeared off the Norman coasts and lay at anchor in a quiet bay, till the men they carried were needed. Not many hours later a watchman on one of the towers perceived a large army approaching from the north-east. When within a mile of the city, it halted, and a herald was sent out, summoning the duke to surrender, in the name of the king his sovereign lord. Instead of the duke, Bernard the Dane came forth to speak with him, and bade him return to his master and tell him the only conditions on which the gates would be opened. They were not hard, but chief amongst them was the stipulation that Louis should enter attended only by his pages, and that his army should remain outside. So well did Bernard act, that he not only contrived to set at rest Louis' suspicions of himself by paying him all the honour possible, but when he was safe in the palace contrived to instil into his mind doubts of Hugh, till the king agreed to break the alliance between them. After he had accomplished this, Bernard threw off the mask, and bade Harold Blue-tooth march from Cherbourg and join the Normans in an attack on the French, who were easily defeated. Harold's next step was to take possession of the duchy on behalf of Richard, but, instead of remaining in it himself as the real governor, merely assisted the Normans to obtain the freedom of their country from the captive king. At a meeting between Louis, Hugh and Richard on the banks of the Epte, the king was forced to surrender the rights he had illegally assumed, and Normandy was declared independent. Then they all went their ways, Louis to Laon, which had undergone a siege from Hugh, and Harold to Denmark, while grand preparations were made for the state entry of Richard into Rouen.

Crowds lined the streets through which Richard was to pass, and from the city gate to the cathedral the whole multitude was chattering and trembling with excitement. After many false alarms the banner of Normandy was seen in the distance framed in the doorway, while brightly polished armour glittered in the sun. A little in advance of his guardians rode Richard on a white horse, prouder of wearing for the first time a coat of mail and a helmet than even of taking possession of his duchy and receiving the homage of his subjects. He was barely thirteen, tall for his age, handsome, with a kind heart and pleasant manners. He had more book-learning, too, than was common with princes of his time, and on wet days could amuse himself with chess, or in reading some of the scrolls laid up in his palace of Rouen. Young though he was, his life had been passed in a hard school, and already he was skilled in judging men, and cautious how he trusted them.

Through the streets he rode smiling, winning as he went the love which was to stand by him to the end of his long life. At the west door of the cathedral he dismounted, and, unfastening his helmet, walked, amid cries of "Long live Richard our Duke," "Hail to the Duke of Normandy", straight up to the High Altar. There he knelt and prayed, while the shouting multitudes held their peace reverently. Then at length he rose from his knees and turned and faced them.

"Four years ago," he said, "you swore oaths of loyalty to me, and now I swear them to you. In war and in peace we will stand together, and with my people by my side I am afraid of nobody. From over the seas the fathers of many of you came with my fathers, but whether you be Bretons, Normans, or Danes, I love you all, and will deal out justice to all of you."

> "Bretons, Normans, and Danes are we,
> "But of us all Danes in our welcome to thee"

was their answer.

X

FREDERICK AND WILHELMINE

It is often very hard to believe that grown-up people were ever little children who played with dolls or spun tops, and felt that they could never be happy again when the rain came pouring down and prevented them from going to a picnic, or having the row on the lake which had been promised them as a birthday treat.

Frederick the Great, the famous king of Prussia, would have played if he could in his childhood, and if his father would have let him. But, unfortunately for Frederick and his elder sister Wilhelmine, and indeed for all the other little princes and princesses, the king of Prussia thought that time spent in games was time wasted, and when, in 1713, he succeeded his old father, everything in the kingdom was turned upside down. Some of his reforms were very wise, some only very meddlesome, as when he forbade the applewomen to sit at their stalls in the market unless they had knitting in their hands, or created an order of Wig Inspectors, who had leave to snatch the wigs off the heads of the passers-by, so as to make sure they bore the government stamp showing that the wigs had paid duty. Another of the king's fancies was to allow only the plainest food to be cooked in the palace, while he refused to permit even the queen to have any hangings that attracted dust. For this second king of Prussia was very clean, in days when washing was thought dangerous, and all through his life he frequently accuses the crown prince Frederick of being dirty.

But king Frederick William's real passion was soldiering. He had served in the Netherlands under Marlborough and prince Eugene when he was a mere boy, and the roar of the guns sounded always in his ears, as his poor little son found to his cost. Unlike other kings, who were always dressed in the finest silks and brocades, Frederick William wore a uniform of blue, with red collar and cuffs, while his breeches and waistcoat were of buff. By his side hung his sword, and in his hand he carried a cane, which he did not scruple to use on the head of any man whom he caught idling in the streets. Most of his spare moments were spent in drilling his soldiers, and he took particular delight in a regiment of Potsdam Guards, formed of the tallest men that could be found, either in Prussia or elsewhere. To his great delight, the Tsar Peter the Great sent him, in the year 1717, a hundred and fifty giants, from seven to eight feet high, in return for the hospitality he had received from the court of Berlin; and every autumn a certain number were regularly expected. The foolish king never guessed that these poor creatures had not half the strength of men of ordinary size, and would never be able to stand the hardships of war. The regiment was his pride, and if he could not enlist soldiers for it by fair means, he would do so by foul. There is a story of a very tall young carpenter, whom the king heard of as living in the town, and was of course very anxious to recruit. So two of his ministers went to the shop, and ordered a coffin of a special length. The carpenter inquired the name of the house to which it was to be sent, but the gentlemen answered that they would call that evening and see it for themselves. About dusk they appeared with some men in attendance, and were shown into the workshop, where the long black thing lay on the ground, with its lid leaning against the wall close by.

"You have made it much too short," exclaimed one of the gentlemen.

"Six feet six inches was the length you said, sir?" replied the carpenter.

"Yes; but that does not measure more than six feet four! You will have to make another."

"Pardon me, sir," answered the young man. "You will find that the full length. I know, for it is just my height"; and so saying he laid himself in the coffin. In an instant the lid was placed upon it and fastened down, and the coffin carried off by the attendants to a safe place. There the screws were undone and the lid lifted, but the man within did not stir.

"Here, get up, my good fellow," cried one of the gentlemen; but there was no answer.

"He has fainted," said someone uneasily, "he wants a taste of brandy"; but when the brandy was brought he could not swallow it. What had happened was plain: the carpenter had died from want of air.

It would have been much happier both for little Fritz and Wilhelmine his sister if the drilling of the army had entirely occupied king Frederick William's time and thoughts; but, unluckily, he felt it to be his duty to lay down rules for the daily life of the crown prince. When he was six, and still in the hands of governesses, a regiment consisting of a hundred little boys was formed, of which Fritz was the captain, and a real colonel commander-in-chief. They were all dressed in a uniform of blue with red facings, and wore cocked hats, and for two years were drilled by a youth of seventeen, till Fritz had learnt his drill properly, and could really command them himself. When this event took place he had already been about a year under three tutors—Duhan (who always remained his friend); von Finkenstein, and Kalkstein; while an old soldier named Von Senning, who had served in Marlborough's wars, taught him fortifications and mathematics.

For of course the king's one idea was to make the crown prince follow in his own footsteps, and to that end he must be strong and hardy. When Frederick William went out to hunt, or to review his troops, the boy was either galloping behind him or seated with a dozen men astride a long pole on wheels, on which it was very difficult to keep your seat when jolting over a rough country. Beer soup was his chief food, whether he liked it or not; and if the king had had his way the child would have been cut off with very little sleep; but this, happily, the doctors would not suffer. As to his lessons, Fritz was to learn all history, especially the history of Brandenburg, and of England and Brunswick—countries which were connected with his illustrious house; French and German, but no Latin; arithmetic, geography, economy "to the roots," a little ancient history, and something of the laws of every kingdom. To these strategy and fortification were shortly added; "For," writes the king, "there is nothing which can bring a prince so much honour as the sword, and he would be despised of all men if he did not love it and seek his sole glory in it." Fritz's religious duties were also strictly attended to, and he was to be brought up a Protestant. "Every morning (except Sunday) he is to get up at 6 o'clock," writes his father, "and after saying his prayers he is to wash his face and hands, but not with soap." This sounds rather odd, as the king was so particular as to cleanliness, and we are told that he washed himself five times a day. But most likely he was afraid of the expense, for at eleven, when his son appears in his presence, the boy is expressly ordered to "wash his face with water, and his hands with soap and water, and to put on a clean shirt." The third washing of hands took place at five, but on this occasion soap is not mentioned.

It must have been very difficult to have been as "clean and neat" as Frederick William required in the few minutes he allowed to his son for dressing himself—for as soon as possible Fritz was taught to do without help. To begin with, however, a valet combed out his hair, and tied it into a pig-tail or "queue" with a piece of tape, but no powder was put on till his morning lessons were over. This must have been a comfort, considering he was to eat his breakfast and drink his tea while the hair-dressing was going on, and that by half-past six everything was to be finished. From eleven to two he remained with the king, amusing himself—if he could—and dining with his Majesty at twelve o'clock. At two his afternoon lessons began, and lasted till five, when he was permitted to go out and ride. He also had half holidays, on Wednesdays and Saturdays, when his morning's work was over, provided that his "repetition" had been satisfactory; and these free hours we may be sure that Fritz spent with his sister Wilhelmine, who, though three years older, was always his loyal companion and friend. Poor little princess, she was small for her age and very delicate, and in years to come she suffered almost as much as Fritz from the harsh treatment both of her father and mother; but do what they might, nothing could break her spirit, or force her to betray her brother's confidence. Wilhelmine was a pretty child, and could use her eyes as well as her tongue. She was also a very good mimic, and could even pretend to faint so cleverly that she frightened those about her so much that the doctor would be sent for to see if she was really dead. This, of course, was exactly what the naughty girl wanted, and the more she took them all in the better she was pleased. No one could be more agreeable than Wilhelmine when she chose, but she was very vain, and it was therefore easy to wound her feelings. When she was nine years old she had a sharp illness, from which she was not expected to recover. At length, however, she took a turn for the better; and the first thing she did was to beg the king to allow her to wear grown-up dresses, and to put on the mantle which in those days meant that a young lady had "come out." Her interest in her new clothes did as much to cure her as the medical treatment of the time, which was so severe that it was a miracle that anyone ever lived through it; and as soon as she could stand she ordered her maids to dress her hair high over a cushion, and to put on her gown of white silk heavy with embroidery, and the much coveted purple velvet mantle.

"I looked at myself in the mirror," she writes in her memoirs, "and decided that they really became me wonderfully well. I next practised moving and walking, so that I might play the part of a great lady. Then I entered the queen's apartments, but unluckily, directly her Majesty saw me she burst out laughing, and exclaimed: 'Good gracious, what a figure! Why she looks like a little dwarf.'" Perhaps the queen's remarks were true; but, none the less, the little girl's feelings were deeply wounded. The two children were very much afraid of the king, and never scrupled to deceive him whenever it was possible. As they grew older, Wilhelmine encouraged her brother in all kinds of disobedience, especially in playing the flute, which his father hated, and in reading and studying French books, which were likewise forbidden. The king wanted him to be a German and a soldier, and nothing more; but to the end of his life Fritz could neither spell nor write his own language properly. The breach thus early made grew always wider by reason of the vexed question of the marriage of both Fritz and Wilhelmine.

THE PRINCESS WILHELMINE WAS STILL in the long clothes of a tiny baby when her mother, like many mothers, began to dream of her future. She was to be beautiful and clever and charming, and she must marry a prince as beautiful and clever and charming as herself, and who could he be but the queen's own nephew, son of her brother, George, prince of Hanover, a boy just two years older than Wilhelmine, and known to us later as the duke of Gloucester, then as the duke of Edinburgh, and lastly as Frederick prince of Wales? And when, on a snowy January day of 1712, the little crown prince entered the world, there was another child to plan for, and was there not a small princess called Emily or Amelia, a newcomer like himself, who would make a suitable bride, say eighteen years hence, for the king of Prussia one day to be? The princess of Hanover, Caroline of Anspach, was written to, and declared that she was delighted to think that some day the bonds already uniting the two countries should be drawn closer still; so the children sent each other presents and pretty notes, and sometimes messages in their mothers' letters when they were too lazy to write for themselves.

Now, in spite of all this, Fritz did not trouble his head much as to the future; the present, he soon found, was quite difficult enough, and besides, he thought much more about his flute—which he was forbidden to play—than about Amelia. But Wilhelmine, who passed most of her time in the palace of Wustershausen, a big castle twenty miles from Berlin, had plenty of time to brood over her coming greatness. Often she was alone there with her governess; but in the summer Fritz and his tutors spent some months at the castle also, and the boy would remain for hours in the day watching for strangers to cross the bridge that spanned the moat.

"You never can tell," he said to Wilhelmine, "whether they will be most frightened at the four eagles" (there were two black and two white) "swirling about their heads, or at the black bears which come tumbling towards them! It is always one or the other, and sometimes it is both; and, anyhow, it is great fun."

But in the year 1727, when Fritz was fifteen, these pleasant things came to an end. No more Wustershausen or Berlin; no more talks with his sister in the childish language they had invented for themselves, no more fishing expeditions to the ponds in the sandy moor that surrounded the palace. The crown prince was major now of the Potsdam Grenadiers, and we may be quite sure that the king never suffered him to neglect his work. Dressed in a smart uniform covered with gold lace, he was to be seen at every muster and every review, leading his men; but, even now, the boy who, thirty years later, was to prove one of the three greatest generals of his century, had no love for war, and would hurry back to Potsdam to exchange his uniform for a loose dressing-gown, and the duties of drilling for a practice on the flute. In this year, too, an event happened which had a great influence on the home life of both Fritz and his sister. This was the sudden death of George I on his way to Hanover, without his having obtained the consent of Parliament to the Double-Marriage Treaty, which the queen of Prussia, Sophia Dorothea, had hoped to have obtained four years earlier. The new king of England, George II, had no particular love for his brother-in-law of Prussia, and for his part Frederick William, though at that time he desired the marriages quite as much as his wife, amply returned his feelings. At length the repeated delays drove him nearly out of his mind with fury, and he vented his anger on the queen (who would have suffered any humiliation rather than give up her project) and on the prince and princess. Henceforth the life of the royal family was made up of violence on the one part and deceit on the other. People began to take "sides," and the quarrel between father and son grew worse daily.

It was to keep him under his own eye, and not in the least to give him pleasure, that, in 1728, Frederick William bade Fritz accompany him to Dresden on a visit to August the Strong, elector of Saxony and king of Poland, and even gave him leave to order a blue coat trimmed with gold lace for himself, and six new liveries for his attendants. The crown prince, who was only now sixteen, must have felt that he had indeed entered into another world, when he contrasted the Saxon court, with its splendid surroundings and incessant amusements, with the bare rooms and coarse food of the palace of Berlin. Other comparisons might be made, and Fritz did not fail to make them. Here he was treated as a welcome guest, and as a person of importance, while at home he was scolded and worried from morning till night. So, instead of the silent, sulky boy Frederick William was accustomed to see about him, there appeared a gracious, smiling young prince, with a pleasant word for everyone, enjoying all the pleasures provided for him, the opera most of all.

ON HIS RETURN TO BERLIN, Fritz fell suddenly ill, and for a while there seemed to be a chance of reconciliation between him and his father. But this reconciliation did not last, and the prince had, or pretended to have, a relapse, in order to avoid going with his father on a tour through Prussia. But, ill or well, he could not escape from the rules the king laid down for him, and they were as strict now as they had been nine years before. A lesson on tactics was to occupy two hours every morning, after which, at noon, he was to dine in company with his tutors major Senning and Colonel von Kalkstein, and the master of the kitchen as well, which sounds rather strange to us. He might, however, invite six friends of his own, and dine or have supper with them in return; but he was always to sleep in the palace, and "to go to bed the instant the retreat sounded." Then the king went away, sure that everything would go on to his liking.

But no sooner had he turned his back on Berlin than a sort of holiday spirit took possession of the palace. "We were perfectly happy," writes Wilhelmine, in her memoirs, and there was no reason that they should ever have been anything else, as the "happiness" mainly consisted in hearing as much music as they wished for, and for Fritz in also playing the flute. From this instrument, which was fated to bring him into so much trouble, the crown prince never parted, and even when hunting with his father he would contrive to lose himself, and hiding behind a large tree or crouching in a thicket, he would play some of the tunes which so delighted his soul. During this memorable month, when the "days passed quietly," the queen gave concerts, aided by famous musicians, Bufardin, the flutist, and Quantz, who was not only a performer but a composer, and others who were celebrated at the Saxon court (whence they came at the queen's request) for their skill on spinet or violin. All this, however, ceased on the reappearance of the king at Wustershausen, and matters fell back into their old grooves: on one side there was suspicion and tyranny, on the other lies and intrigues. Fritz tried to break away from it all by persuading

Kalkstein to ask his father's permission to travel in foreign countries. But Frederick William absolutely refused to let his son quit Prussia, and things were worse than they need have been, owing to the smallness of the house where they were all shut up together. Certainly never had a father and son more different tastes.

"To-morrow I am obliged to hunt, and on Monday I am obliged to hunt again," writes Fritz. He is bored by the court jests and jesters, as well as by the king's guests. As for the days, they seemed perfectly endless, and well they might, seeing that it was no uncommon thing for him to get up at five and go to bed at midnight! No wonder he exclaimed "I had rather beg my bread than live any longer on this footing." Once again Fritz made an effort after a better state of things, and wrote to his father to apologise for any offence he might unwittingly have committed, and to assure him of his respectful duty. He had perhaps been wiser to have let ill alone, for the king only replied by taunts of his "girlishness," and hatred of everything manly—which is all rather funny, when we remember that the object of these reproaches was Frederick the Great—and in general was so unkind and unjust, that both Kalkstein and the other tutor Finkenstein resigned in disgust.

During this same autumn the discussion about the two English marriages was re-opened. As regards the king, he was as anxious as the queen for that of Wilhelmine with the prince of Wales, but, unlike her, he considered Fritz too young and unsteady to take to himself a wife. This did not please king George at all, and in answer to a letter from Sophia Dorothea, queen Caroline wrote that *both* marriages must take place—or neither. This reply put Frederick William in a towering passion. Wilhelmine should marry *somebody*, he said, and that at once. She was nearly twenty now, and had five younger sisters for whom husbands would have to be found. Indeed, he was not at all sure he should not prefer the margrave of Schwedt for a son-in-law, than the stuck-up English prince! So he stormed; and meanwhile the queen, Wilhelmine, and Fritz kept up a secret correspondence with the court of St. James.

About this same year (1729) the crown prince made friends with one of the king's pages, Keith by name, and also with a certain lieutenant Katte. These two young men had the same tastes as himself, and were with him during all his leisure hours. When Fritz could escape from the hated reviews or hunts, in which he was forced to bear his father company, he would hurry back to his own apartments, throw off his tight uniform, slip on a dressing-gown of scarlet and gold brocade, and begin to play on his beloved flute. In his rooms he often found his teacher Quantz awaiting him, and then for a time his troubles were forgotten in the soothing tones of the great flutist. One day both master and pupil were practising together a difficult passage, when Katte rushed in breathless.

"The king is on the stairs," he panted, snatching up flutes and music, and hiding them in the wood closet. In an instant Fritz had flung his dressing-gown behind a screen, and put on his coat; but he could not manage to tie his hair, which he had loosened, and which hung about his face, in a way that the king disliked. The confused bearing of all three naturally attracted Frederick William's attention, and, bursting into a fit of rage that rendered him almost speechless, he kicked down the screen in front of him. "I knew it," he shouted, catching up the dressing-gown, and thrusting it into the fire where he stamped it down with his heavy boot. Then, sweeping a pile of French novels from a little table, he thrust them into the arms of the gentleman-in-waiting, bidding him send them back at once to the bookseller; for even in his wrath the king did not forget to be economical.

After this affair father and son were on worse terms than ever. It was not at all an uncommon thing for Frederick William to throw plates at the heads of his children when they vexed him, and one evening, after dinner, as he was being pushed about in a wheel-chair during an attack of gout, he aimed a blow with his crutch at Wilhelmine. The girl sprang aside, and it fell harmless, but this only increased the king's fury, and he called to the attendants to push his chair quickly so that he might prevent her reaching the door. They dared not disobey, but contrived to find so many obstacles in the way that the princess was able to escape. As to Fritz, he was struck by his father almost daily, and on one occasion, about a month before the prince's eighteenth birthday, when the young man entered the room, his father leaped at his throat, dragged him by the hair, beat him violently with his stick, and forced him to kneel down and beg his pardon—for what offence the crown prince did not know! Not content with this, the king exulted in his son's misery, and even told him that worse was in store.

It is hardly wonderful that under these circumstances the prince felt that his life was in danger, and began to form plans of escape; but they were so badly laid and so transparent, that everybody could guess what was happening, and three or four times he was forced to give them up. His favourite project was to reach France and go next to London, where he was sure of protection, and in all this his principal confidant was his friend Katte. Early in July the king started for Potsdam, taking the crown prince with him. After remaining there a few days, he announced his intention of making a progress by way of Wesel, and this gave Fritz the idea that from Wesel he could gain Holland and cross to England. He managed to obtain a secret interview with Katte, and it was arranged that they should write to each other through a cousin of Katte's, of the same name, who was recruiting near Anspach, as they knew the king intended to stop at this city and visit his daughter who had married the margrave the year before.

The king spent a week at Anspach, during which time he was busy with the affairs of the young couple, whom it would have been much wiser to have left to themselves. Fritz meanwhile was fuming at the delay, but tried to turn it to account by gaining over the page Keith to his service. It was settled between them that young Keith should take advantage of his position to secure some horses, and the crown prince wrote to Katte that he was to go in a few days to the Hague and there inquire for a certain count d'Alberville—for under this name Fritz proposed to travel. Keith was ordered to join him there also, and from the Hague they would slip across almost before their absence was discovered. Unluckily all the hardships he had suffered had not yet turned Fritz into a man. Passionately though he longed to escape from his father's tyranny, he still expected life to be like the French novels he was so fond of, and from one of which the name of count d'Alberville was taken. So, instead of putting on an old suit of clothes, in which he might have passed unnoticed, he ordered a fine new red cloak for himself, and a blue one for young Keith, to wear on the great occasion.

From Anspach they went to visit the duke of Württemberg, and thence set out for Mannheim, where the elector palatine was awaiting them. Fritz had arranged to make his flight from a place called Sinsheim, but, to his dismay, the king announced that he meant to push on to Steinfurth, which was nearer Mannheim. The whole royal party slept in two barns, and more than once Fritz almost gave up his plan in despair, so impossible it seemed for him to steal away without waking somebody. However, they were very tired after their long day's journey, and slept soundly, all except Fritz's valet, Gummersbach, who, hearing a sound soon after two, awoke with a start to see the crown prince dressing himself.

"But your Royal Highness"—stammered Gummersbach, in surprise, rising to his feet.

"If I choose to get up it is no business of yours," replied Fritz, in an angry whisper. "Give me my red cloak, I am going to the king." And he crept softly from the barn, never hearing Gummersbach's answer that the king intended to start at five instead of three. The valet said nothing, but hastened to wake Rochow, the prince's tutor, who was lying on some straw with all his clothes on.

"What is the matter?" cried he.

"Quick! quick! sir, the prince!" was all Gummersbach could answer, and without wasting time in questions Rochow rushed away in the direction of an open green space in front of the farm. Seeing in the dim light the outline of two heavy carriages, he altered his pace, and strolled carelessly up to young Keith, who was holding two horses.

"Whom are these for?" asked Rochow politely.

"They are for myself and the other page to accompany his Majesty," answered the boy.

"Ah, yes, of course; but you should have been informed that his Majesty does not intend to start till five to-day, so you had better take them back to the stables." And, unwilling though he was, Keith was forced to obey, especially as some of the generals in the king's suite had come on the scene, and advanced to one of the carriages against which Fritz was leaning.

"Can we be of any use to your Royal Highness?" asked Rochow respectfully; but, with an oath, the prince brushed him aside, and throwing off the red cloak that covered him, went straight to the place where his father was sleeping. He may have thought that the officers would say nothing in his presence, and indeed they were mostly on his side, and far from anxious to make things worse for him.

"Is it so late?" asked the king, who was still lying on the rough bed, wrapped in a large coat. "Well, your carriage is heavier than mine, so you had better start early."

The prince bowed and went out, but contrived to delay on one pretext or another, so that the king's own carriage was brought up first to the gate of the farm, and soon his Majesty was on the road to Mannheim. All the way the king expected to catch up his son, but even when Fritz was not found at Heidelberg he suspected nothing, and his only uneasiness was in the fear that the prince had entered Mannheim without him. When, however, he reached the city himself, at eight in the evening, and there was still no Fritz, he grew seriously disturbed, and to quiet him, the elector sent some of his servants to look for the crown prince. At half-past ten the whole party appeared, Fritz tired and very sulky, but as determined as ever not to remain a moment more than could be helped in his father's power. He had hoped for a chance of flight along the road, but none presented itself, and now he was resolved to begin all over again. Once more a message was sent to young Keith to be ready with the horses as soon as he received a signal, but the page was not cast in the same mould as his master. In mortal terror of his life, he threw himself at the king's feet, confessed the whole plot, and implored forgiveness. For once in his career Frederick William managed to control his temper; he would have his son closely watched, but he should not be arrested till he was on Prussian soil; yet all through the rest of the tour Fritz was well aware that someone had betrayed him. Immediately on their arrival at Wesel, the prince was put under arrest, and sent, without once being allowed to leave the travelling carriage, to the castle of Spandau, whence he was afterwards removed to Cüstrin. General Buddenbrock was appointed his gaoler, and ordered to shoot him dead in case of a rescue.

AND WHERE WAS WILHELMINE ALL this time, and what was she doing? Well, she was at Berlin, still very weak and sickly from a bad attack of smallpox the year before, and the severity of the treatment which followed it. The king remained always fixed in his determination to find a husband for her; if not the prince of Wales, then the margrave of Schwedt, the margrave of Baireuth, who was young and agreeable, or, best of all, the duke of Weissenfeld, not so young, and perhaps not so agreeable, but the man most favoured by Frederick William. "After all, marriage is not of such great importance," said one of her ladies to the princess, in well-meant consolation. "Nobody makes such a fuss about it elsewhere. A husband that you can turn and twist as you like is an excellent thing to have, and however angry the queen may be now, when once the thing is over she will make up her mind to it. So take my advice, and accept the hand of the duke of Weissenfeld, and you will please everybody." But Wilhelmine did not agree with madame la Ramen. She knew too much about marriage to think that the choice of a husband mattered nothing, and she had not the slightest intention of sacrificing her whole life to the whims of her very changeable father. So she gave a vague answer to the earnest entreaties of madame la Ramen, and let the subject drop.

On the evening of August 11, the princess entered the palace from the garden, where she had passed several hours, feeling excited and melancholy by turns; *why*, she could not imagine, as everything was going on as usual. Therefore, she did not, as usual, go straight to her rooms, but instead, ordered a carriage and drove to Montbijou where a concert was taking place. In this way she missed the strange events that were happening in her mother's apartments. Let Wilhelmine tell her own story; it is a very surprising one:—

"That night the queen was seated before her dressing-table having her hair brushed, with madame von Bülow beside her, when they heard a fearful noise in the next room. This room was used as a kind of museum, and was filled with precious stones and gems, and some very rare and tall Chinese and Japanese vases. Her Majesty thought at first that one of these vases must have been knocked over, and have been broken in pieces on the polished floor, and she bade madame la Ramen go and see who had done it, but, to her amazement, on entering the museum, the lady-in-waiting found everything undisturbed. Scarcely had she rejoined the queen when the noise began afresh, louder than before, and madame la Ramen ran back, accompanied by another of the queen's attendants, only to discover all in perfect order, and the room dark and still. Three times this occurred, and then the noise ceased in the museum altogether, to start again far more loudly in the corridor which led from the queen's apartments to those of the king. At each end of this corridor stood a sentinel, to prevent anyone passing but the servants on duty, so the disturbance was all the more strange.

'Bring lights, and we will pass down the corridor,' said the queen to her ladies, and left her room, followed by all but madame la Ramen, who hid herself, in a great fright. But hardly had they stepped across the threshold when fearful groans and cries broke out around them. The ladies trembled at the sound, and the guards at each end were half-dead with fright; but the queen's calmness made them all ashamed, and when she ordered them to try the doors along the corridor, they obeyed in silence. Each door was locked, and when the key was turned and the room entered, it was empty. Her majesty then questioned the guards, who confessed that the groans had sounded close to them, but they had seen nothing, and with that she was forced to be content, and to return to her own apartments, rather angry at having been disturbed in vain. Next morning she told me the story, and though not in the least superstitious, ordered me to write down the date of the occurrence. I am quite sure that there must be some simple explanation, but it is curious that the affair happened during the very night that my brother was arrested, and a most painful scene between the king and queen afterwards took place in this very corridor."

It was at a ball given by the queen at Montbijou, five days later, that she learned the terrible news. "It was six years since I had danced," says Wilhelmine, "and I flung myself into it without paying attention to anything else, or to the repeated wishes of madame von Bülow, who told me it was time for me to go to bed.

"'Why are you so cross to-night?' I asked, at length; 'I don't know what to make of you!'"

"'Look at the queen,' she replied, 'and you will be answered.' I turned and looked, and grew cold and white at the sight of her, standing rigid in a corner of the ball-room between two of her ladies. In a moment more she bent her head and said good-night to her guests, then walked to her carriage, making a sign to me to follow her. Not a word did we utter all the way to the palace; I thought my brother must be dead, and in this terrible silence and uncertainty my heart began to palpitate so furiously that I felt as if I should be suffocated."

For some time her ladies, under the queen's orders, refused to tell Wilhelmine what had happened, but seeing the poor girl was firmly convinced of the prince's death, madame von Sonsfeld informed her that letters had arrived from the king, stating that the crown prince had been arrested, as he was attempting to escape. Next day they learned that Katte also had been taken prisoner, but Keith cleverly managed to place himself under the protection of the English ambassador to the Hague, lord Chesterfield, and to pass over to England in his suite. When the shock of the news was passed, the first thought of both the queen and Wilhelmine was for the numerous letters they had written to the prince, in which they had said many bitter and imprudent things about the king's behaviour. Wilhelmine hoped they had been burned, as she had always bidden Fritz to do the moment he received them; but the queen feared that they might have been entrusted to Katte (as he was known to have in his care many of the prince's possessions), and in this case they must be got from him at all cost, or the crown prince's head would certainly pay forfeit. The queen was right: the letters were among Katte's papers, with the official seal placed upon them.

In this desperate plight, Sophia Dorothea threw herself upon the generosity of marshal Natzmar, Katte's superior. No direct answer was received, and the queen and Wilhelmine were almost ill with anxiety, when, one day, when the princess was alone with madame von Sonsfeld, the countess von Fink entered bearing a heavy portfolio.

"It is most mysterious," said she, sinking into a chair with her burden; "when I went into my room last night I found this great portfolio, with a chain and seals round it, addressed to the queen, and this note for you, madame. As I did not like to disturb her Majesty I have brought them to you."

Wilhelmine's heart beat with excitement, but she dared not betray herself. She took the note quietly, and read its contents, which were very short. "Have the goodness, madame, to deliver this portfolio to the queen. It contains the letters which she and the princess have written to the crown prince."

Carrying the portfolio, and grumbling all the while as to the unknown risks she might be running, countess von Fink followed Wilhelmine and madame von Sonsfeld into the presence of the queen, whose joy was boundless on receiving the precious letters. But in a few minutes her face clouded over again, as she perceived that many difficulties still lay before her. First, there were the spies by whom the king had surrounded them; they would at once detect the absence of so large an object. Then there was the danger that Katte would mention the letters in the cross-examination he would have to undergo, and once their existence was known, and madame von Fink questioned, the prince's cause was lost, and his mother and sister might have to undergo imprisonment for life. What *could* be done? All day long plan after plan was thought of and rejected, but at length it was Wilhelmine who hit upon one that might do. The portfolio was openly to lie in the queen's apartments as if it had been brought to her for safe custody, and then, with great precautions, the seal could be raised without breaking it, and the chain filed through where it could easily be joined again. Then the letters could be taken out, and others, quite harmless, written and put back in their place. Clever though it all sounded, it would have been impossible to carry out the scheme had it not been for a most lucky accident which had befallen the queen's confidential valet Bock, who was called in to raise the seal. On examining the coat-of-arms on the wax he recognised it as the same engraved on a seal he had picked up four weeks earlier in the garden at Montbijou, and which, he now discovered, belonged to Katte. By this means the wax could be broken and re-sealed without the slightest risk.

The letters were now in the hands of the queen and princess, and were to the full as dangerous as they had expected to find them; but there was no time to spare for lamenting their folly if they were to have others ready to await the king on his return. Of course, there was no need to replace the whole fifteen hundred; but a great deal had to be done, and without delay Wilhelmine and her mother sat down to write a large number, taking care to obtain paper with the proper water-mark of every year. In three days they had seven hundred ready, and in order to give the impression that they wished to conceal the letters, the queen filled up the portfolio with handkerchiefs and various articles of fine linen.

All was now ready for the arrival of the king, and when the day and hour was fixed the queen awaited him in her apartments. As soon as he reached the threshold, he shouted out: "Well, Madame, your wretched son is dead."

"Dead!" repeated the queen, clutching at a chair as she spoke. "Dead! you have had the heart to kill him?"

"Yes, I tell you," was his answer; "and I want the portfolio containing his letters."

Hardly able to walk, the queen went to fetch the portfolio, which the king slashed in pieces and took out the letters. Then, without another word, he walked away.

"Have you heard? Fritz is dead!" said the queen to Wilhelmine, in a terrible voice that seemed dead also. The princess fainted at the horrible news, but when she recovered her senses, madame von Sonsfeld whispered not to be afraid, as she had reason to know that the prince, though strictly guarded, was alive and well. These words put fresh life into the hearts of his mother and sister, and enabled Wilhelmine to bear the blows and kicks which her father showered upon her, till he was dragged off by his other children. Then he confessed that Fritz was still living, and accused Wilhelmine of having been his accomplice in an act of high treason against the king's person. This was more than the poor girl could bear.

"I will marry anyone you like," she cried, "if you will only spare my brother's life—the duke of Weissenfeld, or anybody else; it is all the same to me." But the king was deaf to everything but the sound of his own voice, and did not hear her, and a moment after Katte, pale and calm, passed the window, under the guard of four soldiers, for his examination by the king.

Frederick William behaved with his usual brutality, even kicking the unhappy prisoner, who threw himself at his feet, confessing his own part in the plot, but denying that Wilhelmine had any part in it. He acknowledged, however, that by the prince's orders he had sent the letters to her, and these were closely examined by the minister Grumkow, "in the hope," says Wilhelmine, "of finding something that would condemn us." But the closest scrutiny revealed nothing of the least importance, though the king was still suspicious, and commanded the princess to keep her room till he had time to question her further.

Meanwhile the crown prince was locked up in the fortress of Cüstrin, and obliged to obey a set of those minute rules which Frederick William loved to draw up. "Every morning at eight a basin and a little water, to wash himself with, is to be taken to his cell by a scullion"; and this seems to have been the only washing allowed him by the king, who is always reproaching him for his dirty habits. Two meals, one at twelve and the other at six, were all he was allowed, and "his food is to be cut up before he has it." Several times a day he was visited by the officers in charge, but they were strictly forbidden to speak to him. By-and-bye the king declared that the prisoner had forfeited his right to the Prussian crown, and ordered him to be spoken of as "colonel Frederick."

At last a council was appointed to try both the prince and Katte, and Keith—if they could get him! The trial was long, and at the end of it Katte was condemned to death for intended desertion, but strongly recommended to mercy. With regard to the prince they considered that, as he had been deprived of his military rank and suffered many months of close imprisonment, he was sufficiently punished, especially as he had expressed his willingness "to do all that His Majesty requires or commands." Touching the charge of disobedience, the council declined to pass judgment.

The recommendation to mercy was not heeded. Katte's grandfather, field marshal von Alvensleben, wrote a touching letter begging for his life, and recalling the many occasions on which he himself had risked his own in the service of Prussia. He received a reply stating that Katte deserved "to be torn with red-hot pincers," as was the law in Prussia, "but that, 'out of consideration' for his father and grandfather, his head should be cut off." This document is signed "Your very affectionate king." Probably nothing that Frederick the Great ever endured in his whole life was as bitter as the scene which his father had prepared for him. Katte was to be beheaded under the windows of the crown prince's prison. If the span was too narrow, another place was to be chosen, "but so that the prince can see well." For this purpose the condemned man was to take a two days' journey to Cüstrin, but, perhaps by the mercy of his gaolers, Frederick was told nothing till he was awakened at five o'clock on the morning of November 6, and informed that Katte had been in Cüstrin since the previous day, and was to be executed at seven. The unexpected news upset the prince completely. He wept and wrung his hands, and begged that the execution might be delayed till he could send a courier to the king at Wustershausen. He offered to resign the crown, to suffer perpetual imprisonment, even to sacrifice his own life, if only he might save that of Katte. The officers were full of pity, but they were powerless.

Gently but firmly he was at length forced to the window beneath which the block stood, between the prison and the river Oder. Then Katte appeared, a minister on each side of him, holding his hat under his arm. As he passed the window he looked up, and Frederick flung himself across the bars, crying "Katte! Katte! forgive me."

"There is nothing to forgive, my prince," answered Katte, bowing; and he walked steadily on to his place in the centre of the little group of soldiers, where his sentence was read. He took off his wig, replacing it with a white cap, and opened his shirt collar. A soldier came forward to bind his eyes, but he motioned him away, and knelt quietly on the sand before him, waiting for the sword to fall. But Frederick did not "see well," for he had fainted.

In a few days whispers were heard in the court of Berlin that the crown prince had been "pardoned" by his father for his wickedness in trying to run away—which he never would have thought of doing had he not suffered such abominable treatment. He remained for a little time yet at Cüstrin, but was allowed to have books—and better light to read them by. No doubt the king took for granted that, after the severe lesson his son had received, the "books" would be works on fortifications or strategy, or something useful of that kind. Had he known that philosophical treatises, Aristotle's "Poetica" and Molière's plays, were among them, another explosion would probably have occurred. And what would he have said if it had reached his ears that the prince had written a long poem in French called "Advice to Myself," dedicated to Grumkow, whom he hated? The poem is really not bad, considering, and one cannot help wondering if Grumkow guessed that the royal prisoner was making fun of him. In a little while he was set free, and even nominated to a seat on the council of war, but he was not yet admitted to Berlin. Poor boy! he was only nineteen even now, but he had learned that if he was ever to live at peace with his father he must give up all his own tastes and pleasures, and submit body and soul to the king's will.

During these dreadful months Wilhelmine had been kept entirely in her room, and if we may believe her own account, which perhaps it is better not to do altogether, she was half starved, and thankful to eat a crust which a crow had left on the window-sill. "In general," she says, "the dinner of myself and my lady-in-waiting consisted of bones without any meat on them, and plain water." Besides her anxiety about the fate of her brother, the princess had been tormented with fears as to her own marriage, for the king had made up his mind that she should no longer be on his hands. The queen still obstinately clung to the old project of having the prince of Wales as her son-in-law; but the king contrived to break off the negotiations, greatly to the wrath of Sophia Dorothea, as well as of Wilhelmine herself, who shared her mother's opinion that to accept any husband who was not of royal birth would be impossible to one of her rank.

But who the bridegroom was really to be was a question that remained undecided. Sometimes it seemed as if the choice would fall upon a member of the House of Brandenburg, the margrave of Schwedt; but at the very moment when this appeared most likely the king sent a message to Wilhelmine, by his porter, announcing that she was to become the wife of the fat and elderly duke of Weissenfeld, a prince of the Empire. The princess was terribly upset—partly by the news itself and partly by the messenger whom the king had chosen to break it to her; but the next morning her anger was redoubled, on receiving a second visit from the porter, while she was still in bed, informing her that he had been ordered by His Majesty to prepare her trousseau! Wilhelmine was speechless with rage, and refused to send any answer. Then, shutting herself into her boudoir, or *cabinet*, as it was called, she began to play on her spinet, in order to calm herself a little.

"Four gentlemen are below, madame, and beg that you will do them the honour of seeing them alone," cried madame von Sonsfeld, suddenly opening the door. The princess rose, feeling that something of serious importance was about to happen, and there entered Grumkow, followed by three other ministers. He declared solemnly (what she knew already) that the English marriage was abandoned, and that the king was forced to choose a husband for her from another house; that the fate of the crown prince, now undergoing a strict imprisonment at Cüstrin, depended on the willingness of the princess to obey His Majesty's desire, which Grumkow earnestly hoped she would do, as otherwise it would be his painful duty to carry her off at once to the fortress of Memel. Finally, he announced that the king's choice had fallen on the hereditary prince of Baireuth—rich, young, and a cousin of her own. After begging for a short time for consideration, Wilhelmine agreed to do as her father wished, and on his return to Berlin, a few days later, he behaved to her with much affection—for the first time for many years. The queen, on the contrary, vowed she would no longer look on Wilhelmine as a daughter, and on the sudden appearance at Berlin of the prince of Baireuth, on the eve of a great review, was so rude to him that he told her politely, but with spirit, that if she objected so much to receiving him into her family he would withdraw his request for the hand of her daughter. The queen saw that she had met her match, and accordingly changed her behaviour.

When she had once seen the prince, Wilhelmine's sadness began to disappear, and she began to think that her future life might be tolerably happy. The bridegroom had a pleasant, frank face, and good manners; he was besides tall and well-made, and had a good education. The betrothal took place at seven o'clock on June 3, 1731, in the palace, and the king, who had got his own way, was quite charming and affectionate, and gave his daughter a magnificent toilette service of gold, besides other presents. The marriage itself was not to be till November—for what reason we are not told, but most probably the delay was owing to some underhand schemes of the queen, who hoped that it might still be broken off. However, the prince of Baireuth was appointed colonel of a Prussian regiment, which gave him an excuse for staying in the neighbourhood, and the morning after the betrothal he asked Wilhelmine if he might see her alone. The few words that he spoke did him honour, and must have sounded strange indeed in the ears of the princess. He only wished, he said, for her happiness, and would do all in his power to secure it, and to deserve the trust which she and her father had given him. Affection had hitherto played such a small part in Wilhelmine's life, that she did not know what to answer; but it must have thawed her poor frozen heart a little, for that evening at supper she "pulled a cracker" with the prince. But this sign of good spirits was more than the queen could bear, and she bade her daughter follow her out of the room, scolding her roundly, as they went, for her want of modesty.

The long months passed somehow, and to the relief of everybody (except the queen) the wedding-day (fixed for November 20) arrived. "When dinner was over," says Wilhelmine, "the king ordered the queen to begin to dress me, for it was already four o'clock, and the ceremony was fixed for seven. The queen declared that she meant to do my hair herself, but she was not clever with her fingers, and could not manage it. Then her ladies tried their hands, but as soon as they had dressed it properly the queen would pull it about, so that it had to be done all over again. At last, however, between them they contrived to make twenty-four large curls, each as thick as your arm, with a royal crown poised on top. The weight was dreadful, and I could hardly hold my head up. Then they put on my dress, which was of cloth of silver, trimmed with Spanish point picked out with gold, my train, twelve yards long, being held up by four ladies." Hardly able to stir under all this grandeur, the bride moved as best she could through six magnificent galleries, in the last of which the ceremony was performed. A ball then followed, but as Wilhelmine could not possibly have danced to save her life owing to the weight of her clothes, the bridegroom opened it with her sister the margravine of Anspach.

The festivities were kept up for several days, and on the 23rd another ball took place, at which seven hundred people were present. This time Wilhelmine who, as we know, loved dancing, did not allow her dress to interfere, and she was in the middle of a minuet when Grumkow approached her.

"Your feet seem to dance of themselves, madame," he said roughly; "don't you see that strangers are present?"

Wilhelmine stopped and stared at a young man whose face was unknown to her.

"Go and embrace the crown prince," said Grumkow.

And she went.

XI

Une Reine Malheureuse

On the day that the whole of Lisbon was convulsed by the most terrible earthquake that Europe has ever seen—and by the tidal wave that followed after it—a little daughter was born, far away in Vienna, to the empress Maria Theresa. The baby, who bore the names of Marie Antoinette Josepha Jeanne, was the youngest of several children; and three of her brothers, as well as her father Francis, wore the Imperial crown. From the first she was her father's favourite, and, as far as he was able to find leisure for her, his companion. Of course, being emperor, there were a great many duties which he had to perform, but he was not so clever at business as his wife, who was the heiress of Austria and Hungary.

"We will die for our *king* Maria Theresa," shouted the Hungarian parliament, when she first appeared before them; and a "king" she was till the day of her death.

The empress was a good mother, and was very fond of her children; but she could not have them much with her when they were little. Sometimes a whole week would slip by without her seeing them, but they had an excellent doctor of their own, who visited them daily, and made careful reports about their health. Maria Theresa was also most anxious about their being properly taught, but unluckily she was deceived in their governesses, who were good-natured, lazy people. "The children were so clever," these ladies would say one to the other, "they really could do without learning lessons like other girls. And besides, were they not princesses, and what need had they to be always poring over books?" So Marie Antoinette and her sisters bade fair to grow up in perfect ignorance of everything except Italian, in which Metastasio the poet was their master.

This state of things might have gone on much longer had not Marie Antoinette remarked one day, in her mother's hearing, that her copies were always pencilled for her before she wrote them. This startled the empress, and, in her usual energetic manner, she began making inquiries as to the methods of teaching pursued by her daughter's governesses. The end of it was that these ladies were dismissed, and the Comtesse de Brandès, a clever and trustworthy woman, took charge of the education of the young archduchess. The change was very much for the better, but it came rather late for Marie Antoinette. She had never been forced to fix her attention steadily upon anything, or to do anything that she did not like. The slightest sound would distract her thoughts, and she would break off in the midst of the "History of the Thirty Years' War," or the account of the appearance of John Sobieski before the walls of Vienna, to wonder if she would be allowed to appear at the approaching fête, or what operas would be given in the coming week. For Marie Antoinette, like all her family, was extremely fond of music, and though she could never play well herself on any instrument, she had a sweet voice, which was carefully cultivated. When she was nearly seven years old there was great excitement in the palace of Schönbrünn, near Vienna, at the news that a little boy called Mozart, younger even than Marie Antoinette, was coming from Salzburg to play to them. "What instrument did he play on? Oh! both the harpsichord (a sort of piano), and the violin. And he could *compose* too! Think of that, at six years old! Would Wednesday never come, that they might hear him!"

Wednesday *did* come, after long waiting, and there entered a little figure in court dress, with a wig and sword all complete. He was followed by his father and mother, and sister Marianne, who, though five years older than himself, was far more shy than he was. Wolfgang, indeed, was not shy at all: it was his music he was thinking of, not himself; he came forward towards the harpsichord, stopping, when he remembered his manners, to make a funny little bow right and left. The archdukes and their sisters gazed at him as if he was a being from another world, and could hardly contain their delight when the emperor mentioned a short composition which the boy was to play with one finger. It could not have been very interesting, but it was a very difficult thing to do, and Wolfgang did it to perfection. When it was over, he wriggled down off his high stool, and bowed three times, waiting for the emperor to tell him what he wished for next. Francis praised his cleverness, then, taking up a piece of silk from a chair, he said: "See, I will arrange this over the keys, and you must play me a minuet without looking at the notes." This was just the sort of thing that pleased Wolfgang; he gave a little laugh of satisfaction, and wriggled on to his stool again. In a moment the notes rang out clear, and the children looked at each other and longed to dance to them.

"Well done, my boy," cried the emperor; "now you shall choose." Then Wolfgang turned to a composer attached to the court who had been eagerly watching his fingers.

"I will play a concerto of yours, and you must turn over for me." And when the concerto was over, and the Emperor inquired how he had liked the performance, the musician answered in the heartiest tones, that never had it sounded so well.

"I think so, too," said the empress, and signed to the child to go over to her. In his haste to obey he slipped on the shining floor, and fell down, his sword clattering as if it had been a man's. Marie Antoinette, who was nearest to him, ran to pick him up, and he thanked her with a smile, saying: "You are very kind; I should like to marry you." Then, without waiting for a reply, walked with careful steps up to the empress, and jumped on her lap.

Wolfgang was a great man when he returned to Salzburg, and everybody he saw asked the same questions about the imperial family.

"And when you had finished, what did her majesty say to you?"

"She said, 'Are you tired?'"

"And what did you answer?"

"I said 'No, your majesty.'"

"Did she say nothing more?"

"She said 'You play very well.'"

"And what did you reply to *that*?"

"I said, 'Thank you, your majesty.'"

FOR SOME TIME AFTER LITTLE Mozart went away the beautifully painted stool in front of the harpsichord was never empty; but by-and-by the children's zeal wore off, and their mother was too busy to see that they practised daily. They passed most of their time at Schönbrünn, which both the emperor and empress preferred to Vienna, and it was so near the capital that ministers and ambassadors could easily drive out to consult them when needful. In their leisure moments, which were few, it rested them to watch the growth of their flowers, or to plan alterations in their garden, while the empress would sometimes go to see the poor in their cottages, and take Marie Antoinette with her.

But, in the summer of 1765, when the little archduchess was nine years old, a break suddenly occurred in their peaceful, happy life. The emperor was obliged to go to Innsprück, and had already bidden farewell to his family and entered his carriage, when he suddenly ordered the coachman to stop.

"Be kind enough to bring me, the Archduchess Marie Antoinette," he said to the equerry; and soon the little girl was flying down the road. "Good-bye, my darling, good-bye," he whispered, taking her in his arms; "now run home again." And as she disappeared round a corner he remarked to his equerry: "I just wanted to see her once more."

It was as if he had guessed what would befall him, for, shortly after, news was received that he had died on his journey. The empress had loved her husband dearly, but she was not the sort of person to shut herself up with her grief, and before the year was out an event happened which occupied all her thoughts. This was a hint let fall by Louis XV, king of France, of a marriage, by-and-bye, between his grandson the dauphin and Marie Antoinette. The plan was to be kept entirely secret for the present, but the empress was greatly pleased, unlike the bridegroom's mother, or his aunt the strong-willed madame Adelaide. The dauphine, mother of the young Louis, was a Saxon princess, and wished her son to marry his Saxon cousin. The dauphin, a good-natured, heavy, ill-mannered youth, did not wish to marry anybody, or indeed do anything except hunt—but he was not consulted. Still, out of respect to his daughter-in-law (and perhaps because he was a little afraid of her), the French king kept a profound silence on the matter to all but the empress, till things were suddenly altered by the death of the dauphine in 1767. Then, no one knew how, the marriage began to be spoken of in Paris, and much more openly at Vienna, to the great embarrassment of the French ambassador. Louis XV had already an Austrian great-granddaughter, for the emperor Joseph II had some years before married the Infanta Isabel, and they had one little girl, named Maria Theresa, after her grandmother. Unfortunately the young empress was seized with smallpox, which was the scourge of those times, and died, while her sister-in-law, the Archduchess Josepha, likewise fell a victim to the same disease a few days later, just as she was starting off to be married. Joseph, in terror lest his little girl should be the next victim, had her inoculated, as people were before vaccination was introduced, and wrote to tell Louis XV, who was very anxious about her, that she was getting on very well. With his letter went one from the little archduchess herself.

"I know, dear grandpapa, that you love me, so I write to tell you that I am quite well, and that I had only fifty spots, which I am very glad of. How I wish I could show them to you, and hug you, for I am very fond of you."

Now, although not a word had been said to Marie Antoinette as to the fate that was in store for her, she was quite clever enough to guess a great deal that was happening. In the first place two French actors arrived in Vienna to teach her how to speak clearly and prettily. They were followed by the abbé de Vermond, who instructed her in the history of France and its literature, while the celebrated Noverre gave her lessons in dancing and the French mode of curtseying, which was far more difficult to learn than the curtsey practised in Vienna. Marie Antoinette delighted in the hours she spent over her dancing, and those passed in playing on the clavecin, under Glück, whose opera of "Orfeo" had just been finished; but her new teachers found the same fault that the old ones had done, that she must have everything told her like a child if it was to dwell in her memory. She never got impatient or cross, in fact she tried to turn everything into a joke; but the abbé discovered her to be ignorant and inattentive, and though she had plenty of good sense, she disliked being made to think. And in all this she was not different from a hundred thousand other little girls!

At length, in September 1768, the King of France made a formal proposal for the hand of the archduchess, who was not yet thirteen years old, and the empress wrote to count Mercy d'Argenteau, her ambassador in Paris, to give orders for the trousseau, on which she was prepared to lay out 16,000*l*. As the wedding was not to take place for a year and a half at any rate, this seems a little early to begin, but there was so much beautiful lace to be made, and wonderful embroidery to be done, that the workers did not think the time any too long. Then her brother Joseph II often came into her private sitting-room in the evening and talked to her about European politics, of which, he truly said, she ought to know something, or the abbé de Vermond was bidden to join the family in the evening and relate the lives of the French queens, and the genealogy of the Bourbons and Valois, besides the names of the chief officers of state and of the great nobles. All these things Marie Antoinette picked up quickly; and as for the army, the abbé used to say she would soon know every colonel of every regiment. Besides this sort of education, the empress felt that her daughter must learn how to take her place in the world, so once or twice a week she was allowed to have parties of ten or twelve in her own rooms, at which she presided, and here they would play *cavagnol* or other fashionable card games, for in those days cards were played every night, and large sums were staked.

The wedding-day drew nearer and nearer, and the empress's heart sometimes failed her at the thought of the child she was sending forth alone. As she was very busy all day, she made her daughter sleep during the last weeks in her room at night, and here she warned her against all the temptations she might find in the court, and read to her out of a little book which her husband had once written for his children. Very useful was the counsel he gave, the dangers he foresaw being mostly those which beset Marie Antoinette during her married life, and led to her downfall. "Beware," he said "of making friends quickly, or of allowing pleasure to become a business when it should only be an amusement. Beware of flattering tongues, and of persuading yourself that things may be innocent when really they are harmful. Do not let the world absorb you, till you forget that you are mortal, but put aside two days in every year to think of death."

As the young archduchess read these words her soul grew serious within her, and she promised her mother that she would keep the book always, and strive to act as her father would have wished. And so she did; but she was young and alone, and if court life is difficult everywhere, in France it was harder than anywhere else.

For three days in Holy Week Marie Antoinette went into retreat, and when she returned to the palace for Easter she had to give audience to the principal Austrian and Hungarian nobles, and to reply in Latin (probably carefully learnt for the occasion) to an address of the University. Next, the empress held a crowded court, and in the midst of it the French ambassador presented the archduchess with a letter from the dauphin, together with his portrait set in diamonds, which was hung at once round her neck by the countess of Trautmannsdorf, who was in attendance. Then, much to the relief of the bride, they went to the theatre, to see a French play. There only remained one more ceremony to be performed, and this, considering that the archduchess was the youngest of a very large family, was merely formal, and in the presence of a number of witnesses she signed a paper renouncing her claim to any Austrian, Hungarian, or Bohemian territory. This done, a few balls and banquets were given in her honour, and, on April 19, her marriage by proxy took place in the church of the Augustinians, her brother, the archduke Ferdinand, taking the oaths instead of the bridegroom. The papal nuncio, or special envoy, gave the blessing, and little Marie Antoinette was dauphine of France.

HER PROGRESS FROM VIENNA, UNDER the care of the prince of Stahremberg, was a series of *fêtes*. On an island of the Rhine the ladies and gentlemen of her suite awaited her in a magnificent pavilion, and here she took off her Viennese clothes, even her stockings, and put on one of her beautiful trousseau dresses, sent straight from Paris. The prince of Stahremberg delivered her into the charge of the comte de Noailles, and bade her farewell. Then the dauphine entered one of the carriages which had been built for her in Paris. In those days the carriages were worth seeing, for each was a work of art. Those intended for the use of Marie Antoinette were things of wonder and beauty, and had astonished even Paris, where splendid coaches were to be seen all day in the streets. One was covered entirely with crimson velvet on which the emblems of spring, summer, autumn, and winter, had been worked in gold thread, while a wreath of flowers, in gold and enamel, ran along the top; the other was also decorated with flowers in their natural colours, and the body of the carriage was in blue, with pictures representing earth, air, fire, and water, embroidered in silver. At that period carriages cost great sums of money, for the paintings of them were done by good artists, and they were handed on from father to son. Strange to say, many of them escaped the fury of the mob in the French Revolution, and brightened the Paris of the Restoration. But a curious fate was in store for them after all. One night, in the year 1848, a young lady living in Paris with her family, was beckoned out of the room by the old *courrier*.

"If you will come out with me, I will show you something you will never forget," said he, "only you must say nothing." The girl promised, and wrapping herself in a cloak and hood, went with the old man to the place du Carrousel, behind the Tuileries. Here a huge fire was burning, and all along the walls the lovely coaches were ranged, to be dragged one by one into the midst of the fire. For a while the girl looked on, as if fascinated by the work of destruction, then suddenly she turned away. "Oh, what a dreadful, dreadful pity!" she cried; "I wish I had never come. Oh, take me home at once."

But we have wandered far down the years from Marie Antoinette, whom we left driving across the bridge to the French town of Strasburg. The carriage could only go very slowly, for, besides the regiments of cavalry which lined the streets, crowds of people stood on every bit of available ground. Guns fired, bells pealed, voices shouted, and Marie Antoinette enjoyed the deafening noise, and smiled and bowed and waved her hand, and looked so pleased and happy that the cries of welcome grew louder and more heartfelt than before. At last she reached the archbishop's palace, where all the great Church officials were drawn up to receive her, headed by her host, the cardinal de Rohan himself; by his side stood his nephew and helper, prince Louis de Rohan, who afterwards did Marie Antoinette a cruel wrong. Gaily the dauphine entered the palace, where she at once held a reception, to which only ladies were admitted, and to each of these she said a few pleasant words and begged to know their names. Next she dined in public, and glad she must have felt of a little rest and food; but she was not allowed to sit long over her dinner, for she had to visit the theatre, drive about the illuminated streets, and attend a ball, before she went to bed. It was a day that would have tired most girls, but Marie Antoinette loved pleasure, and seemed to thrive on it, and it was with regret that next day she took leave of the hospitable city, which never forgot her or her pretty manners. "Ah!" the people would say to each other, when the dark days came by-and-bye, "she was better than beautiful, and had a heart of gold. Did you not hear when monsieur le maire addressed her in German, how she would have none of it, and answered, 'You must not speak to me in German, Monsieur, for now I understand nothing but French'? Ah, poor thing, poor thing!"

The May trees were in blossom and the lilacs and laburnums bloomed in the gardens when Marie Antoinette arrived at the little town of Compiègne which the king, the royal family, and his cousins, the princes of the blood, had reached the day before. The first person whom she met was the duc de Choiseul, the king's minister, sent to welcome her by the king.

"I shall never forget," said the dauphine, holding out her hand for Choiseul to kiss, "I shall never forget that it is you who have made my happiness."

"And that of France," answered the minister. And then the royal carriage drove out and the king dismounted, followed by his daughters, and Marie Antoinette fell on her knees before him, as her mother had bidden her. But Louis raised her and kissed her, and presented the dauphin, who took far less interest in the bride than his grandfather. For some reason or other, the court of France had not expected the future queen to be more than tolerably good-looking, and when she entered the royal apartments where the princes of the blood were awaiting her, led by the king and the dauphin, they were all startled by her beauty. It was not only the brilliant complexion, the fair hair with hardly a touch of powder, or the bright blue eyes which they admired, it was the sort of radiance of expression, the life and power of enjoyment, shown in the pictures painted at that time. And she had charms besides, which in the French court were more dearly prized than mere loveliness; she had an air of distinction and dignity not always possessed by people of high birth. She was tall for her age, and held herself well, and could answer the fine compliments that were then in fashion, with equal grace and courtesy.

The ceremony of presentation that now took place would have been rather alarming to most young princesses. One by one the king introduced his cousins. First the duc d'Orléans and his son the duc de Chartres (hereafter to become Philippe Egalité, and lose his head on the guillotine), then the whole Condé family, and the duc de Penthièvre and his son, and the lovely princesse de Lamballe; then those who were more remote. After each one had bowed or curtseyed, he or she sat on an armchair and when all the armchairs were full, as in a game, the duc d'Orléans, the senior prince of the blood, rose, bowed again, and backed to the door, followed by the rest in order of precedence.

The following morning a number of splendid carriages drawn by six or eight long-tailed horses, might have been seen on the road from Compiègne to Paris. The king's coach, containing the bride and bridegroom, drew up at the doors of the Carmelite convent at St. Denis, where the princess Louise was a professed nun. Here they entered, accompanied by madame Adelaide, madame Victoire, and madame Sophie, who were anxious to take this opportunity of seeing their sister, for the Carmelite rule was very strict, and visitors, even royal ones, were rare. The gentle *sœur* Louise was delighted with her new niece, and still more pleased when she learnt that it was she and not the king, who had wished to pay the visit, while on her side Marie Antoinette had a sense of rest in the presence of the nun, which she never felt when with the other princesses. But the king soon rose, good-byes were said, and the carriages rolled along outside Paris to La Muette in the Bois de Boulogne, where the dauphin's younger brothers, the comte de Provence and the comte d'Artois were ready to receive them. The elder boy was serious and heavy, like the dauphin, but the younger was bright and gay, and at once made friends with his sister-in-law. But best of all were the two little princesses, madame Clotilde, the king's favourite, and madame Elizabeth, the girl who in after years stood by Marie Antoinette in all her trials, and followed her to the guillotine. However, no shadows lay over that warm May day when the dauphine set out from La Muette for Versailles, for the celebration of her marriage in the chapel. The

Swiss Guards were drawn up before the palace, the same corps which, twenty-two years after, were cut down before the Tuileries in defending Marie Antoinette and her husband, and they presented arms as she got down from her carriage, and went to change her dress in the rooms which she was temporarily to occupy.

At one o'clock she appeared again, dressed in a white brocade dress, looped back over panniers. Holding her hand high in the air walked the dauphin, wearing the robes of the Order of the St. Esprit, glittering with diamonds and gold. Although more than a year older than the archduchess, he looked like a clumsy boy by her side, and instead of his gorgeous garments lending him dignity they seemed to smother him. After the princes of the blood and their attendants came the bridegroom's two brothers, then followed the king leading princess Clotilde, mesdames his daughters, and a train of seventy of the noblest ladies of France. The blessing was given by the archbishop of Paris, grand almoner to the king, and then the royal family signed the register, but their writing was so very bad that it could hardly be read.

The rest of the day was passed in the manner usual at royal weddings: fêtes were held during the afternoon; at six, card tables were set, and the public were admitted to stare at them while they were playing at *cavagnol* or *lansquenet;* at half-past nine they had supper in the new hall of the opera house. Marie Antoinette went through it all with the life and spirit she put into everything, though she could hardly have helped feeling irritated with the bored face of her bridegroom. Next day seemed very long indeed to her—and to him also. Etiquette did not allow him to hunt, and he cared for nothing else; and though she tried to forget that she had a husband, and only to think of the gaiety about her, yet the gloomy youth at her side weighed down her spirits, and no doubt all the excitement of the last few days had tired her. When, the next morning, the dauphin set out with a beaming countenance to hunt with the king, she felt quite relieved, and glad to spend a few quiet hours with her dog and her lady-in-waiting. Still, just now she was not allowed much time to feel lonely, for she seemed always dressing and undressing to go to some brilliant festivity. One evening a great ball was given, at which even madame Clotilde was allowed to appear, and a young princess of Lorraine, Marie Antoinette's cousin, was present. For two hundred years the French nobles had always been jealous of the dukes of Lorraine, and never lost any chance of being rude to them; so when they heard that the king had allotted the princess a place in the first state quadrille, they ordered their wives and daughters to stay at home. Of course the ladies were all bitterly angry, and wept tears of disappointment; but they sobbed in vain, and it was only when a special order from the king arrived, that the injured nobles were forced to give way—to the great delight of their families.

The marriage rejoicings were to end by a display of fireworks given by the City of Paris, intended to be the most wonderful ever seen. They were to be sent up from the Place Louis XV which later changed its name to the Place de la Revolution, and then to the Place de la Concorde, and the wide space was filled with wooden platforms for the spectators, grouped round a Temple of Hymen. After streams of flame from the mouths of the dolphins, and rockets and fire-balls had fascinated the people, the scene was to be crowned by the ascent of the temple into the air, where it was to burst into a thousand fiery fragments. Holding their breath, the dense crowds watched the temple rising into the sky, and a gasp of admiration followed its explosion. So intent were they in gazing at the spectacle that they never noticed that one of the burning rockets had fallen on a platform standing at the back till the wood was flaming up behind them. Had they kept their presence of mind they might all have got safely away, but the panic spread as quickly as the fire, and there was a general rush to the side where the carriages stood, as that was the only part of the Place not blocked by the wooden buildings. In their mad flight they dashed up against the horses, which, already excited by the noise of the fireworks, plunged and tried to bolt; many of the fugitives were trampled under their feet, or fell, for others to fall over them. Some struggled through, but, blinded with terror, could not see where they were going, and stumbled over the bank into the river, which ran close by. Now, owing to an accidental delay, the dauphine, who was to drive to the Place Louis XV with mesdames, had been delayed in starting, and only arrived when the panic was at its height. She was horror-stricken at the sights and sounds around her, and when she found there was nothing to be done at the moment, directed the coachman to return to the palace. All night long the cries and groans rang in her ears, and as soon as it was daylight both she and the dauphin sent all the money they had to the chief of the police, begging him to lay it out for the good of the sufferers from the fire.

From these, and many other acts of kindness, the bride became very popular with the Parisians, over whom she was some day to rule; and her mother was forced to write and warn her not to put too much faith in their loyalty, or to think herself the piece of perfection they called her, for they were very fickle, and easily threw down their old idols, to worship new ones in their stead. Marie Antoinette replied dutifully to her mother's letters, but, being young, put little faith in her counsels. What the empress said might be true of *most people*, she thought, but it could never be true of *her*. So she smiled and danced, and beamed with happiness—till the crash came, and she laid her head down on the Place Louis XV, where the guillotine was erected.

Like the king's own mother, the little duchesse de Bourgogne, and Louis XIV, she became the pet and plaything of the dauphin's grandfather. Louis XV enjoyed being treated by her in a friendly, unceremonious fashion, and her spirits and gaiety roused him from the boredom which had been the bane of his life. "Mon papa," she called him when they were alone, and she would fling herself into his arms, and tell all that she had heard and seen, and the amusements she had invented. How that when they were next at Fontainebleau she meant to have donkey rides with her friends every day in the forest, and then she would take long walks, as she used to do at Schönbrünn—nobody at Versailles seemed to have any legs at all; and by-and-bye, when the bad weather came, she would have singing lessons again, and study the harp. Perhaps she might even read some history, if the snow was not hard enough for sledging! Yet, in spite of Marie Antoinette's power of being happy, she had many difficulties, to fight against, though she was often unconscious of the fact. Mesdames, with whom she passed much of her time, were fond of her and kind to her, but unluckily the eldest of the three, madame Adelaide, had the strongest will and the worst temper, and the other two were afraid of opposing her, lest they should make her angry. Besides being strong-willed and bad-tempered, madame Adelaide had very little common-sense and a great deal of pride, and often gave the dauphine advice which got her into trouble. Then, at first, the dauphin, who was very shy, and not at all clever, held aloof from her, and left her to pass her time as best she could while he was away hunting. But after a while his timidity wore off, they became good friends, and he consulted her and asked her opinion on all sorts of subjects. When a couple of years had passed, he had grown so far like other people that he would be present at the little dances of intimate friends which Marie Antoinette gave once a week in her own apartments, and allowed proverbs and comedies to be played in his own rooms, which amused them much and cost but little. Sometimes

Marie Antoinette herself would act, with her brother-in-law the comte de Provence, or they would have music, when fat and friendly princess Clotilde would accompany herself on the guitar, and Marie Antoinette would sing also. At length, to the dauphin's great delight, she declared her intention of hunting on horseback, which no dauphine had done for hundreds of years. When every other amusement failed there were cards—always cards—which the king's aunts preferred to everything else.

The years sped gaily on to the young dauphine, who never heard, or did not heed, the rumblings of the discontent of the starving and down-trodden people. She herself was always kind to them, not merely in words but in taking trouble, which is much harder work. Yet the flattery she received from the friends who were constantly with her had worked her evil. She fancied herself all-powerful, and became vexed and impatient if her wishes were not immediately carried out. She began to meddle in politics, too, of which she knew absolutely nothing, and in this, though she would have been shocked to think it, she worked positive harm.

In May, 1774, a change came into her life. The king had been taken ill of small-pox about a fortnight earlier in the cottage of the Little Trianon, where he was having supper, and was hastily removed in a carriage to the palace of Versailles. It was curious to note the total indifference with which his subjects, especially the Parisians, received the news of his danger. Louis the Well-Beloved, as the child of five had been named, was passing away, and Louis the Wished-for was to take his place. Nobody cared—nobody pretended to care—except his daughters. Only Marie Antoinette, to whom he had always been kind, was really sorry, and offered to stay with him and mesdames; but, being forbidden, she shut herself up in her own room, where her sisters and brothers-in-law, bewildered with the strangeness of it all, gathered around her. The dauphine felt bewildered too, in the midst of her grief.

"I feel as if the skies were falling on me," she said. As for the dauphin, he had given orders that the moment the king died the carriage should be ready to go to Choisy.

So they waited, watching the lighted candle in the window of the sick room, which was to be extinguished the moment the king had ceased to breathe. He could not see the sunset—that they knew; but there was something awful in that solemn silence. Suddenly a noise was heard outside, and madame de Noailles entered.

"The courtiers are in the Œil-de-Boeuf, Madame," she exclaimed; "will your Majesties deign to go there to receive them?"

Arm-in-arm, the queen of eighteen and the king of nineteen advanced into the room, where the duc de Bouillon, grand chamberlain, came forward to meet them. As they paused in the doorway he threw himself on one knee: "The king is dead," he said. "Long live the king!"

MANY YEARS AGO, AN OLD lady who had passed her hundredth birthday, told the writer of this story that on a cold day in January, 1793, she went to a children's party in London. The house was large, and was filled with little boys and girls all eager to begin to dance on the beautifully polished floor. The musicians had already tuned up, and the eager faces of the little guests were turned towards the door, waiting for their hostess to enter. At length she came, dressed in black, her eyes red with weeping. "Children," she said, "you must all go home. I have just heard the king of France is dead."

The king was Louis le Désiré, the husband of Marie Antoinette, who had died on the guillotine.

XII

The "Little Queen"

A queen at seven and a widow at twelve. Who can guess that riddle? Yet there have been very few little girls in Europe who could be described in such a way, and, out of those, fewer still who were not mere dolls, but left a mark on the history of the time, and therefore of the time to come.

AT THE CLOSE OF THE year of grace 1395 a group of children were living in the Hôtel de St. Pol, on the banks of the Seine in Paris. They were all pretty—their mother Isabeau de Bavière, queen of France, was as famous for her beauty as for her wickedness—but the prettiest of all was Isabel, the eldest daughter, with her large brown eyes and pink and white skin. Charles VI, the father of these little princes and princesses, was subject to terrible fits of gloom, which in later years deepened into madness. Still, he always had a special love for Isabel, who was everybody's favourite, even her mother's, though it was not to be expected that the queen would give up any of her own pleasures in order to look after her children. By-and-by two little sisters, years younger than any of these, princess Michelle, hereafter to be duchess of Burgundy, and little princess Katherine, who became the wife of Henry V and queen of England, were so neglected by their servants (who thought they might safely follow the queen's example) that the poor little things were half-starved and clad in dirty rags. But at the time we are speaking of matters were not so bad. Queen Isabeau was proud of princess Isabel, and gave her masters to teach her music and the old romances. The child was quick and fond of books, and would often leave the games which she had been playing with her brothers and sit in the small dark rooms with carved ceilings and tapestry hangings, embroidered in *fleurs-de-lis*, listening to the old stories of Sir Galahad and the Holy Grail, or the adventures of Huon of Bordeaux. In the dark evenings she would lie on a silken cushion on the floor of the great hall, her fingers absently thrust in the hair of the small greyhound that was curled up against her, her mind wrapped up in the lays sung by the minstrels to charm away the gloom of the king.

In the midst of this quiet life there one day entered the gates of Paris a goodly array of ambassadors from England to demand from Charles VI the hand of the princess Isabel on behalf of Richard II, king of England. The envoys had not set forth without fierce protest from the English people, who still remembered Crécy and Poitiers, won by Richard's own father when still a boy, and hated the thought of an alliance with their foes. Besides this, they had all loved Richard's first wife, Anne of Bohemia, who had only died the year before; and though it was necessary for him to marry again, and have a son to wear the crown after him, they did not wish him to forget so soon, still less for his choice to fall on a French princess, and a mere baby! Richard summoned parliament to meet and talk over the matter, and the famous chronicler Sir John Froissart, who had newly entered England, was present at the debates. But whether his subjects approved or not, the king was determined to have his way. He was half French himself, he always declared; for was he not born at Bordeaux, and did he not love the songs and the poetry that came from France? And then, though perhaps he may have kept this reason in the background, where else could he find a bride endowed with such great riches? And Richard was always extravagant and always in debt.

OF COURSE RICHARD HAD NOT called his parliament together without first finding out the mind of the French king on the subject. The first messenger who was sent to Charles received for answer that the princess was already betrothed to the son of the duke of Brittany, that it would be five or six years at least before she was of marriageable age, and that Richard was twenty-two years older than she. But Richard, who now and then behaved like a spoilt baby, only gave a scornful laugh when he read Charles's letter. Had not the king another daughter who would make as good a duchess of Brittany as Isabel? And as for the rest—and with a shrug of his shoulders he turned away and began to talk with Sir John Froissart about the next yearly meeting of the *jongleurs*, or minstrels, to be held at his court.

Now these matters had been carefully concealed from the princess Isabel, who had no idea that the splendidly arrayed and armed body of five hundred men riding along the banks of the Seine towards the Hôtel de St. Pol had come to decide her fate.

"Look, look!" she cried to her brothers and sisters as they all crowded at the small window. "Who can they be? One has a mitre; is he a bishop, think you? or an archbishop? And the others? I know not the devices on their shields, but they are richly dressed, and they hold themselves proudly. And, see, they are entering the gateway. Oh, Louis, you are the dauphin! I wonder if they will send for you!"

After all, it was not Louis but Isabel, who was summoned, and in a few words learned from her great-uncle the duke of Burgundy the object of this magnificent embassy. Isabel listened in surprise, but it was not the first time that she had heard talk of her marriage; so she showed no signs of shyness, and bade her maids put on with all haste her light blue velvet dress, the colour of France, and clasp the loose folds with her jewelled belt. Then, escorted by her uncle, she entered the great hall, and, standing by her mother's side, awaited the appearance of the envoys.

"Who can know how such a child will behave?" the council of regency, who governed France during Charles's fits of madness, had asked of the English nobles when they had begged for an interview with the princess herself. But the earl marshal, looking at the tall and dignified young lady before him, felt that they need not have been afraid. This was no child, beautiful indeed, but caring for nothing except sweet confections and puppets, but a girl whose face and manner showed marks of thought and of careful training in the ways of courts.

"Madam, if it please God, you shall be our lady and queen," said the earl marshal, falling on one knee, and Isabel answered, "Sir, if it please God and my lord and father that I be queen of England, I shall be content, for I know that I shall be a great lady." So saying she signed to him to rise from his knee, and, taking his hand, led him to the queen her mother, who was well pleased with her reply.

So Isabel's fate was settled, and as the poor French king was not in a state to talk about business, it was the duke of Burgundy with whom the ambassadors held daily discussions. It was decided that, though the earl marshal should represent Richard in the marriage ceremony, which, at the urgent request of the English king, was to take place at once, the young bride should remain in Paris another year, to get her trousseau and be taught the duties of the "great lady" she was to be. Among these "duties" we may be sure the learning of English was included, and also the practice of music, which Richard loved. No doubt she managed to find out something of her future husband from the count of St. Pol, who was his brother-in-law, and she would only hear the many good things that could truly be said of him: of his grace, his beauty, his cleverness, and his gallantry when as a boy of fifteen he faced the rebel archers of Wat Tyler and Jack Straw, and won them over to his side. Of his wilfulness, his extravagance, and his heedlessness there was no need to tell her; and indeed, whatever were his faults, Richard was always true and loving to her.

THE YEAR THAT WAS TO pass between the marriage by proxy and the real marriage most likely seemed as long to the "queen of England," as she was now called, as it would have done to any little girl of her age. But at length it was announced that at the end of October Richard would cross over to Calais, which was to be English ground for nearly two hundred years longer. The king, who, unlike his people, much desired a peace with France, sailed with a noble company across the Channel, for at his express wish his famous uncle, John of Gaunt, duke of Lancaster, with his third duchess, the duke and duchess of York, and the duke and duchess of Gloucester, with their two daughters, sailed with him. It was with great unwillingness that Gloucester obeyed the summons of the king to attend his marriage. He hated his nephew for many reasons, and Richard was not slow to perceive and return his feelings. Well he knew that his uncle was an ambitious man, who would fain have seen his daughter queen of England; and, besides, the duke longed to go to war with France, and lost no chance of exciting the passions of the English people and making the French alliance more unpopular than it was already. Perhaps Gloucester had cherished secret hopes of being left behind to rule the kingdom while Richard was away; but if so he was disappointed, for the king's cousin, Henry earl of Derby (afterwards Henry IV), was declared regent.

It was on October 27, 1396, that the kings of France and England met in a plain outside Calais. Everything had been carefully planned beforehand, and the two sovereigns quitted their lodgings at precisely the same moment and walked slowly to the appointed place, which must be reached at exactly the same time, as it would be unfitting for one king to look more eager than the other! Tents splendidly furnished had been prepared for them, and all around stood eight hundred French and English knights, their drawn swords shining bright in the autumn sunshine. From one direction came Charles, with Richard's two uncles, Lancaster and Gloucester, on each side of him, while from the other Richard was escorted by the dukes of Burgundy and Berri, brothers of the late king. "At the moment of the meeting," says the chronicler, "the eight hundred knights fell on their knees; the two kings swept off their hats and bowed, then took each other by the hand, and so entered the French king's tent, while the four dukes followed them." Here another welcome awaited Richard, for he was received by the duke of Orleans, brother of Charles, and the duke of Bourbon, his cousin. But as soon as they had greeted the bridegroom these two left the tent to join the dukes outside, and at length Charles and Richard were alone and could talk over business.

Next day—the feast of St. Simon and St. Jude—a grand banquet was given by Charles, and when it was over presents were exchanged between the kings, a ceremony which kept them employed until the little bride arrived, attended by the duke of Orleans (who had gone to fetch her) and a great suite. Some of the ladies were drawn in the long carriages, like furniture vans, that were fashionable in the days of Charles VI, while Isabel herself and her young maids of honour were mounted on beautiful horses, with gorgeous velvet trappings, embroidered in gold. The "queen of England" wore a golden crown, which must have felt very uncomfortable on horseback, and her dress was blazing with precious stones. She had ridden a long way and was very tired, but she greeted her uncles gaily as they lifted her from her horse, and went forward to speak to the duchess of Lancaster and Gloucester. Then she entered the tent, where Richard sat awaiting her.

It was not until Isabel had knelt twice before him, as she had been told to do, that Richard got up, took her in his arms, and kissed her. When he set her down, she looked at him, anxious to see what her future husband was like. She found his eyes fixed upon *her*, and they both smiled, well pleased with their first sight of each other. He was not at all like what Isabel had expected: a man of thirty—almost an *old* man, too old to care for anything but serious matters, such as making laws and governing his kingdom. Why, the king was quite *young* and very, very handsome, with his dark blue eyes and golden hair, and a complexion as white and fair as her own. He could laugh, too, and be merry, she was sure. Oh no, she could never be afraid of *him*, and some day she might even be able to chatter to him as she did to Louis. And Richard read her thoughts in her face and was content with what fate had brought him.

The marriage did not take place till four days later, on All Saints' Day, and, curiously enough, neither the king nor queen of France was present at it. Since they had bidden farewell to their daughter, after her meeting with Richard, they had stayed quietly at the little town of St. Omer, though they had news of Isabel from the duke of Orleans and the duke of Burgundy, who went over to see her at Calais, before she sailed for England. It was the first time that Isabel had ever been upon the sea, and she did not like crossing, for though the wind was in their favour, it must have been very high, as the ship reached Dover in three hours. Two days later she dismounted at the palace of Eltham in Kent, and at last had time to rest from her journey.

IN THOSE DAYS HOUSES WERE few and there were no coal fires to make smoke, so Isabel was able to see in the distance the towers of Westminster Abbey, where by-and-by she would be crowned. Between the Abbey and Eltham stretched the gorse-covered common of Blackheath, the scene of some of Richard's youthful deeds, and the tall trees of Greenwich Park. And when she was tired of looking at the view, and wandering through the gardens with her maids of honour and madame de Coucy, her lady-in-waiting, she would summon them to her own rooms to watch the unpacking of her trousseau. This of itself was a wonderful sight. It not only included dresses of velvet covered with fur and jewels and embroideries for grand occasions, but gowns of the finest scarlet or green or white cloth for every day. The sleeves were very long, and so was the train; but this could be drawn through the belt and tucked up when the wearer wanted to play or run races, as we may be certain Isabel often did. When they had finished admiring her clothes and jewels, there were the rich stuffs and tapestries to be arranged on the different walls or hung on the different beds; and, better than all, had not Isabel brought with her a store of figs and sweet things of her own choosing, which she bade her waiting women set out on little silver plates before her friends?

But after a few days these joys were interrupted, for it was necessary that Isabel should make a progress through the City of London and show herself to her new subjects, who hated her so much, though she did not guess the fact. So she left Eltham under a strong escort and rode to Greenwich, where she stepped on board the royal barge, and was rowed down to Kennington, near Lambeth. Richard was delighted to welcome her here in the old palace which had belonged to his father, the Black Prince, and where he himself had lived for a while with his mother when she became a widow. The next morning Isabel rose early, for she knew she must be carefully dressed so as to look her best to her husband's people. Her long bright hair was brushed till it shone, and over it a fine white veil hung from a golden circlet. Luckily the day was fine and warm, for of course the hood which she usually wore out of doors had to be laid aside. Then her richest robe of velvet edged with ermine and covered with gold embroidery was put on, with a jacket of the same colour over it, and her golden shoes with the long pointed turned-up toes were fastened, and very fair she seemed to her ladies and her husband as she was placed on her white palfrey, covered like herself with gold.

Her face was so full of happiness as she rode along by the side of the king, mounted also on a white horse, whose housings or trappings tinkled with silver bells, that the hearts of many who most bitterly disliked the French marriage melted towards her. Behind followed the king's uncles and great nobles, all wearing their special badges or coats of arms, and accompanied by their retainers. The procession passed through Southwark and came at last to London Bridge, which, though made of stone and not yet cumbered with houses, was filled with such a dense crowd that there was hardly room for the king and the queen to move, even at a foot's pace. Then an accident happened, as it was sure to do. Something touched a horse; he grew frightened and kicked; the throng pressed back on each other; someone stumbled and fell. There were no policemen or soldiers lining the way to keep order or to give help, and by the time the procession had crossed the bridge nine persons had been trampled to death.

In Isabel's day, and for long, long after, the street which we call the Strand was filled with the palaces of great noblemen with their large gardens sloping down to the river and barges moored to the bank; for the streets were so narrow and so dirty that no one willingly went through them even on horseback or in a carriage. However, on the day that Isabel first saw them the fronts of the houses were draped with rich hangings and crowded with shouting people, while every now and then a platform might be seen on which a show of some kind would be given or a company of minstrels would sing a song. Altogether, pleased and touched though she was with her welcome, Isabel must have been glad when the houses were left behind and Westminster was reached—Westminster, not as we know it now, with houses everywhere, but as it was when Guinevere went a-maying, with broad fields and pleasant streams, and in the distance northwards the russet leaves of a forest. But queens are not so fortunate as their subjects, and have little time to rest themselves, and Isabel's days for some time to come were spent in receiving graciously and smilingly as she well knew how, the homage of all who came to pay their respects. Soon after there followed a tournament which lasted fourteen days, held in the open space of Smithfield, where the victor claimed his prize from the hands of the queen. The tournament over, the preparations were begun in good earnest for Isabel's coronation.

At length the festivities were finished and life went on quietly as before, Isabel remained in the palace at Westminster, and daily rode out past the marshy ground which is now Conduit Street, where flag flowers and forget-me-nots and marsh marigolds might be plucked in spring, and wildfowl were shot when the weather grew colder. Or sometimes she would accompany the king and his friends to a grand hunt after boar or deer in the woods that lay about the stream called the West Bourne, whence the chase would often lead them eastwards to the heathery spaces beyond what was afterwards the Moorgate. When it grew too dark or too wet for these sports, Richard would bid the queen play to him, and he could correct her faults as well as any master; or she would try and speak English to him, and they would both laugh heartily over the blunders she made.

Thus the days went by, and Richard was so good and kind to her that Isabel was perfectly happy, and thought him the most wonderful person in all the world. She did her utmost to please him and to take an interest in all he told her, and she noticed with pride that he never treated her as a little girl, but talked to her as he might have done to a grown-up woman. Inside the palace all was peace; but outside the people had begun to murmur again, and faces grew dark at the sound of Richard's name, and men spoke of the debts that were daily increasing and the taxes that were ever growing. But if Richard took no heed of these signs, there was one person who never failed to watch and listen, and every now and then to put in a careless word, which somehow always made matters worse. This was the duke of Gloucester, uncle to the king, and a great favourite of the Londoners. He, like them, wished for war with France, and lost no opportunity of letting his views be known on the subject. When things seemed ripe the duke sent for the earl of March, next heir to the kingdom, to his castle of Pleshy in Essex, and there unfolded to him a plot which he and the earl of Arundel had woven between them.

It was not without some hesitation that the duke of Gloucester told his tale to the earl of March, for he knew that his great-nephew was a true and loyal man, and that he dearly loved the king his cousin.

But he had prepared a bait which he thought could not fail to land the most obstinate fish, only he resolved not to speak of that till the end of his story. Therefore he began by relating all Richard's acts of misgovernment—and they were many—and the burdens laid on his subjects, which were many also.

The two earls nodded their heads. What Gloucester said was nothing but truth, and well they knew it. But how to find a remedy? *That*, as they say, needed sharper wits than theirs. Then Gloucester proceeded, choosing his words carefully, but in spite of all his prudence he saw March beginning to move uneasily.

"I do not think I understand," he said, and Gloucester repeated that the patience of English people had come to an end, that they would bear no more, and demanded (for so his tale went) that Richard and his queen should be taken possession of, and kept for life as honoured prisoners in separate palaces. This news struck the earl dumb with amazement, but before he could speak Gloucester added that, after asking counsel of many wise and powerful men, they had determined that, as soon as Richard was deposed, March should be declared king.

A dead silence followed. The earl burned to tell his tempter what he thought of such treachery; but in those times speech was not always safe, so he held his peace. Gloucester, however, read in his face something of what was passing in his mind, and entreated him to ponder the matter, and above all things to keep it secret, or the lives of many of his friends would be endangered. This March joyfully promised, and instantly returning to London obtained leave from Richard to go and govern Ireland, of which he had just been made viceroy. Every man among the conspirators was not, however, as loyal as March. The plot was betrayed to the king, who instantly summoned his two uncles, Lancaster and York, and his brother-in-law the count de St. Pol lately sent by Charles VI to see the queen. The king laid the matter before all three and asked their advice how to prevent the success of the conspiracy. The two dukes could not deny the truth of what the king told them—for the scheme that was being planned had come to their ears also; but they spoke soothing words, saying that Gloucester ever threatened more than he meant or could do, and assuring Richard that, even if he really cherished such an evil purpose, they would see that it was not carried out. Then, to avoid taking sides against either brother or nephew, they retired hastily to their castles, leaving Richard to fight his own battles as best he could.

THE WAY WHICH HE CHOSE has left a dark stain on his memory. He felt helpless and alone, and there were not wanting people about him to whisper that he would never be secure on his throne as long as Gloucester lived. Still Richard knew too well that if he dared to arrest him publicly his own doom would be sealed, for all London would at once fly to arms. Therefore, taking some men with him on whom he could rely, Richard rode down into Essex to the duke's house of Pleshy, and with fair words requested his company to the Tower of London. Gloucester went without misgiving—would he not be in the City which adored him?—and was lodged in splendid apartments close to the king, on pretence, perhaps, of caring the better, for his uncle who was at that time suffering from illness. This may also have sufficed for a pretext to keep the duke in his room, thus hiding his presence. But a night or two later he was hurried over to Calais, doubtless by the river, which flowed conveniently past the fortress, and handed over to the governor by the earl marshal, now duke of Norfolk.

"What have I done to be so treated?" the duke inquired indignantly of Norfolk, and the earl marshal answered soothingly that "the king his master was a little angry with him, and had given orders that the duke was to be locked up for the present in his good town of Calais, and, sorry as he himself was to displease his grace, he was forced to carry out his orders." Gloucester understood, and without further parley begged that a priest might be sent for, to hear his confession and give him absolution. The rite over, he was preparing to dine when four men entered the apartment. The duke had not expected them so soon, but he made no resistance. What would have been the use? He was speedily strangled, and a messenger sent over to tell Richard that his uncle was dead. "As to the manner of his death, in France no man cared," says the chronicler; but the Londoners were furious, and the dukes of Lancaster and York trembled for their lives, though they afterwards found that it was to their interest to make peace with the king. More troubles followed this act of treachery; several nobles were condemned to banishment or execution, and a fierce quarrel broke out between Henry of Bolingbroke, duke of Hereford (son to John of Gaunt), and Mowbray duke of Norfolk. A court of chivalry to decide the matter was summoned to meet at Windsor, and we can imagine Isabel's excitement as she watched the assembling of the barons, knights, and bannerets of England in the courtyard of the castle. The scene is described by Shakespeare in the opening of the play of "Richard II" (though he places it in London), and you can all read it for yourselves. After much talk judgment was passed that the quarrel should be fought out at Coventry on September 16, in presence of the king, a body of representatives of the house of commons, and the people.

On the day appointed the dukes rode to their places clad in the heavy armour of the time. "God speed the right!" cried Norfolk, and Henry of Bolingbroke solemnly made the sign of the cross. Each had his lance in rest, and leaned forward, listening for the expected signal; the trumpets were already raised for sounding the charge, when the king's warder was suddenly thrown down between the combatants.

> "Hold," he cried; "our kingdom's earth should not be soiled
> With the dear blood that it has fostered;
> Therefore we banish you our territories:
> You, cousin Hereford, upon pain of life,
> Till twice five summers have enriched our fields.
> Norfolk, for thee remains a heavier doom:
> The hopeless word of 'Never to return'
> Breathe I against thee upon pain of life."

"Those whom the gods will to destroy they first infatuate." Surely the old Latin proverb was never more true than in this act of Richard II. He thought to rid himself of two powerful nobles, and instead he turned them into two undying enemies, and he soon learned with dismay that Hereford had been welcomed at the French Court. Then came news which caused the king bitter grief; the earl of March, whom he so dearly loved, had died in Ireland. Matters there needed a master's eye, and Richard knew not whom to trust. At last, troubled as were the affairs of England, the king felt that he must go himself and try to settle things. And Henry duke of Hereford, on the other side of the Channel, watched it all, and knew that his chance would soon come.

After the sentence had been passed on the banished lords, Richard had sent prince Henry of Monmouth (son of Hereford) and his sisters to Windsor, where the widowed duchess of Gloucester and her two daughters had been living ever since the death of the duke. It was, we may believe, with great unwillingness that the duchess consented to dwell under the roof of her husband's murderer; but she dared not disobey the king, and reminded herself that Isabel not only was innocent of the crime, but ignorant of it, as she was of all Richard's evil deeds. The "little queen," who daily grew more beautiful and womanly, only knew that her aunt had lost her husband, and judged her grief by what she herself would feel at the death of Richard. So she busied herself in doing all the kindnesses she could to the duchess and her daughters, though these young ladies were some years older than herself, and did not care to play the games in which prince Henry, her devoted friend, and his sisters Blanche and Philippa delighted. Henry was about her own age, but the little girls were younger, and Isabel, who had in the days that now seemed so long ago taken care of her own brothers and sisters, no doubt mothered these children also, and saw that they learned their lessons, especially French, and that their manners were good. The duke of Hereford had three other sons, but they were not sent to Windsor.

But games and lessons and everything else was forgotten when one day Richard came into the queen's "bower," as a lady's boudoir was then called, and told her that he must leave her and proceed at once to Ireland, where he was much needed. Isabel wept and clung to him, and besought him to take her with him; but he shook his head gently, and said that Ireland was no place for ladies, still less for queens, and that she must stay at home and look to her household. He went on to say that he had been greatly wroth at discovering the state that the lady de Coucy had taken on herself, and had dismissed her from her charge about the queen, and bade her to go back to France. In her stead he had given her place to his niece, the young and widowed countess of March, who would shortly arrive with her two small children, and join the sad company in the castle.

LEFT ALONE, THE QUEEN REMAINED sitting in her carved high-backed chair, gazing straight before her, but seeing nothing. Her thoughts wandered away through the past year, and to the Christmas which she and Richard had kept in the bishop's palace at Lichfield, and to the journey they had made during the summer, riding under shady trees and hedges gay with honeysuckle and wild roses, and over downs sweet with gorse and bright with heather, amongst the towns of the west country, where they had seen splendid cathedrals and stately abbeys, and listened to the people talking a strange speech, which even Richard, clever as he was, could not understand! How happy they had both been, laughing over all their adventures, and what merry evenings they had passed in the tents that Richard had ordered to be spread for the night, wherever Isabel fancied. And how wonderful it was to visit the places where Guinevere had lived, and Arthur had fought his last battle! And now, now he was going to leave her, and travel over the seas, where he might suffer shipwreck, and run into dangers that she might never know. Oh no! It was impossible! She could never bear it.

But it had to be.

On April 25, St. Mark's Day, Richard and Isabel went hand in hand to St. George's chapel at Windsor, kneeling side by side while a solemn Mass was sung and one of the collects chanted by the king himself. When the service was over they left the church as they came, Isabel with her face white and drawn, with her eyes bright and tearless, and walking steadily. Outside the great door was set a table with wine and food, and together they ate, for the king did not mean to return again into the castle, but to ride straight into the west. When they had eaten, or pretended to eat, the king lifted up the queen in his arms, and holding her to his heart he kissed her many times, saying, "Farewell, madame, until we meet again," not knowing that it was farewell for ever. Then he rode away without looking back, his young cousins, Henry of Monmouth and Humphrey duke of Gloucester, riding behind him.

The queen stood watching till the cavalcade was out of sight, then slowly turned and walked towards the castle, none daring to speak to her. She mounted the narrow stone staircase like one in a dream, and shutting her door flung herself on her bed, with a burst of weeping. Kind lady March heard her sobs and longed to comfort her; but she too knew what sorrow was, and for some hours left Isabel alone with her grief. For a fortnight the queen was too ill to move from her room, and suffered no one except lady March and her old French maid to attend on her. But one morning the sun shone for her once more, for in came lady March carrying a letter tied with silk and bearing the royal arms, which Richard had sent by a special messenger from Milford Haven.

"He had been thinking of her, as he knew she had been thinking of him," he wrote, "while he rode along the same roads on which they had travelled last year together. But she must keep up a good heart, and not grieve if she heard nought of him, for the seas were rough, and not easy for boats to cross, but to remember that he loved her always."

Perhaps, if the earl of March had lived to rule Ireland, things might have turned out differently, or at any rate Richard's ruin might have been staved off a little longer. As it was, the expedition to Ireland only hurried on the calamity. The murmurs of the Londoners, which had hitherto been low, now became loud, and men shook their heads and reminded each other of the fate of Edward II. "Trade grows daily worse," said they, "and no honest dealer can carry his wares along the roads without fear of robbers and outlaws, while should the thief be caught justice is never done on him." At length a meeting was held, and it was decided that Henry, now duke of Lancaster by the death of his father, should be invited to come from France and seize the crown. Most likely Henry had expected such a message, but he was too cautious to accept the invitation at once, and he merely replied that he must take a day to consult with his friends. The envoy, however, had noticed a sudden sparkle in his eye, and had little doubt of the answer, and a few days later Henry, with an escort of ships, was seen sailing up the English coast.

The news spread like lightning, and as soon as it was known that he had landed at Ravenspur, in Yorkshire, men flocked to join him. Richard alone remained ignorant of the enemy at his gates, and when, three weeks after, a boat managed to cross bearing the evil tidings and the king took ship for Holyhead, it was only to learn that Henry was advancing to meet him with an army of 60,000 men. The king had entrenched himself in Flint Castle when Henry knocked at the entrance.

"Who goes there?" cried a voice from within, and the newcomer answered:

"I am Henry of Lancaster, and I have come to claim my heritage, which the king has taken for himself. And so you can tell him."

The man within the gate hastened across the courtyard and up the stairs, and entering the hall where Richard and his knights were holding counsel he said to him:

"Sire, it is your cousin the earl of Derby who knocks, and he demands that you shall restore to him all that belongs to the duchy of Lancaster."

Now as to this matter Henry spoke truly, for Richard had indeed taken the money and lands that belonged of right to his cousin, and had spent them upon his ill-fated expedition to Ireland. Therefore he looked uncomfortably at his councillors and inquired of them what he should do.

"Sire, he speaks well," replied the knights, "and it is our advice that you listen to him, for he is much loved throughout the kingdom, and especially by the Londoners, who sent for him beyond the sea to make cause with him against you."

"Then open the gate," said Richard, "and I will speak with him."

So two knights arose and went across the courtyard of the castle and through the small door which was in the great gate, and bowed themselves before Henry and his friends, taking care to bear themselves politely and graciously, for they knew that the strength did not lie on their side.

"My lord the king will gladly see you and speak with you," said the oldest of the two, "and he prays you to enter."

"Thus will I do," answered Henry, and entered forthwith, thinking nothing of the danger he ran, for the king might have straightway put him to death. He walked across the hall, up to the chair where Richard was seated, and the king changed colour at the sight of him. Not that he was in bodily fear, for no Plantagenet was ever a coward, but because he knew in his heart that he had done his cousin grievous wrong. "Have you breakfasted?" asked Henry without further greeting.

"Not yet," replied the king, who had expected bitter reproaches, and half thought this must be a jest; "it is still early. But why do you ask me?"

"You had better eat something at once," answered his cousin, "for you have a long journey before you."

"A journey?" said Richard; "and where to, I pray?"

"To London," replied Henry; "therefore I counsel you to eat and drink, that the ride may seem more merry."

Richard understood; resistance was useless; so he commanded food to be brought, and ate and drank without haste and composedly.

The castle gates were thrown open wide, and a multitude of soldiers and archers pressed in and advanced to the doors, but Henry ordered them to stand back, and bade them do damage to none, for the castle with all in it was under his protection. After that he fetched the king into the courtyard, and while the horses were saddled they talked together in a corner.

Now Richard had a greyhound of great size and beauty called Math, which he loved much, and the dog would suffer none but the king to touch him. When he rode out Math was always by his side, and often the two would play together in the hall, and Math would put his two huge paws on the king's shoulders. And when Math beheld the horses ready saddled, and being led to the spot where Richard and his cousin were standing, he sprang up, and came with quick bounds towards them. Richard held out his hand to his favourite, but the dog passed him by, and, going to the side of Henry, reared himself on his hind legs and rubbed his head against the duke's cheek.

"What is he doing?" asked Henry, who had never seen Math before.

"Cousin," answered the king, "that caress holds a great meaning for you and a little one for me."

"What is your interpretation of it?" inquired Henry, looking puzzled.

"My greyhound hails you to-day king of England, as you will be when I am deposed, and my crown taken from me. Keep him with you; he will serve you well."

Henry answered nothing; perhaps in his heart he may have felt a little ashamed; but the dog stayed with him, and did not leave him till the day of his death.

MEANWHILE, AT THE FIRST WHISPER of invasion, the duke of York, who had been left regent, had removed the queen from Windsor to the stronger castle of Wallingford. The poor girl thought nothing of her own danger, but was wild with despair at the idea that the crown of England might be placed on the usurper's head and the rightful king be ignorant of the fact. Soon arrived the news that Richard had fallen into the hands of the duke of Lancaster, and was to be taken to London. Luckily she never heard that at Lichfield, where he was probably lodged in the same house where they had passed their happy Christmas so short a time ago, he had tried to escape, but was recaptured in the garden. After this his guards were doubled during the long ride to the Tower.

If Henry was in London, Isabel was clearly not safe at Wallingford, and the regent took her by lonely roads and obscure villages to the castle of Leeds in Kent. Here she was within reach of the coast, and could, if needful, be sent over to France. It was at Leeds that Isabel received a messenger from the Londoners to the effect that the lady de Coucy (who had lingered about her mistress in spite of Richard's order) and all French attendants of the queen should be despatched to Dover and conveyed to Boulogne. By the envoy's desire the lady de Coucy was summoned to the queen's presence, and found to her surprise a plain man in the dress of a citizen standing by the window.

"Madame," he said, without taking the trouble to bow, "bid your maids get ready your packages, for you must quit this place without delay. But beware of telling anyone that you do not go of your own free will; instead, say that your husband and daughter need you. Your life hangs on your silence and obedience, and the less you hear and see the better for you. You will have an escort as far as Dover, where you will find a ship to put you ashore at Boulogne."

"I will obey your orders, good sir," answered the lady de Coucy, who had listened trembling; and she lost no time in making her preparations and in bidding the queen farewell. Indeed, she was in such a haste to be gone that she would hardly wait to hear the loving messages which Isabel sent to her father and mother, or allow her to take leave of the faithful servants who had come with the queen from France, but hurried them down into the courtyard, where horses of all sorts were saddled and bridled. A troop of soldiers was in readiness to accompany them to Dover, but on their arrival there the fugitives—for they were nothing less—found to their dismay that they were expected to pay heavily for the honour, "each according to his condition," as Froissart says. Right thankful were they to get on board the vessel which was to land them on French soil. Once in France the lady de Coucy hastened to Paris, and it was from her that Charles learned, for the first time, the peril of his daughter.

At their departure poor Isabel felt more lonely than she had done since she had bidden her parents farewell before her marriage. Far more lonely, for *then* she had Richard, and *now* the new English attendants which "the Londoners" placed about her were forbidden even to mention his name. So her days were spent in torturing thoughts and her nights in evil dreams; she could hardly have been more wretched had she known he was in the Tower. The suspense would have been terrible for a grown-up woman, and for a girl under twelve it was almost unbearable; but her grief would have been deeper still if she had known that Richard had prayed to have his wife with him in his captivity, and had been refused.

Shut up in the Tower, Richard had plenty of time to look back on the events of the twenty-two years that his reign had lasted and to note the folly and extravagance which had led to his ruin. Some friends he still had, and of these the earl of Salisbury was the chief; but a little while after this an effort made by the earl to assassinate Henry only ended in his own death and in the death of the king he was so anxious to save. The advice of Richard's attendants was to resign at once, lest worse should befall them, and, bitter though it was to him, the king felt that the counsel was good. Therefore he sent a message to Henry, now living in his own house on the banks of the Thames, to say he would like to speak with him. The duke, with a company of knights in attendance, arrived in a barge, and was conducted to the king. Humbly Richard confessed all the wrongs he had done him, and declared himself ready to abdicate the throne

ANDREW LANG AND LEONORA BLANCHE LANG

in his favour. Henry replied that this must be done in the presence of parliament and with the consent of its representatives; but in three days a sufficient number of these could be assembled for the purpose. Not being a generous man, he did not stop there, but went on to point out that if Richard had followed in the steps of his grandfather, Edward III, and of his father, the Black Prince, all would have been well; instead, he had chosen to go his own way without considering his people. "Still," cried Henry—and perhaps at the moment he meant what he said—"out of pity I will defend you and preserve your life from the hatred of the Londoners, who would have you die."

"I thank you, cousin," replied Richard; "I have more faith in you than in the whole of England."

AFTER REMAINING FOR TWO HOURS with Richard the duke of Lancaster returned home, and sent out letters to all his relations of Plantagenet blood and to the nobles, Churchmen, and citizens of London, summoning them to meet at Westminster. When they arrived he rode to the Tower with a great company, who, leaving their horses outside, entered the fortress. Here Richard awaited them in the great hall, wearing on his head the crown of his coronation and holding the sceptre in his hand, while the royal mantle flowed from his shoulders. "For twenty-two years," he said, standing on the steps of the dais and looking steadfastly into the faces of the men around him—"for twenty-two years I have been king of England, duke of Aquitaine, and lord of Ireland. I now resign crown, sceptre, and heritage into the hands of my cousin Henry duke of Lancaster, and in the presence of you all I pray him to accept them." Then he held out the sceptre to Henry, who stood near him, and taking off the crown placed it before him, saying as he did so, "Henry, dear cousin and duke of Lancaster, I give you this crown, with all its duties and privileges," and the duke of Lancaster received that also and handed it to the archbishop. This done, Richard—king no longer—returned to his apartments, and the company who had witnessed the act of abdication rode silently back to their own houses, while the sceptre and the crown were deposited for safety in the treasury of Westminster Abbey. The bitterest moment of Richard's life had come. He had, through his own fault he knew, been forced to yield up the inheritance that had descended without a break from father to son for 200 years. He had worn out the patience of his subjects, till he stood alone, and they refused him even the comfort of his wife's presence. Ah! *she* was faithful, and would suffer with his pain! And in thinking of Isabel for a while he forgot himself.

He had done what was required, and the last acts of the drama were gone through without him. Perhaps Henry was merciful; perhaps he did not care to risk his throne by showing the people their rightful king, of whose beauty and boyish gallantry they had once been so proud. In any case it was Henry who presided at the parliament held at Westminster, "outside London," in September 1399, and demanded that he should be declared king on the ground of three claims which he set forth: First, by right of conquest; second, by heirship; and third, by the resignation of Richard in his favour, in presence of nobles, bishops, and citizens gathered in the Tower. "You shall be our king; we will have none other!" they cried, and twice more Henry repeated the same question and received the same answer. Then Henry sat himself on the throne covered with cloth of gold, and the people stretched out their hands and swore fealty to him. Before parliament separated, October 8 was fixed for the coronation.

At nine o'clock on the appointed day the royal procession left the palace. The sword of justice was borne by Henry Percy earl of Northumberland; the sword of the Church by the young prince of Wales; while the earl of Westmoreland, marshal of England, carried the sceptre. Seats had been erected in the Abbey for the nobles and clergy, and in their midst was a raised platform, on which was a vacant chair draped with cloth of gold. Henry walked up the steps and took possession of the throne, while the archbishop turned to the four sides of the platform and demanded if it was the wish of that assembly that Henry duke of Lancaster should be crowned king. "It is, it is!" they cried as before; so Henry came down from the throne and walked to the High Altar, and the crown of Edward the Confessor was put on his head, and he was anointed in six places. Then deacon's robes were placed on him, signifying that he would defend the Church, and the sword of justice was blessed, and Henry IV was proclaimed king.

In spite of the dark whispers that had been heard during the past year as to the fate of Edward II, it is doubtful if Richard's life would not have been spared but for the plot made by the earl of Salisbury for assassinating Henry. The plot failed because Henry did not appear at the tournament; but, nothing daunted, Salisbury persuaded a man named Maudlin, who had a strong likeness to Richard, to personate the deposed king, and sent word to Isabel that her husband was marching to rescue her at the head of a large army. The queen, who knew by this time that Henry had been proclaimed king of England, believed all that was told her, and instantly left Sunning Hill, near Reading, where she had been staying for some time, and joined the body of troops commanded by the earl of Kent, nephew of Richard. Happy and excited, and full of hope, she knew no fatigue; but her spirits fell a little as they drew near Cirencester without either letter or message from her beloved husband. Once inside the gates the mayor betrayed them to Henry, and, while Kent and Salisbury were beheaded at once, Isabel was sent, strictly guarded, to Havering-atte-Bower, not far from London. Here three French attendants were all the company allowed her—a maid, a physician and confessor, and her chamberlain; but these like the rest of her household were forbidden to mention the late king; even the two gentlemen sent over by Charles VI to inquire into the condition of his daughter received orders from Henry himself to keep silence on this subject, though they were assured that Isabel would be kept in all the state befitting a queen dowager. They found her at Havering surrounded by Richard's relations, "who honourably kept her company," as Froissart tells us. There were the duchess of Ireland, sister of lady de Coucy and wife of Robert de Vere; the duchess of Gloucester, whose little son had lately died on his voyage from Ireland, her daughters, and several other ladies. Isabel looked up eagerly when the Sieur Charles de Labreth and the Sieur de Hangiers were ushered in, and was about to question them eagerly on the matter next her heart when M. de Labreth slightly shook his head. Isabel had grown apt in reading signs. She understood, and the brightness left her face; but she begged them to tell her all they knew about her father and mother, her brothers and sisters, and what had become of her old servants and friends who had returned to Paris. The envoys, very ill at ease, feeling themselves surrounded by spies, did not stay long, but rode back through London to Eltham, where they took leave of Henry, who gave them fine jewels and fair words.

In the end that which was bound to happen did happen. At the first news of the conspiracy of the earl of Salisbury, Richard had been hastily removed from the Tower of London to Pontefract Castle, in Yorkshire, and there, early in February 1400, he met his death. *How* is not exactly known: stories of all kinds went abroad, and, to make sure—a vain precaution—that no pretenders should hereafter spring up, his body was brought to London and carried in procession through the City. Four black horses led by two grooms drew the open car, and, four knights in mourning rode behind it. Slowly they travelled along Cheapside, while twenty thousand people pressed around to gaze their last upon the beautiful face of their dead king, who looked scarcely older than on the day on which he had faced Wat Tyler. "Some were moved to pity," says Froissart, "but others declared that he had brought his fate on himself, and felt no sorrow for him." And the body passed on, unconscious alike of friend or foe, till it lay for a while in the church of St. Paul's, and then found rest at Langley.

In these days it is difficult to understand how no whisper of her husband's death reached Isabel, but it was several weeks before Henry allowed the fact to be broken to her. She had thought that she was prepared for every misfortune and every grief that could befall her, but at twelve one does not easily give up hope, and by the despair that took possession of her the "little queen" at last knew that she had expected "something" might happen to bring them together again.

Considering all that had passed, it seems scarcely possible that Henry IV should have been so stupid as to think that he could bring about his dearest wish and unite in marriage Henry prince of Wales with the young queen dowager. His accession to the throne had been attended with so little difficulty that he had ceased to reckon with opposition—he remembered that prince Harry and Isabel had played together while he was in exile, and forgot that he had usurped her husband's crown and countenanced his murder. The horror with which Isabel rejected his first proposals did not open his eyes to his folly, and during the two years and a half that she remained in England he spared no effort to bend her to his will. But Isabel was as determined as he, and in her refusal was supported by the French council of regency—for at this time her father was insane.

After much consideration and many messages passing between London and Paris it was finally settled that Isabel should be restored to France and allowed to live with her family. But in all these transactions the meanness of Henry's nature came out. When we remember that Richard had appropriated the revenues of the lands of Lancaster to defray the expenses of the Irish expedition we may perhaps find some excuse for his division of Isabel's jewels amongst his children (though a large number of them had been given her in France); but he pretended that he had ordered their return, which was plainly untrue, and declined to give her and her attendants proper clothes for their journey. The French court was far more indignant with his conduct than Isabel, who, still stricken with grief and wearied with imprisonment, was longing to be back in her own country. At the end of May Isabel set out from Havering with a great train of ladies, the noblest in the land. They rode slowly, for the roads were bad, and in the towns people crowded to see them and to wonder at the beauty and sad face of the "little queen," whose six years of sovereignty had held more of sorrow than the lifetime of many of those who watched her. Through the green fields and past the country houses at Tottenham and Hackney she went, till at length she reached the Tower, and her cheeks grew white as she glanced at the great hall which was the scene of Richard's abdication. Happy memories there were, too, of her early married life, and of her progress through the City; but these did not bear thinking about, and she hastily turned and spoke some kindly words to the old countess of Hereford, who was behind her.

During the six weeks that Isabel remained in the Tower Henry renewed his son's suit, and urged truly that nowhere would Isabel find a more gallant husband. The prince of Wales, boy though he was, had always admired and loved Isabel; "there was no princess like her," he thought, "and now that she was free why should she not be queen of England again?" And so she might have been had not the shadow of Richard lain between them; once more she refused, though she liked the youth well, and would have been content to know that years after she was dead he would marry her sister Katherine. It was only on French soil that Isabel parted with tears from her English ladies, to whom she gave as remembrances the few jewels she had left. Then she was delivered by Sir Thomas Percy to the count de St. Pol, who was waiting with a company of high-born damsels sent to attend on her, and by him she was conducted to the dukes of Burgundy and Bourbon, with an armed force at their back.

So the merry little girl of seven years old came home again, sad, widowed, and penniless, for Henry had refused to restore her dowry or to make her the customary allowance. This behaviour so enraged her uncle, Louis duke of Orleans, that he is said to have challenged Henry to fight a duel, but Henry had replied that no king ever fought with a subject, even one of royal blood. Isabel herself cared little about the matter. She found, on arriving in Paris, that things were changed very much for the worse. Her father's fits of madness were more frequent and more severe, her mother was more bent on pleasure, and her children were more neglected than before. Isabel did what she could, we may be sure; but the queen of France, though she omitted to perform her own duty, would not suffer it to be done by other people; and Isabel, finding she could be of little use, passed most of her time with her uncle, the duke of Orleans, and his wife, Violante Visconti.

Now the duke of Orleans had a son, Charles, three years younger than the "queen of England," and it was his cherished plan to marry him to his niece. The two cousins had much in common; they both loved music, and old romances, and songs, and Charles had already begun to write some of those poems that sound sweet in our ears today. Of course the boy was too young for a marriage to be spoken of at present, but after a while it became understood that the ceremony of betrothal would shortly take place. Isabel had not given her consent (in those times that counted for little) without a long struggle. The memory of Richard was still green in her heart, but she was alone in the world. Nobody wanted her except her uncle and aunt, and her friend Charles. Oh yes! and one other, but she would not think of him. Charles was her friend, and in a way she loved him; so, to his great joy, she promised to be his wife, and when she burst into tears during the magnificent ceremony of betrothal he imagined that she was tired with all the feasting, and he led her away to rest and read her the little song he had written all about themselves.

A year after the betrothal the duke of Orleans was stabbed by the duke of Burgundy in the streets of Paris. No notice was taken of the murder, so Isabel and her mother-in-law dressed themselves in deep mourning and, mounting in front of the carriage, which was drawn by white horses with black housings, they drove weeping to the Hôtel de St. Pol, where the king was, followed by a long train of servants and attendants. But Charles was in no state to settle these questions, for any excitement only brought on a paroxysm. The duke's murder remained unavenged, and a year afterwards his widow died, deeply mourned by her son and by Isabel, to whom in the last years she had been a true mother.

It was only in 1408 that Isabel was really married to her cousin, and the one year that was left to her to live was a very happy one. If she had not forgotten Richard, Charles had grown to be part of herself, and once more she was heard to laugh and jest as of old. But in September 1409 a little daughter was born, and in a few hours after the mother lay dead with her baby beside her. At first it was thought her husband would die too, so frantic was his grief, as the poems in which he poured out his heart bear witness. But after a while he roused himself to care for the child, and later to fight for his country, and was taken prisoner at Agincourt by Isabel's old suitor, Henry V. Orleans was brought to England, and in the Tower, where he was imprisoned for twenty-three years, he had ample time to think about his lost wife—of her life in that very Tower, of her body resting quietly in the abbey of St. Lammer at Blois. It lay in the abbey for over two hundred years, and was found, in the reign of Louis XIII, perfect as in life, the linen clothes having been wrapped in quicksilver. By this time the Valois had passed away from the throne of France, and their cousins the Bourbons reigned in their stead, and by them Isabel's body was reverently brought from Blois and laid in the sepulchre of the dukes of Orleans.

XIII

Two Little Girls and Their Mother

And what became of the Ladies Blanche and Philippa, the playmates of the "Little Queen"? Well, Blanche's life was, unlike that of her friend, a very happy one; but she and the "Little Queen" died, strange to say, in the same year, leaving behind a son and a daughter. Philippa lived many years longer, but she had no children, and her husband was restless and quarrelsome, and always at war with his neighbours; and Philippa had often to govern the kingdom in his absence, and ruled a great deal better than he did himself. But this all happened "by-and-by," and we must begin at the beginning.

Towards the end of Edward III's reign there died Humphrey de Bohun, the great earl of Hereford, leaving a widow and two daughters. These little girls, whose names were Eleanor and Mary, were the richest heiresses in England, and many greedy eyes were cast upon them and the vast estates which they were to share. Mary was a mere baby at her father's death, and Eleanor only a few years older, so for a while they lived quietly at home with their mother; but as soon as Eleanor was old enough to marry, the king's youngest son, Thomas of Woodstock, then earl of Buckingham, and later duke of Gloucester, came forward as a wooer. His offer was accepted by the countess of Hereford, and after the ceremony was completed he took his young bride to Pleshy in Essex, one of her own estates. Mary remained with her mother, under the care of John of Gaunt, duke of Lancaster, who was her guardian.

Now, rich though he had become through his marriage, the earl of Buckingham was not content, and longed to become richer still and more powerful than either of his elder brothers, Lancaster and York. So, under pretext that he was frequently obliged to be away at the wars, and that his wife was very lonely during his absence, he prevailed on the duke of Lancaster to allow Mary de Bohun (at this time about eleven years old) to come to Pleshy and keep her sister company. Once at Pleshy, Buckingham believed that his persuasive tongue would easily turn the girl's thoughts to a religious life,—for she was quiet and gentle, and liked music and books better than tournaments and dances,—and when she had become a nun, her money and lands would go to him and his children. Thus he plotted in his secret heart, for he was too wary to take any man into his confidence; but he constantly sent for the nuns from the convent of St. Clare "to attend her and tutor her in matters of religion, continually blaming the married state." Great, we may feel sure, was his delight when he saw that "the young lady seemed to incline to their doctrine, and thought not of marriage."

Careful as was the earl to hide his plans, whispers got abroad as to the frequent visits of the nuns to Pleshy, and reached the ears of the duke of Lancaster. It happened that Lancaster also had a son, a handsome and promising youth, called Henry of Bolingbroke, earl of Derby, and, says Froissart, "the duke had for some time considered that he could not choose a more desirable wife for him than the lady who was intended for a nun, as her estates were very large and her birth suitable to any rank; but he did not take any steps in the matter till his brother of Buckingham had set out on his expedition to France. When Buckingham had crossed the sea, the duke of Lancaster had the young lady conducted to Arundel castle, for the aunt of the two heiresses was the sister of Richard, earl of Arundel. At the desire of the duke of Lancaster, and for the advancement of her niece, this lady went to Pleshy, where she remained with the countess of Buckingham and her sister fifteen days. On her departure, she managed so well that she carried the lady Mary with her to Arundel, where the betrothal between her and Henry took place." "The earl of Buckingham," ends the chronicler, "felt no desire to laugh when he heard these tidings; and when he learned that his brothers had all been concerned in this affair he became melancholy, and never after loved the duke of Lancaster, as he had hitherto done."

We do not know exactly what Eleanor thought about it all. Most likely she was delighted that her beautiful young sister should get a husband whom she could love, though she was too much afraid of the earl of Buckingham to approve openly. The bride went back at once to her mother, and a large sum was allowed by her guardian for her expenses, though Mary cared but little for the fine clothes and extra servants that were given her, and busied herself with her books and music as before. If she wanted amusement, were there not the minstrels and *jongleurs*, singers and dancers, whom young king Richard had brought over from France; and could she wish anything better than to sit and listen to their songs, while she sat close to the window to get light for her embroidery?

As Mary's fourteenth birthday approached, an ever-increasing stir might be noticed in the castle. Travelling merchants drew up in the courtyard, accompanied by pack-horses laden with rare silks and velvets and laces. These were carried into lady Derby's bower, and she and her mother spent hours in fingering the stuffs and determining which to take and which to leave. Jewellers too rode down from London, with an escort of armed servants, for highwaymen were much to be dreaded on the lonely heaths; and then at last came the journey to Arundel, where Henry was waiting for Mary; and her wedding day drew near.

Unlike some of the marriages common in those times, as well as these, this wedding was not merely a matter of riches on one side and high rank on the other. Henry and Mary loved each other dearly, and nothing ever came between them. Mary was always ready to be pleased with everything and everybody, and made friends at once with her sisters-in-law: Philippa, two years older than herself, and by-and-by to be queen of Portugal; and Elizabeth, about her own age, who soon after married the earl of Huntingdon, half-brother of the king. The chapel of Arundel must have been a fair sight during the ceremony, with all the gallant young nobles and their youthful wives, and no handsomer pair was present than king Richard with his queen, Anne of Bohemia, now a bride of two years' standing. Knowing Mary de Bohun's passionate love of music, Richard had brought his court minstrels with him, and sweetly they sang through the banquet which followed the marriage. And never once did the bride's thoughts stray back to the nuns of St. Clare, or her heart "blame the marriage state."

When the rejoicings were over, the earl and countess of Derby bade their friends farewell, and journeyed down to the hilly west country, to their home in Monmouth castle, where the little river Monmow flows into the Wye. Mary would gladly have stayed there for ever, but soon Henry was called away to fight, and her mother came to keep her company. In a little while she had another companion also, who took up all her time and attention, her baby, Henry of Monmouth, afterwards Henry V. Thus the years came and went, and the earl of Derby was sometimes at home, but more often travelling. At one moment he joined the band of Teutonic knights who were fighting some pagan tribes on the south-east coasts of the Baltic, with the hope of converting them. Then he sailed for Morocco, and later visited Austria, and altogether he must have had many interesting adventures

ANDREW LANG AND LEONORA BLANCHE LANG

to tell his wife whenever he returned to England. Meanwhile four little boys were growing up under their mother's care, and in 1392 his eldest daughter was born in Peterborough, where lady Derby was then living, and was christened Blanche after her grandmother. More than a year later Blanche had a little sister to play with, and to her was given the name of Philippa, after the Queen of Edward III.

Henry of Monmouth, the eldest of the six children, was only seven years old when, in 1395, his mother died after a short illness, and the countess of Hereford took her place. Lady Hereford was a very different woman from Mary, and thought that children should be kept at a distance, so, though she meant to be kind to them, they missed their mother deeply. Mary had never been too busy to listen to them, or to play with them, or to sing them old songs, but now everyone was in too much of a hurry to pay them any attention. Soon they were removed into Lincolnshire, and shortly afterwards Henry, whom the rest considered a man and full of wisdom, was sent to Leicester, and little John to his kinswoman the lady Margaret Plantagenet.

In this manner things continued for a year, and when the day of their mother's death came round again, the countess of Hereford ordered fresh suits of deep mourning to be prepared for herself and her little granddaughters, and set forth with a train of servants to the Abbey at Leicester, where Mary de Bohun was buried. Blanche and Philippa, who were now only three and four, had forgotten what their mother was like, and the long hours passed kneeling in the black-hung chapel must have seemed endless to them, and very trying to their poor little backs; but they were delighted to see Henry again and to watch the twenty-four poor women, who each received a warm black cloak, in memory of the dead lady who was twenty-four when she died. And they hung about Henry and admired him, while he on his part told them how much he had learned since he last saw them, and bade them take heed to their lessons, and learn courtly ways and manners. Then they returned to Bytham, and the next morning, when they looked round for their dark dresses, they had vanished, and instead gay scarlet frocks edged with green lay in their place. If they went out to walk in the stately garden, or accompanied their grandmother on a visit to some neighbour in the big stuffy coach, they were wrapped up in hoods and cloaks to match if the weather was cold, while on the occasions that a great lord or noble lady spent a few days at Bytham cloth of gold and ermine capes were put on their small figures, and golden coronets upon their heads, in case they should be summoned into the hall to pay their respects. A few months after their journey to Leicester their grandmother considered it was time that they should each be given special attendants, and sometimes even a house of their own. One would have thought that with the number of servants already in the castle two or three nurses and governesses would have been enough for little girls of three or four, but children in those times were treated very differently. The ladies Blanche and Philippa had cooks and scullions, pages and waiting-maids, and a steward called John Green, who kept all the servants in order. They also had a head-governess, and a knight of the chamber, named Sir Hugh Waterton, in whom their father placed absolute trust. Indeed they were sent to pass a whole year in his house at Eton, which must have been very large if it was able to hold all his servants as well as theirs, and when they left they paid some visits to their relations, before joining their father in his beautiful home at Bishopsgate, on the outskirts of London. Rich people changed their houses very often then, for though they were rich they were not clean, and the houses became unhealthy.

In spite of his long absences, the earl of Derby had always been very fond of his children, and Blanche and Philippa were enchanted to go and live with him again, and to watch their two eldest brothers, Henry and Thomas, taking their daily riding lessons, while their father, who next to king Richard was the best horseman of the day, corrected their faults. How Philippa longed to have a pony too, and to jump the barricades with them. She was sure *she* would not fall off any more than Thomas did—why should she? Of course Henry was different, she could never sit as *he* did; why, he did not *move* when Black Roland gave that plunge! but her father said she was too little and must wait awhile, and wait she did. But when Blanche was married, and Philippa, though only nine, was, "the first Lady of England," what a store of horses and saddles and housings her stables could show!

Whatever attention was paid to their manners, neither Blanche nor Philippa seems to have learnt anything, though it is very certain that had their mother lived she would have taught them as she had taught Henry. But when the "Little Queen" came to Court, and people talked of the songs she knew, and the tales she had by heart, and the poetry she could repeat, the earl of Derby felt ashamed of the ignorance of his own little girls. So he ordered some alphabets for them, and very costly they were, for there was no printing then, and books were all written and copied mostly by the monks, who often put beautiful pictures in them. The children were both clever, and anxious to imitate the queen, to whom they paid frequent visits, and as *she* could dance and play the lute, of course *they* must do so too. But it was more difficult for Blanche to do her lessons than her sister, as she was constantly sent for by her father to be present at some banquet to his friends, and though she was no more than six, the child knew how to behave like a grown-up woman, and never showed when she was tired or bored.

But all this came to an end a few months later, when the King suddenly banished the earl of Derby for ten years, just after he had created his cousin duke of Hereford. At Richard's wish, the little girls and their brother Henry, now an undergraduate of Queen's College, Oxford, were sent to Windsor Castle, to be brought up with queen Isabel. The king was always fond of children, and treated them all kindly, Henry in particular. And Henry never forgot this, and one of his first acts after succeeding to the throne was to bring Richard's body up from its resting-place at Langley, and bury it with honours in Westminster Abbey.

AFTER RICHARD II HAD ABDICATED and died, and Henry, now duke of Lancaster, was crowned as king Henry IV, the princess Blanche was forced by her father to take her mother's place entirely. It was she of whom the knights had to ask leave before fighting in a tournament, and it was she who gave the prize to the victor. How glad Blanche felt for the months she had passed by the side of the "Little Queen", when she had learned from her how such things ought to be done! And Blanche's thoughts would go back to her former playfellow, and all the troubles she was passing through, and tears of sorrow would fill her eyes, for the princess was always faithful and loving to her friends.

IT WAS EARLY IN 1401 that the emperor sent over messengers from Germany to ask for the hand of the princess Blanche for his son Lewis. Henry IV had just returned from fighting some Welsh rebels, and he would much have liked to have kept his little girl with him for a few years longer; but the marriage pleased him, and he readily gave his consent. In general, as we know, the bride was suffered to remain at home for some time after the ceremony of betrothal, but the emperor desired that Blanche should come over at once to her new country, so she was bidden to begin her preparations as soon as possible.

The two little sisters were very sad when they heard their father's decision. They had never been separated in their lives, and how strange and dreadful it would feel not to be able to talk together about all that interested them! Of course they knew they would be married "some day," but "some day" is always a long way off, and meantime there were journeys and tournaments and music, and all manner of delightful things in the world, especially horses.

"Oh, you *must* give a prize to that grey horse!" Philippa would whisper in Blanche's ear, as she sat by her side at the lists at a tourney.

"But how can I," asked Blanche, "if the knight that rides him is not the victor?"

"Oh, he *must* be when he has a horse like that," Philippa would answer. Then the trumpet would sound, and the eyes of both children would be fixed on the field. *Now* it was Philippa whose lot it would be to give the prize, and Blanche would be far away amongst strangers.

The young leaves were out, and the "ways and the woods smelt sweet," when the day of parting actually came. "They say the lord Lewis is good and kind, and has many books and a number of minstrels about him," observed Philippa, who always tried to make the best of things. "You will write and tell me what he is like, and about your palace, and your wedding. Oh, and you will promise to be married in the dress of cloth of gold that you bought from master Richard Whittington, who had the black cat which made his fortune? It is so much, much more beautiful than any of the rest!" Then good-bye was said, and Blanche began her journey with the household that her father had formed for her. The countess of Salisbury was her lady-in-waiting, and Henry could not have made a better choice. Blanche's old friend John Green was to go too, and the child's heavy heart grew a little lighter as she remembered that here was someone who knew all about her, and who could talk of Philippa and her brothers as well as she could herself. And besides the servants and attendants of every degree, her uncle the duke of Somerset was in charge of the party, together with the bishop of Worcester, who was to perform the marriage.

It was high summer before Blanche reached Cologne, for travelling was slow in those days, and many times she stopped to rest and to receive guests who came to give their homage to the daughter-in-law of the emperor. But at length the town was in sight, and a halt was called, so that Blanche might be gaily dressed in one of her grand new dresses, while her golden coronet was placed upon her flowing hair and her collar of pearls was hung round her neck. Then she mounted the white horse with silver trappings which had been sent expressly for her, and wondered as she did so what Philippa would have thought of him. The emperor was not present at Cologne, for business had kept him elsewhere, but his son Lewis, the bridegroom, was awaiting her at the gate, with an escort of nobles behind him. He looked, as Philippa had said, good and kind and very pleased to see her, and that was all that Blanche cared for, as, unlike queen Isabel, she had no wish to be "a great lady." But her attendants felt that a slight had been put on their king and their country, and murmured among themselves at the emperor's absence. However they were wise enough to hold their peace in the presence of the Germans, and not to mar the wedding festivities with cross faces. And Blanche was married three days later in Dick Whittington's famous gold brocade, and once more she gave away the prizes at a tourney.

Perhaps the feelings of the English might have been soothed if they had seen the welcome given their princess by the emperor in his palace of Heidelberg, and his admiration of her beauty. She touched his heart by her modesty and unselfishness, and he felt he had done well in choosing his son's wife. Blanche was grateful for his kindness, and soon loved him and her husband dearly, while she was never tired of standing at the windows of the castle, whose ruins you may see to-day, looking over the broad Rhine and the vine-clad mountains. Here she had more time for reading, too, as there were no great Court ceremonies that needed her presence, and her husband would tell her tales of bygone emperors, and teach her how to speak his native tongue, which she found much more difficult than French.

"How *can* I remember all those different endings?" she cried, "and by the time I come to the verb, I have quite forgotten what I was going to say! and Lewis—who bade her call him "Ludwig"—would laugh, and relate to her the brave deeds of Henry the Fowler, or recite some verses of the "Lay of the Nibelungs," till Blanche would stop her ears at the cruelties of Brunhilda and Chriemhild. Or if the days were fine the husband and wife would go out together, and visit some church or citizen's house that was being built, and Lewis, who had much skill in these things, would show Blanche the wonderful carving or bid her mark the fine proportions of the architecture. Blanche—the "electoral princess"—would have liked to stay in Heidelberg, but after awhile she was obliged to leave Cologne to go to Alsace, and preside over a Court again. She always did what came in her way pleasantly and graciously, but she was very sorry to give up her happy life, with its books and music and church-building, and pass her time in public ceremonies, even though the little Court of Alsace was much quieter and more homely than that of either Richard II or her own father. But the climate did not agree with her, and as she grew older she also grew more delicate. This she managed to conceal from her husband who was busy with many things, fearing to distress him, and she kept gay words and a smile for everyone as long as she possibly could. But at length she grew too weak to ride or walk, and by-and-by lay amongst pillows at her window gazing at the mountains, and now and then saying a word to her husband, who never left her when he could help it.

One day, early in May, when the birds were singing and the streams gurgling, he returned from a long journey to find Blanche lying with a little son beside her and a look of rapture on her face.

"Ah, you will get better now!" he cried joyfully, noting the happiness in her eyes; but she said nothing, only kissed his hand, and drew it towards the baby. And she was right: from that moment she grew worse, and a few days later she was dead, leaving this one child behind her. Hardly sixteen! yet how well and nobly she had filled the place and done the duties that had been given her!

THE NEWS OF BLANCHE'S DEATH was a terrible grief to her father in England, and to her sister Philippa, who had been for nearly three years queen of Denmark. It was not that they ever saw her—perhaps they never would—but they felt she was *there*, thinking about them and caring for them; and what joyful days those were when a special courier or travelling knight brought them letters from her! Yet as she read with streaming eyes what her brother-in-law, "the lord Lewis," had written, Philippa's heart ached for herself, as well as for the dead girl. Blanche's life at least had been happy from first to last, but to Philippa some bad days had already come, and others were casting shadows before them.

Except for parting from Blanche, Philippa had also had a happy childhood, and she being very lively and full of plans, nobody ever felt dull in her presence. No sooner had Blanche set out on her journey to Cologne than Henry was obliged to go into Wales, and he left Philippa and her second brother, John, duke of Bedford, together with the children of the late earl of March, under the care of Sir Hugh Waterton at Berkhamstead Castle. It was summer, and the pretty Hertfordshire commons were golden with gorse and sweet with bushes of wild roses and honeysuckle, and, strictly guarded though they were, Philippa and the rest had many a merry gallop over the grass, for her love of horses had become a passion with her. Sometimes, when they were tired of playing, she and John used to walk soberly up and down the alleys in the castle garden, talking of their new stepmother—for even before the departure of Blanche Henry had been married "by proxy" to the widowed duchess of Bretagne, Jane of Navarre.

"She *sounded* kind in the letter she wrote," said Philippa in a doubtful tone, "and if Blanche had been here I should not have been afraid. But suppose she should be like the stepmothers in the nursery tales, and send me down into the kitchen to do scullion's work!"

"And do you think the king would not miss you and bring you back?" asked John mockingly. "Oh, Philippa, what nonsense you talk, and what a bad scullion you would make!" and they both laughed, and Philippa's tears, which had been very near her eyes, went back to their proper place. "Besides," continued John, "remember that she will not be here for many months yet, and during all that time *you* will have to take Blanche's place, and preside at the pageants and tourneys. And then, when she *does* come, she will bring her daughters, the ladies Blanche and Marguérite, with her."

"Just like the nursery tales," thought Philippa to herself; but before she could say more the little Mortimers ran up to say that the sun was now sinking, and they could have a game of hoodman blind without getting too hot. And in chasing her cousins all over the garden Philippa forgot the terrors of a stepmother.

She need not, however, have been afraid. When queen Jane and her daughters arrived at Winchester, wearied with their long, cold, and muddy ride all the way from Falmouth, their hearts warmed to the handsome, bright-faced child standing a little behind her father in the hall of the castle. Philippa's own fears melted away like snow as she saw how pale and tired they all looked, and with genuine kindness (mixed perhaps with a feeling of importance) she ordered hot possets to be brought instantly to warm them, and begged them to be seated in the great chimney-place till supper was ready.

Though her new subjects never forgave queen Jane for having a large train of French people ever about her, which was foolish and ill-judged on her part, she always showed great wisdom in her dealings with her husband's daughter. She knew that, owing to her mother's early death and her sister's marriage, Philippa had had a great deal more liberty than most princesses of her age, and that it would be very hard for her to be banished from court festivities, or to remain in the background like her own little girls. Perhaps she, too, had read some of the nursery tales, which are the same all over the world, and remembered about cruel stepmothers and ill-treated stepdaughters; but at any rate, as far as possible, she left Philippa alone, and the child saw this and was grateful. She was quite content with her life and her playfellows, and tried to forget the marriage which had been arranged for her at Berkhamstead, and which threatened to put an end to it all!

While they had been living in Hertfordshire an embassy had arrived from Margaret, queen of Norway, Sweden, and Denmark, seeking a wife for Eric, her great-nephew and successor. Considering that it was only six years since the three kingdoms had been united in one, and that Eric, changeable, weak and hasty, showed small signs of following in his aunt's footsteps, and being able to hold the kingdom together, we cannot help wondering why Henry did not refuse Margaret's offer and wait for a better match. But, curiously enough, he seemed quite satisfied, and only stipulated that three years should pass before the contract was fulfilled. Philippa breathed a sigh of thankfulness. There was so little traffic with the North in those days that it seemed strange and far away; and besides, she was very happy as she was, and did not want to be married at all. But three years! Oh, that was an eternity! and as at present the marriage only meant, as far as she was concerned, the title of "Queen of Denmark" and an establishment of her own, with as many horses as she could wish for, she enjoyed the pleasures she had, and shut her eyes to the price that must be paid for them. By-and-by there came the moment when her trousseau had to be got ready, but Philippa took far more heed of the housings and trappings of her horses, and of the cushions for her coaches, than of her own gowns, which queen Jane, whose taste was not bound down by strict fashion, ordered after her own fancy. In those days court dresses were embroidered with precious stones, and cost immense sums, and Philippa's wedding dress of cloth of gold, with the stomacher of pearls, cost the enormous sum of 250*l.* She was surprised and delighted when she saw it, and only wished Blanche could see it too, for she *thought*, though she was not quite sure, that it was even finer than the gold brocade of Master Whittington.

All these things and a great many more having been prepared for her benefit, Philippa set out to pay some farewell visits to the friends and relations she was never likely to see again. Between each visit she went back to her father at Eltham, for she wished to spend as much time as possible with him and the queen, who was now very lonely, as her own two daughters had returned to Brittany. Philippa's very last visit was to the bishop of Durham, and after that was ended the king and his four sons, together with the Swedish ambassadors who had been sent to escort the bride, took her to Lynn in Norfolk. From here, says the chronicler Stow, "in the month of May, 1406, dame Philip, the youngest daughter of king Henry, accompanied by divers lords spiritual and temporal, was shipped to the North and so conveyed to Denmark, where she was married to the king of that country in a city called London." The vessel in which Philippa sailed was, of course, very different from anything *we* can imagine, and even when fitted up for a princess must have been very uncomfortable. It was the largest in the English navy, but would have looked very small in our eyes, and must have rolled terribly. The admiral of the North Sea was in command, and he placed on board some of the unwieldy cannon then used, in case pirates or foreign ships should be met with; but no mishap of any sort occurred, and Philippa landed safe in Sweden, where queen Margaret and the young king Eric gave her a hearty welcome. After a short rest they journeyed to Lund (or "London" as Stow calls it), the old Swedish Capital in the very south of the country, where Philippa's marriage and her coronation took place.

From the day that Philippa set foot on board the vessel she left her childhood behind her. She felt that she was going, alone and for ever, to a land of which she knew nothing, with a language and customs entirely strange to her. It was enough to make a brave man sad, and Philippa was barely thirteen, yet she dared not show her grief or her fears for the sake of her father and brothers who were watching her anxiously. So she smiled and chattered up to the very last moment, and then came a storm of tears, as she clung silently to one after the other. However, she had contrived to banish all traces of sorrow by the time she reached Sweden, and queen Margaret saw with pleasure the good sense and dignity which marked her behaviour. A girl who cared only for amusement would have been a bad wife for the young king, and have encouraged him to be more idle than he was already. But Philippa, she was sure, was made of different stuff, and would some day walk in her own footsteps—if only she was sensible and would listen to her counsel! Philippa *did* listen, and it speaks highly for her that, though for the last five years she had been suffered to do very much as she liked, and had lived more with horses than with books, she now, by the queen's wish, went meekly back to her lessons, and spent several hours a day in learning the history and Sagas (old stories) and languages of the three countries over which she was now queen. Margaret herself, queen of all three kingdoms, taught her the special laws and customs of each, and Philippa, to her surprise and delight, took an interest in everything, and tried with all her might to do the things that Eric her husband left undone—which were many. Very soon the people came to know this, and they thanked her in their hearts and loved her dearly.

So matters went on for six years, and though Philippa was not very happy with her husband, and had no children to comfort her, there was always queen Margaret to go to for help, and consolation. But in 1412 Margaret died, and then Philippa felt lonely indeed. However, she still strove to help her subjects, and had more power than most queens, because the king was always fighting with his neighbours, and left her to rule as she thought best. When her cares pressed heavily she used to go for a holiday to a Swedish convent, and there got strength to carry on her work. And thus, in harness, she died in 1430 at the age of thirty-seven; and nine years later king Eric, who had at last wearied out the patience of his people, was driven from the throne.

ANDREW LANG AND LEONORA BLANCHE LANG

XIV

The Troubles of the Princess Elizabeth

W hat reign in English history do you like best to read about?"
I think that if you were to put this question to twenty children
you would get the same answer from at least fifteen.

"Oh, Queen Elizabeth's, *of course!*" And in many ways they would be
quite right. After the long struggle of the Wars of the Roses, which had,
a hundred years before, exhausted the country, the people were losing the
feeling of uncertainty and anxiety that had possessed them for so many
years, and were eager to see the world and to make new paths in many
directions. The young men were so daring and gallant, so sure of their
right to capture any ship laden with treasure they might meet on the high
seas, so convinced that all other nations—and Spaniards in particular—
which attacked *them*, were nothing but pirates and freebooters, whose fit
end was "walking the plank" into the sea, or being "strung up on the yard
arm," that, as we read their stories, we begin to believe it too! And when
we leave Drake and Frobisher and the rest behind, and turn to sir Walter
Raleigh throwing down his cloak in the mud for the queen to tread on,
and the dying sir Philip Sidney, on the field of Zutphen, refusing the water
he so much needed because the wounded soldier beside him needed it still
more, we think that, after all, those days were really better than these, and
life more exciting. If, too, we should chance to love books better than tales
of war, we shall meet with our old friends again in the beautiful songs that
almost every gentleman of those times seemed able to make—Sidney, and
Raleigh, and many another knight, as well as Shakespeare, and Marlowe,
and Ben Jonson. The short velvet tunics and the small feathered hats,
which was the ordinary dress of the young men of the period, set off, as we
see in their portraits, the tall spare figures and faces with carefully trimmed
pointed beards of the courtiers who thronged about the queen. While the
head and crown of them all, restless, energetic, courageous as any man
among them, was Elizabeth herself.

Yes, there is a great deal to be said for the children's choice.

BUT PERHAPS YOU WOULD LIKE to hear something of the life the
queen led before she ascended the throne, which was not until she was

twenty-five. As, no doubt, you all know, Henry VIII had put away his wife Katharine of Aragon, aunt of the emperor Charles V, in order to marry the beautiful maid of honour Anne Boleyn; and his daughter Mary had shared her mother's fate. It was all very cruel and unjust—and in their hearts every one felt it to be so; but Henry managed to get his own way, and in January, 1533, made Anne Boleyn his wife.

It was on September 7, in that same year, that Elizabeth was born in the palace of Greenwich, in a room that was known as the "Chamber of the Virgins," from the stories told on the tapestries that covered the walls. The king was greatly disappointed that the baby did not prove to be a boy, but as that could not be helped he determined to make the christening as splendid as possible. So, as it was customary that the ceremony should take place a very few days after the child's birth, all the royal secretaries and officers of state were busy from morning till night, writing letters and sending out messengers to bid the king's guests assemble at the palace on the afternoon of September 10, to attend "the high and mighty princess" to the convent of the Grey Friars, where she was to be given the name of her grandmother, Elizabeth of York.

AT ONE O'CLOCK THE LORD mayor and aldermen and city council dined together, in their robes of state; but the dinner did not last as long as usual, as the barges which were to row them to Greenwich were moored by the river bank, and they knew Henry too well to keep him waiting. The palace and courtyard were crowded with people when they arrived, and a few minutes later the procession was formed. Bishops wore their mitres and grasped their pastoral staffs, nobles were clad in long robes of velvet and fur, while coronets circled their heads. Each took his place according to his rank, and when the baby appeared in the arms of the old duchess of Norfolk, with a canopy over her head and her train carried behind her, the procession set forth, the earl of Essex going first, holding the gilt basin, followed by the marquis of Exeter and the marquis of Dorset bearing the taper and the salt, while to lady Mary Howard was entrusted the chrisom containing the holy oil. In this order the splendid company passed down the road which led from the palace and the convent, between walls hung with tapestry and over a carpet of thickly-strewn rushes.

BUT IN SPITE OF THE grandeur of Henry's preparations, the godparents of the baby were neither kings nor queens, but only

Cranmer, the newly-made archbishop of Canterbury, the old duchess of Norfolk, and lady Dorset. Henry knew full well that it would have been vain to invite any of the sovereigns of Europe to stand as sponsors to his second daughter: they were all too deeply offended at his divorce from Katharine of Aragon and at the quarrel with the Pope. He did not, however, vex himself in the matter, and took pleasure in seeing that the ceremony was as magnificent as if the child had had a royal princess for a mother, instead of the daughter of a mere country gentleman. At the close of the service the Garter King-at-Arms advanced to the steps of the altar, and facing the assembled congregation cried with a loud voice: "God of His infinite goodness send a prosperous life and long to the high and mighty Princess Elizabeth of England." Then a blast of trumpets sounded through the air, and the first act of little Elizabeth's public existence began among the noise and glitter that she loved to the end.

By this time it was growing dark, and everybody was hungry. As the church was not very far from the palace, it might have been expected that the company would return there and sit down to a great banquet; but this was not Henry's plan. Instead, he had ordered that wafers, comfits and various kinds of light cakes should be handed round in church, with goblets full of hypocras to wash them down. When this was over, and the christening presents given, the procession re-formed in the same order, and lighted by five hundred torches set out for the palace by the river side, where their barges were awaiting them.

FOR THREE MONTHS THE BABY was left with her mother at Greenwich, under the care of her godmother, the duchess of Norfolk, and lady Bryan, kinswoman to Anne Boleyn, who had brought up princess Mary. After that she was taken to Hatfield, in Hertfordshire, and then moved to the country palace of the bishop of Winchester, in the little village of Chelsea. The bishop's consent does not seem to have been asked, for the king never troubled himself to inquire whether the owners of these houses cared to be invaded by a vast number of strangers. If *he* wished it, that was enough, and the poor bishop had to give up his own business, and spend all his time in making arrangements for the heiress of England—for so she was now declared to be—the rights of Mary being set aside. Right glad must he have been when the king's restless temper removed the baby again into Hertfordshire, to a house at Langley, and sought to provide her with a husband. The prince chosen, first of a long line of suitors, was Charles duke of Orleans, the third son of Francis I of France. The match was in some ways a good one; but Henry wanted so many things which the French king could not grant that the plan had to be given up. In any case it could hardly have come to pass, as the boy died before his bride had reached her twelfth birthday.

Having contrived to get rid of one wife when he was tired of her, Henry saw no reason why he should not dispose of his second for the same cause. Therefore, when he took a fancy to wed Jane Seymour, maid of honour to Anne, he thought no shame to accuse the queen of all sorts of crimes. One day the booming of the Tower guns told that the Traitors' gate leading down to the Thames had been opened, and Anne, whose life had been passed in pleasure and gaiety, stepped out of the barge; the laughter had died out of her eyes and the colour from her face. Well she knew the fate that awaited her, and in her heart she felt it was just. Had she not in like manner supplanted queen Katharine, and thrust her and her daughter from their rightful place? Thus she may have thought as her guards led her to her cell, from which she walked on May 19 to the scaffold on Tower Hill.

"The young lady," says Thomas Heywood, "lost a mother before she could do any more but smile upon her." But ten days later her vacant throne was filled by Jane Seymour, whose brothers, Edward earl of Hertford and sir Thomas Seymour, were constantly seen at Court. Elizabeth, no longer heiress of the crown, had been sent down to Hunsdon, in Hertfordshire, under the care of lady Bryan and her kinsman Shelton, and here she was left, forgotten by everyone, and without any money being allowed for her support. As for clothes, she had really none, "neither gown, nor petticoat, nor no manner of linen, nor kerchiefs, nor rails (or nightgowns), nor sleeves, nor many other things needed for a child of nearly three years old." Neither, according to the rest of lady Bryan's letter to the king's minister, Thomas Cromwell, does she seem to have been provided with proper food. Lady Bryan evidently did not get on well with master Shelton, who shared her charge, and complains that he knows nothing about children, and wished Elizabeth to dine and sup every day with the rest of the household, and that "it would be hard to restrain her grace from divers meats and fruits and wines that she would see on the table." No doubt it was hard, for Elizabeth was always rather greedy, and set much store by what she ate and drank. Just at this time, too, simple food was specially necessary for her, as she had "great pain with her great teeth which come very slowly forth"; and most likely she was rather cross and fretful, as children are apt to be when they have toothache; so lady Bryan is sorry for her, and "suffers her grace to have her will," more than she would give her at other times. But when her teeth are "well graft," or cut, her governess trusts to God "to have her grace after another fashion than she is yet, for she is as toward (or clever) a child and as gentle of conditions as ever I saw in my life."

It was not only lady Bryan whose soul was filled with pity at the forlorn situation of the little girl, whose birth had been made the occasion of such rejoicings. Her sister, princess Mary, now restored to favour, also entreated the king on her behalf, but we are not told if their letters produced the changes prayed for.

ONE DAY IN OCTOBER, 1537, when Elizabeth was just four and Mary about twenty-one, a messenger rode up to the house at Hunsdon, clad in the king's livery, and craved permission to deliver a letter to the princess. He was shown into the hall, and there, in a few moments, the two sisters appeared. Bowing low before them, the man held out the folded paper, bound with a silken thread and sealed with the royal arms of England. Mary took it, guessing full well at its contents, which were, indeed, what she had supposed. A boy had been born to the queen, Jane Seymour, and the king summoned the prince's sisters to repair without delay to Westminster in order to be present at the christening of the "Noble Impe."

Elizabeth, full of excitement, listened open-mouthed as princess Mary told her that they had a little brother, and were to ride next morning to London to see him in the palace. Like her father Henry VIII, whom she resembled in many ways, the little princess loved movement of any kind, and all her life was never so happy as in journeying from place to place, as the number of beds she is supposed to have slept in testify. Like the king also, she loved fine clothes; and the old chroniclers never fail to describe what the king wore in the splendid pageants in which he delighted. His taste seems to have been very showy and rather bad. At one time he is dressed in crimson turned up with green, at another he is gorgeous in a mixture of red and purple. Elizabeth, we may be sure, was arrayed in something very fine, as she proudly carried the chrisom containing the holy oil, with which the baby was to be anointed. Princess Mary, his godmother, held him at the font, and when the ceremony was over, and they left the chapel, the king's two daughters went into the room where lay the dying queen.

FROM THAT DAY ELIZABETH HAD a new interest in life. She felt as if the little prince belonged to her, and when he gave signs of talking, she was sent for to London by the king "to teach and direct him." She made him a little shirt as a birthday present, and as he grew older she taught him easy games, and told him stories out of books. By-and-by she begun to repeat to him simple sentences in French, or Latin, or Italian, and when his tutors took him away, or she grew tired of being governess, she would practise her music on the viols, or try some new stitch in needlework.

In this way time slipped by, and Elizabeth had passed her sixth birthday, when it became known at Court that the king was about to wed a fourth wife, and that his choice had fallen on princess Anne of Cleves. This new event was of the deepest interest to Elizabeth, and she at once, with her father's permission, wrote the bride a funny stiff note, "to shew the zeal with which she devoted her respect to her as her queen, and her entire obedience to her as her mother."

This letter gave great pleasure to the German bride, and laid the foundation of a lasting friendship between the two. For though rather big and clumsy, and not at all to Henry's taste, Anne was very kind-hearted, and grateful to the little girl for her welcome. All the more did she value Elizabeth's affection because it was plain, from nearly the first moment, that the king had taken a violent dislike to her, and though she knew he would not dare to cut off *her* head, as he had done Anne Boleyn's, because she had powerful relations, yet she felt sure he would find some excuse to put her away. And so he did after a very few months; but during all that time Anne busied herself with the interests and lessons of the young princess, and when the decree of divorce was at last pronounced, begged earnestly that Elizabeth might still be allowed to visit her, as "to have had the princess for a daughter would be a greater happiness than to be queen."

IN READING ABOUT ELIZABETH IN later years we feel as if she much preferred the company of men to women; but in her childhood it was different, and the three stepmothers with whom she was brought in contact were all very fond of her. Jane Seymour, of course, she hardly knew, and besides, Elizabeth was only four when she died. But when the pretty and lively Katharine Howard stepped speedily into the place of the "Flanders Mare" (for so, it is said, Henry called the stout Anne of Cleves), she insisted that the child should take part in all her wedding fêtes, and being herself a cousin of Anne Boleyn, Elizabeth's mother, gave the princess the place of honour at the banquets. Elizabeth, no doubt, was flattered and pleased at the honours heaped on her, but in her secret heart she would rather have been with Anne of Cleves.

Henry's marriage with Katharine Howard came to an end even more swiftly than his marriages were wont to do. This one only lasted six months, and after the queen's execution, which took place in February 1542, Elizabeth was sent to rejoin her sister Mary in the old palace of Havering-atte-Bower. Here she remained in peace for a whole year, as the king was too busy with affairs of state, with rebellions in Ireland and a war with Scotland, to think about her, or even about a new wife. Still, marriage, either for himself or somebody else, was never far from Henry's mind, and soon after he not only offered Elizabeth's hand to the young earl of Arran, who did not trouble himself even to return an answer, but tried to obtain that of the baby queen of Scotland, Mary Stuart, for prince Edward. We all know how ill this plan succeeded, and that in the end, when Henry was dead and the English had again invaded Scotland, queen Mary was hurried by guardians over to France, and Edward VI left to seek another bride. "We like the match well enough, but not the manner of the wooing," said the Scots, so Mary became queen of France as well as queen of Scotland.

But all these things were still four years ahead, and Henry had yet to marry his sixth and last wife, Katharine Parr, the rich widow of lord Latimer.

This event took place during the year 1543, when Katharine had been only a few months a widow. Unlike three out of her five predecessors her ancestry was as noble as that of the king himself, to whom, indeed, she was fourth cousin. Her mother had brought her up carefully and taught her to write her own language well, besides having her instructed in those of other countries. She insisted, too, on the child spending much of her time at needlework, which Katharine particularly hated, and escaped whenever she could. However, in spite of her dislike, she grew very clever with her fingers, and some beautiful pieces of embroidery still remain to show her skill. Katharine was fair and gentle, and full of sense and kindness, and as she was known to be a great heiress, her suitors were many. Before she was twenty she had been twice married, and had several stepchildren, and as she was often at Court, where many of her relations filled important offices, she was no stranger to Henry, who had great respect for her judgment. At Lord Latimer's death she was only thirty, and hardly was he buried when sir Thomas Seymour, the king's handsome and unscrupulous brother-in-law, began to woo her for his wife. Perhaps it was because he was so different from either of her previous husbands that lady Latimer fell in love with him, but before the marriage could be accomplished Henry stepped in, and Seymour retired in haste. He knew better than to cross his sovereign's path! So six months after Latimer's death, his widow became queen of England, and Elizabeth went to live with her fourth stepmother.

ALL HER LIFE ELIZABETH WAS able, when she thought it worth her while, to make herself pleasant in whatever company she might be in; tyrannical and self-willed as she often proved in after-years, she invariably managed to control her temper and thrust her own wishes aside if she found that it was her interest to do so. She had learned this in a hard school; but luckily she had the gift of attracting friends and keeping them, and as a child there was not one of her mother's successors on the throne—little though they had in common—who did not delight in Elizabeth's presence. Queen Katharine at once obtained the king's consent to fetch her to Whitehall, and to give her rooms next to the queen's own. Here the princess, now ten years old, could work under Katharine's eye, with her brother Edward, and, as Heywood says, "Most of the frequent tongues of Christendom they now made theirs: Greek, Latin, Italian, Spanish, Dutch, were no strangers," and by the time she was twelve Elizabeth knew a little about mathematics, astronomy and geometry; but history was her favourite study, and many were the hours she passed with old chronicles in her lap. Love of music she inherited from her father, who composed anthems, which you may still hear sung; and needlework had always been a pleasure to her, so that she had plenty to do all day. Now, every one would declare that so much time spent over books was very bad for her, but Elizabeth never seemed any the worse, and could ride over heavy roads from dawn to dark without the least fatigue. If you wish to see a specimen of her labours you can find one in the British Museum, where lies a little book she made for her stepmother when she was staying at Hertford, which bears the date December 20, 1545! It is a translation in French, Latin and Italian, done by Elizabeth herself, of some meditations and prayers written by the queen, and copied by the princess in a beautiful clear hand. The cover appears to be made of closely worked stitches of crimson silk on canvas, with the initials K. P. raised in blue and silver, which time has sadly tarnished. Perhaps it was meant for a Christmas present and a surprise for the queen, who must have been very pleased with her gift.

Prince Edward was a delicate child, and most likely for that reason he was sent down by his father to live at Hatfield House, with Elizabeth to keep him company. Hatfield had formerly belonged to the bishops of Ely; but a mere question of possession mattered no more to Henry than it had done to Ahab before him, and, like Ahab, he took for his own the land he coveted, and gave the unwilling bishops other property in exchange. Here in the park, through which the river Lea ran on its way to join the Thames, Edward and Elizabeth could wander as they pleased, while inside the beautiful house, part of which had been built in the reign of Edward IV, they did their lessons with the excellent tutors the king had chosen for them. One of these, Sir Anthony Cooke, was allowed to have his daughters with him, and these young ladies, afterwards as famous for their learning as their father, were destined to be closely bound up in Elizabeth's life, as the wives of Bacon and of Burleigh. So, "these tender young plants, being past the sappy age," as Heywood poetically calls them, spent some happy months, till an event happened which changed everything for everybody.

On January 30, 1547, Elizabeth was at Enfield, where she had been passing the last few weeks, when to her surprise she beheld, as dusk was falling, her brother, whom she imagined to be at Hertford, riding up to the house with his uncle, Edward Seymour earl of Hertford on one side, and sir Anthony Brown on the other. The prince glanced up at the window and waved his hand as she leant out, but Elizabeth, who was quick to notice, thought that, even in the dim light, the faces of his escort looked excited and disturbed. In a few minutes they were all in the room, where a bright fire was blazing on the huge hearth, and then, hat in hand, the earl told them both that their father was dead, and that his son was now king of England.

THE BROTHER AND SISTER GAZED at each other in silence. Then Elizabeth buried her head on Edward's shoulder, and they wept bitterly and truly. As yet neither of them had suffered much from Henry's faults, and though Edward had been his favourite just because he was a boy and his successor, he had been proud of Elizabeth's talents and her likeness to himself. Thus, while many in England who had trembled for their heads felt his death to be a deliverance, to two out of his three children it was a real sorrow. Poor Mary had suffered too much, both on her own account and on her mother's, to have any feeling but a dull wonder as to her future.

The reading of the king's will did something, however, to soothe her bitter recollections, for it placed her in the position which was hers by right, heiress of the kingdom should her brother die childless, and in like manner Elizabeth was to succeed her. Meanwhile, they both had three thousand a year to live on—quite a large sum in those days—and ten thousand pounds as dowry, if they married with the consent of the young king and his council.

THE MOMENT THAT HENRY WAS dead Katharine Parr left the palace and went to her country house at Chelsea—close to where Cheyne pier now stands; and here she was immediately joined by Elizabeth, at the request of the council of regency. Katharine had been in every way a good wife to Henry, and had nursed him with a care and skill shown by nobody else during the last long months of his illness. He depended on her entirely for the soothing of his many pains, yet it was at this very time that he listened to the schemes of her enemies, who were anxious to remove her from the king's presence, and consented to a bill of attainder being brought against her, by which she would have lost her head. Accident revealed the plot to Katharine, and by her cleverness she managed to avert the danger—though she never breathed freely again as long as the king was alive.

The old friendship between Katharine and her stepchildren was destined to receive a severe shock, and in this matter the two princesses were in the right, and the queen wholly wrong. It came about in this way.

As far as we can gather from the rather confused accounts, sir Thomas Seymour, Katharine Parr's old lover, a man as greedy and ambitious as he was handsome, had taken advantage of Henry's affection for him to try to win the heart of the princess Elizabeth, not long before the king's death. As she was at that time living at Hertford, under the care of a vulgar and untrustworthy governess, Mrs. Ashley, it would have been easy for Seymour to ride to and fro without anyone in London being the wiser. Certain it is that, from whatever motive, he was most anxious to marry her, and a month after her father's death wrote, it is said, a proposal to the princess in person—a very strange thing to do in those days, and one which would assuredly bring down on him the wrath of the council. But Elizabeth was quite able to manage her own affairs, and answered that she had no intention of marrying anybody for the present, and was surprised at the subject being mentioned so soon after the death of her father, for whom she should wear mourning two years at least.

Although Seymour thought highly of his own charms, he had a certain sort of prudence and sense, and he saw that for the time nothing further could be gained from Elizabeth. He therefore at once turned his attention to the rich widow whom the king had formerly torn from him, and with whom he felt pretty sure of success. He was not mistaken; and deep indeed must have been Katharine's love for him, as she consented to throw aside all the modesty and good manners for which she was famed and to accept him as a husband a fortnight after the king's burial, and only four days after he had been refused by Elizabeth, with her knowledge and by her advice.

The marriage seems to have followed soon after, but was kept secret for a time.

It is difficult to say whether Mary or Elizabeth was more angry when these things came to light. Elizabeth had, as we know, been almost a daughter to Katharine, but she and queen Mary had always been good friends, and many little presents had passed between them. At her coronation Katharine had given the princess, only three years younger than herself, a splendid bracelet of rubies set in gold, and when Mary was living at Hunsdon a royal messenger was often to be seen trotting down the London road, bearing fur to trim a court train, a new French coif for the hair, or even a cheese of a sort which Katharine herself had found good eating. Mary accepted them all gratefully and gladly, and passed some of her spare hours, which were many, in embroidering a cushion for the closet of her stepmother.

And now, in a moment, everything was changed, and both princesses saw, not only the insult to their father's memory in this hasty re-marriage, but also the fact that royalty itself was humbled in the conduct of the queen, who should have been an example to all. Mary wrote at once to her sister, praying her to mark her disapproval of the queen's conduct by leaving her house and taking up her abode at Hunsdon. Elizabeth, however, though not yet fourteen, showed signs of the prudence which marked her in after-life, and answered that having been placed at Chelsea by order of the king's council, it would not become her to set herself up against them. Besides, she feared to seem ungrateful for the previous kindness of the queen.

But though living under the protection of the queen-dowager, either at Chelsea or in the country village of Hanworth, Elizabeth had her own servants and officers of the household, amounting in all to a hundred and twenty people. It was very unlucky in every way that the governess chosen to be her companion should have been her kinswoman, Mrs. Ashley, a good-natured, vulgar-minded woman, who was never so happy as when she was weaving a mystery. Of course Katharine took care that the princess passed many hours in the day in lessons from the best tutors that could be found, but still there was plenty of time left when the governess, whose duty kept her always by the girl's side, could tell her all manner of silly stories and encourage her foolish fancies. At length, about Whitsuntide 1548, the queen's ill-health put an end to this state of things, and Elizabeth was sent down, with all her servants, to the castle of Cheshunt, then under the command of sir Anthony Denny; and from there she wrote a letter to her stepmother, thanking her for the great kindness she had ever received from her, and signing it "your humble daughter Elizabeth." After this, they wrote frequently to each other during the following three months, which proved to be the last of Katharine's life. By the end of the summer she was dead, leaving a little daughter behind her, and bequeathing to Elizabeth half of the beautiful jewels she possessed.

Elizabeth's sorrow was great; but when Mrs. Ashley asked if she would not write a letter to the widower, now baron Sudeley and lord high admiral of England, the princess at once refused, saying "he did not need it." He did not, indeed! for a very short time after the queen's death he came down to see Elizabeth, and to try and obtain from her a promise of marriage, which the girl, now fifteen, refused to give. But he still continued to plot to obtain possession of the princess, and, what he valued much more, of her lands. At length his brother the protector thought it was time to interfere. The admiral was arrested on a charge of high treason, committed to the Tower, and executed by order of the council in March 1549. Seymour's downfall brought about that of many others. Mrs. Ashley, her husband, and the princess's treasurer Parry, were all thrown into prison, on suspicion of having helped the admiral in his schemes to marry Elizabeth, and she herself was in deep disgrace at Court. For a whole year she was kept as a sort of prisoner at Hatfield, under the watchful eye of sir Robert and Lady Tyrwhit, and she would have been very dull indeed had it not been for her books. However, as we know, Henry had been careful to give his children the best teaching, and the celebrated sir John Cheke and William Grindall, who had formerly been tutors to Edward and Elizabeth, were now replaced by the still more famous Roger Ascham.

Perhaps Elizabeth was not *quite* so learned as Roger Ascham describes her in a letter to an old friend in Germany. Tutors sometimes think their favourite pupils cleverer than is really the case, and do not always know how much they themselves help them in their compositions or translations. But there is no reason to doubt that, like sir Thomas More's daughters, her cousin lady Jane Grey, and her early playfellows, the daughters of sir Anthony Cooke, Elizabeth understood a number of languages and had read an amount of history which would astonish the young ladies of the present day. At that time Greek was a comparatively new study, though Latin was as necessary as French is now, for it was the tongue which all educated people could write and speak. The princess, according to Ascham, could talk it "with ease, propriety and judgment," but her Greek, when she tried to express herself in it, was only "pretty good." It does not strike Ascham that during this part of her life she cared much for music, though she had been fond of it as a child, and, by her father's wish, she had then given so much time to it that she played very well upon various instruments. Cicero and Livy she read with her tutor, and began the day with some chapters of the Greek Testament. Afterwards they would read two or three scenes of a tragedy of Sophocles, specially chosen by Ascham not only for the beauty of their style, but for the lessons of patience and unselfishness that they taught—lessons which it is feared Elizabeth did not lay greatly to heart.

Scholar though he was, and writing to another scholar, it was not only about Elizabeth's *mind* that Ascham concerned himself. The princess, he says, much prefers "simple dress to show and splendour; treating with contempt the fashion of elaborate hair dressing and the wearing of jewels."

We smile as we read his words when we think of the queen whom we know. It is very likely that the king's council, who heard everything that passed at Hatfield or Ashridge, did not allow Elizabeth enough money for fine clothes or gold chains; but at that time, and for some period after, her garments were made in the plainest style, and she wore no ornaments. No sooner, however, did she ascend the throne than all this was completely changed, and she was henceforth seen only in the magnificent garments in which she was frequently painted; and there is even an old story, that has found its way into our history books, telling us how, after her death, three thousand dresses were discovered in her wardrobes, "as well as a vast number of wigs."

ALL THIS TIME SOMERSET THE protector had strictly forbidden the king to see his sister or to hear from her. But receiving, we may suppose, good reports of her conduct, both from Ascham and the Tyrwhits, he though it might be well to allow both her and her brother a little more liberty, and gave Edward leave to ask Elizabeth to send him her portrait, and even to make her a present of Hatfield. Elizabeth was delighted to be able once more to exchange letters with the young king, and writes him a letter of thanks in her best style, to accompany her picture.

"For the face, I grant I might well blush to offer, but the mind I shall never be ashamed to present. For though from the face of the picture the colours may fade by time, may fade by weather, may be spotted by chance; yet the other (her mind) nor Time with her swift wings shall overtake, nor the misty clouds with their lowerings may darken, nor Chance with her slippery foot may overthrow.

"Of this, although the proof could not be great, because the occasions have been but small, notwithstanding as a dog hath a day, so may I perchance, have time to declare it in deeds, where now I do write them but in words."

ELIZABETH MUST HAVE BEEN VERY pleased with herself when she read over her letter before sealing it and binding it round with silk. Not one of her tutors could have expressed his feelings with greater elegance, and Edward no doubt agreed with her, though most likely a brother of these days, even if he happened to be a king or prince, would have burst out laughing before he was half through, and have thrown the letter in the fire.

ALL THAT SUMMER, PART OF which was spent among the woods and commons of Ashridge near Berkhamstead, Elizabeth hoped in vain to be sent for to Court, but for some reason the summons was delayed till March 1551. A messenger in the king's livery arrived one day at the house, and the princess was almost beside herself with joy as she read the contents of the letter he brought. Then she sprang up and gave orders that a new riding dress should be got ready, and her favourite horse groomed and rubbed down till you could see your face in his skin, and her steward himself was bidden to look to the trappings lest the gold and silver should have got tarnished since last the housings were used. And when March 17 came, she set forth early along the country roads, and at the entrance to London was met by a gallant company of knights and ladies, waiting to receive her. Oh! what pleasure it was to ride through those narrow streets again and to look at the gabled houses, every window and gallery of which was thronged with people! Many times in after years did Elizabeth make royal progresses through the city, but never once was her heart as glad as now. She had escaped from the solitude which she hated so much, and come back to a life of colour and movement.

And so she reached St. James's Palace, and was led to her room.

Here she rested all the next day, while Mary in her turn made an entry, surrounded by an escort very different to look upon from Elizabeth's. The princess and her ladies were all alike dressed in black, while rosaries hung from their girdles and crosses from their necks. There was no mistaking the meaning of these signs, and though they did honour to Mary's courage, it was hardly a civil way of answering her brother's invitation, and it irritated the council against her, which there was no need to do.

IT WAS ON THE DAY after Mary's entrance that Elizabeth again mounted her horse, and in the midst of the company of nobles and ladies rode across St. James's Park to the palace of Westminster, where the king received her with open arms.

"My sweet sister Temperance," he called her, with a laugh, when he noted the extreme plainness of her dress and the total absence of jewels; in these respects a great contrast to the ladies in her company. But it is probable that in choosing such simple clothes the princess had acted from an instinct which told her that by so doing she would gain for herself the goodwill of the all-powerful council, with whom she had been, as we know, for two years in disgrace. And if this was her motive, she had reasoned rightly, for according to her cousin, lady Jane Grey's tutor, "her maidenly apparel made the noblemen's wives and daughters ashamed to be dressed like peacocks, being more moved with her most virtuous example than with all that ever Paul or Peter wrote touching that matter."

Perhaps the good Dr. Aylmer did not know much about the hearts of women, or the influence of a fashion that is set by a princess. In any case, the change in the dresses—and feelings—of the noble ladies did not last long, for in a few months we find them all, Elizabeth excepted, "with their hair frounsed, curled and double curled," to greet Mary of Guise, the queen-dowager of Scotland, who passed through England on her way from France. Edward, now fourteen, gave her a royal reception, and we may be sure that he would not allow his "dearest sister" to remain in the background. When the fêtes were over, the princess returned to Hatfield, triumphant in knowing that she had gained her end, and established her place in the affections of the people.

THE HOUSEHOLD FORMED FOR ELIZABETH was suitable to her rank, and she had a large income on which to support it. From an account book that she has left behind her it is easy to see that even at this time of her life she was beginning to suffer from the stinginess which, curiously enough, was always at war with her love of splendour. She hardly spent anything on herself, and only gave away a few pounds a year—not a great deal for a princess with no one but herself to think of!

Meanwhile grave events were taking place in Edward's Court. The earl of Warwick, soon to be duke of Northumberland, had long hated Somerset, and now contrived to get him committed for the second time to the Tower. Somerset is said to have implored Elizabeth, whom a short time before he had treated so harshly, to beseech Edward to grant him pardon; but the princess replied that owing to her youth her words would be held of little value, and that, besides, those about the king "took good care to prevent her from approaching the Court." This was quite true, and whether she wished to save Somerset or not, certain it is that she had no power to do so.

So, in January 1552, the protector's head fell on Tower Hill, and Northumberland, who succeeded to his place, began secretly to prepare a marriage between his youngest son, lord Guildford Dudley, with the king's beautiful and learned young cousin, lady Jane Grey, whose grandmother, the duchess of Suffolk, was Henry VIII's youngest sister. Edward's own health was failing rapidly, and often after being present at the council, or at some state banquet, he was too tired to care about anything, so that it was easy, as Elizabeth had said, to keep his two sisters from him. Northumberland even managed to persuade the boy that it was his duty to pass over Mary, the natural heir to the crown, on account of her religion, and in this design he was greatly helped by the princess's foolish behaviour. As for Elizabeth, the case was more difficult. At first he thought of arranging a marriage for her with a Danish prince, and when this failed he fell back on some Acts of Parliament excluding her from the throne which had never been revoked, although, of course, if Elizabeth had no right to succeed to the crown on account of her father's previous marriage (as some now said), the same thing applied to Edward.

The object of all these plots and plans concocted by Northumberland was plain to be seen: it was to have his daughter-in-law, lady Jane Grey, declared heir to the throne; and he so worked on the king, who was too weak to oppose him, that Edward was induced, shortly before he died (on July 6, 1553), to appoint his cousin his successor.

As FREQUENTLY HAPPENED IN THOSE times, the fact of the king's death was kept a secret for some days, and during this period Northumberland tried to get both the princesses into his power by sending letters to say that Edward greatly wished to see them once more. If they had come—and Mary nearly fell a victim to his treachery—the Tower would have speedily been their lodging, and probably the scaffold their portion, but they happily escaped the snare. Next, he tried to buy the consent of Elizabeth, promising both money and lands if she would give up her rights. In this, however, he was foiled by the princess, who answered, with tact, that while Mary was alive she had no rights to resign.

WHILE THIS WAS GOING ON the sixteen-year-old Jane was forced by her father-in-law into a position she was quite unfitted for, and which she very much disliked. She loved her young husband dearly, and was perfectly happy with him and her books, taking no part or interest in politics. Suddenly, she was visited at Sion House near Brentford, to which she had gone at her father-in-law's request, by a number of powerful nobles of Northumberland's party, who informed her that the king was dead, and had left his kingdom to her, so that the Protestant religion might be well guarded. Then all the gentlemen present fell on their knees before the bewildered girl and swore to die in her defence.

Jane was overwhelmed. She grasped hastily at a chair that was near her, and then sank fainting to the ground. The duchess of Northumberland, who was present with some other ladies, dashed water in her face and loosened her stiff, tight dress, and soon she grew better, and was able to sit up. Rising slowly to her feet she looked at the little group before her, and said: "My lords, sure never was queen so little fit as I Yet, if so it must be, and the right to reign is indeed mine, God will give me the grace and power to govern to His glory and the good of the realm!"

Little heed did those who heard her so submissively take of her words. She had done what they wished, and that was all that mattered: the rest was their affair. So, leaving Jane to her own thoughts, they departed and went their own ways. A day or two later, on a blazing July afternoon, their victim was taken in a barge from Chelsea to the Tower, and there, mounting the stairs, her train carried by her grandmother the duchess of Suffolk, once queen of France, the crown was held out to her by the royal treasurer. Then, and then only, the death of Edward was publicly announced, and a letter, which, it was pretended, had been written by Jane, was distributed among the citizens of London, stating the grounds for setting aside the princesses and putting the granddaughter of Henry's younger sister in their place.

It did not take long for Northumberland to find out that he had laid his plans without reckoning with the will of the people or the courage of the princesses. The country had seen through him, and even gave him credit for more evil than he had actually done, for a rumour went abroad that he had poisoned Edward to serve his own ends. This adventurer, high as he had risen, should never dictate to Englishmen. Why, most likely even lady Jane herself, or "queen" as he would have the world call her, would come to a bad end when it suited him! No! No! No Northumberland for *them!* and Mary's religion and cold, shy manners were forgotten, and gentlemen called together their friends and followers and marched towards London.

Northumberland was no match for them, and knew it; and what was more, he knew that he had no ally in Jane herself. His energy was not of the kind that increases with difficulties, and when he heard that Jane's grandfather, the duke of Suffolk, had signed with his own hand the order for the proclamation of queen Mary, he rightly judged that all was lost, and tried to escape. But it was too late, and next day he was charged with high treason and lodged in the Tower.

Nobody cares what became of Northumberland, as he only got what he deserved; but every one must mourn for the Nine Days Queen, who never could have been a danger either to Mary or Elizabeth.

July was not yet over when Elizabeth, now nearly twenty, was bidden to leave Hatfield and ride by her sister's side in her state entry into the city. So far the two sisters had always got on fairly well together; still, Elizabeth misdoubted the temper of the Catholic party, and rode through the lanes and over the commons with an escort of two thousand armed men. That night she lay at Somerset House (now her own property), on the banks of the Thames, and the next morning went out to Wanstead, on the North Road down which Mary would come. It had not taken the princess long to discover that at present she herself ran no risks, so she dismissed half her guard, and with five hundred gentlemen dressed in white and green, and a large number of ladies, she passed smiling through the crowded streets, which rang with shouts of welcome. No one seemed to remember the king, who still lay unburied; but so much had happened since he died, that everybody, even including his "sweet sister Temperance," had forgotten him for the moment.

The first breach between Mary and her subjects, and also her sister, was not long in coming. The ways and services of the old religion were speedily restored, and Elizabeth was given to understand that she was expected to attend mass. This she refused to do, and thereby increased her popularity tenfold; but she seems to have allowed Mary secretly to think that it was possible she might some day change her mind, and, in order to keep her sister in a good humour, requested to be given Catholic books to read and priests to teach her.

In this way matters went on till September, when Mary's coronation took place. Elizabeth drove the day before, in the state procession to Westminster, in a coach drawn by six white horses decorated with white and silver to match her dress, Anne of Cleves being seated by her side. All through the ceremonies she was given her proper place as the heiress to the throne, and even publicly prayed for.

Unluckily, this happy state of things did not last long, and the different views of religion held by the two sisters were embittered by many whose interest it was that there should be constant quarrels between them. A plot was set on foot to marry Elizabeth to her cousin,

Courtenay earl of Devon—who had already been refused as a husband by Mary herself. This was encouraged by Noailles, the French ambassador, for his own purposes; but Elizabeth, who feared her friends more than her foes, sought to escape from it all, and to retire at once to Ashridge in Hertfordshire.

Here she received a letter from Mary begging her to come at once to St. James's Palace; but, knowing as she did that sir Thomas Wyatt was doing his best to stir up a revolt against the queen, Elizabeth thought it more prudent to make the most of an illness under which she was suffering, and remain where she was. She likewise put Ashridge in a state to stand a siege, should it be necessary, filling the castle with provisions and armed men.

IT WAS WYATT'S REBELLION THAT sealed the fate of lady Jane Grey and her husband, and made Elizabeth tremble for her own head. The Nine Days Queen had hitherto been warmly defended by Mary herself, in spite of the assurances, which had been so frequently whispered in her ears, that her throne would never be safe during the life of such a claimant. Now, with the successes of Wyatt among the men of Kent, these whispers became louder, and this time Mary listened to them. Not that she believed her young cousin to have any share in Wyatt's treasonable schemes; she knew her too well for that. But as long as she lived she would be used as a handle for all plotters, so, with deep and real regret, Mary signed the warrant that was placed before her, and within a few days Jane was beheaded in the square of the Tower, the only woman who was not executed on Tower Hill. She and her husband had never met since they had been arrested; but now Mary sent a messenger to lady Jane, granting permission for a farewell interview. But lady Jane refused. "What," she asked, "would be gained by their bidding each other farewell on earth, when they would so shortly meet in heaven?" It may be that she feared for *his* courage more than her own, for she stood unseen at her window while he was led forth to the scaffold on Tower Hill, and remained there till his body was brought back. Then her own turn came, and cheerfully she left her cell and walked the few steps that lay between her prison and the green. Here she paused in front of the block, and turning, spoke to those who were gathered round:

"The plot of the duke of Northumberland was none of my seeking," she said, "but by the counsel of those who appeared to have better understanding of the matter than I As to the desire of such dignity by me, I wash my hands thereof before God and all you Christian people this day."

After that, she begged those present to help her with their prayers, and repeated a psalm, and then, kneeling, laid her head on the block.

IF LADY JANE WAS THE most important victim of all these conspiracies, she was by no means the only one, for Wyatt and other leaders were shortly to pay the same penalty, not, however, without declaring that all they had done was with the knowledge and consent of the princess Elizabeth, and of Courtenay earl of Devon. Mary had no difficulty in believing this; Elizabeth's own conduct had for the last few months given rise to suspicions, so a company of gentlemen, headed by the princess's kinsman lord William Howard, and including a certain Dr. Wendy, who had formerly attended Henry VIII, were sent down to Ashridge to see how far the princess's illness was real, and to bring her to London if possible. It was ten o'clock at night when they arrived, and Elizabeth refused to admit them; but they politely insisted, and she was obliged to open her door.

No trace of guilt or fear, or indeed of anything but impatience, could be read in her face, as the queen's messengers entered her apartment.

"Is the haste such," she said, "that it might not have pleased you to come in the morning?"

The ambassadors held it wiser not to state how great "the haste" was, but they only answered that they were sorry to see her grace in such a case, referring, of course, to her supposed illness.

"*I* am not glad at all to see *you* at this time of night," she replied; and went on to say that "she feared her weakness to be so great that she should not be able to travel and to endure the journey without peril of life, and therefore desired some longer respite until she had recovered her strength."

In this matter neither Howard her great-uncle, nor her old friend Wendy the doctor, agreed with her. It is true that anxiety for herself, if not sorrow for the fate of lady Jane Grey, about whom she seems to have cared nothing, had thrown her into some sort of fever, but it was quite plain that there was nothing to prevent her undertaking the short journey. In order, however, that no risks might be run the thirty-three miles that lay between Ashridge and Westminster were divided into five stages, and every night she was to sleep in some gentleman's house. A week later she started in a litter, and when, several days after, she entered Aldgate, the curtains were thrown back at her bidding, so that the people, who had always loved her, might be touched by the sight of her thin pale face. But well or ill, when the moment came in which courage was needed, Elizabeth was always herself, and her bows and smiles betrayed no fear as, dressed in white, she was carried through the city, with an escort of scarlet-coated gentlemen riding in front.

Rooms were given her in Whitehall, and here she hoped to see the queen, and be able to convince her of the innocence she so loudly proclaimed to everyone. But to her great disappointment and secret terror, Mary refused her an interview, and ordered her to be taken at once to the palace of Westminster and placed in an apartment which had no entrance except through the guard-room. A certain number of personal attendants were allowed her, and through them she heard with dismay that Courtenay had been lodged in the Tower, and every day was examined for some time as to his share in Wyatt's conspiracy.

For three weeks Elizabeth waited, not knowing exactly how much the council knew, but remembering, with dread, two notes which she had written with her own hand to Wyatt. She guessed truly that all the weight of Spain would be thrown in the balance against her, for the emperor Charles V had neither forgotten nor forgiven the divorce of his aunt, and, besides, his son Philip was already betrothed to the queen.

At last, one Saturday, ten members of the council visited her, and told her that a barge was in waiting at the stairs, which would take her to the Tower. Elizabeth received the news without flinching, though she felt as if the nails were being knocked into her coffin, but begged permission to finish a letter to the queen which she had just begun. This the council could not well refuse; but the princess made her letter so *very* long that the tide ran out too far for her to embark, and as Sunday was a day when no work was done, her gaolers were obliged to wait until Monday.

On Monday, however, even Elizabeth could invent no more pretexts for delay, and entered her barge with as good a grace as might be. But when the rowers shipped their oars at the Traitors' Gate, she objected that it was no entrance for *her*, who was innocent.

"You have no choice," said one of the lords who was with her, and stooped to lay his cloak as a carpet on the muddy steps. With an angry gesture Elizabeth dashed it aside, and sat down on a wet stone, as if she intended to sit there for ever. The lieutenant of the Tower, who was awaiting his prisoner at the top, prayed her to come in out of the rain and cold, which at last she consented to do, and was conducted by him to her prison, a room that led only into the lieutenant's own house on one side, and a narrow outside gallery on the other, used by the prisoners for air and exercise. Here Elizabeth's suitor, sir Thomas Seymour, had been lodged before his execution, and here Arabella Stuart would be confined, in years that were yet to come.

For two months Elizabeth's imprisonment lasted, though the extreme strictness with which she was kept was afterwards relaxed, and she was suffered to walk in a little garden under a strong escort, and to receive flowers from the children belonging to the servants about the Tower, with whom she had made friends. At first she had, like Courtenay, constantly to undergo examinations as to her guilt, but she somehow managed to gain over the earl of Arundel, hitherto one of her most bitter enemies, and henceforth she had no warmer partisan. She seems to have answered the questions put to her with her usual cleverness, as the Spanish ambassador writes that though "they had enough matter against Courtenay to make his punishment certain, they had not yet been able to obtain matter sufficient for Elizabeth's conviction," partly owing to the fact that several witnesses were in hiding.

It was in May that the queen sent an unexpected summons to Elizabeth that she was to join her at Richmond, where she was passing the Whitsun holidays; and how beautiful the flowers and trees must have looked in the eyes of the prisoner, accustomed for so many weeks to nothing but the walls of the Tower, with the bitter memories they contained! She did not stay there long, however, for the queen, irritated at Elizabeth's firm refusal to marry the prince of Savoy, sent her in a few days to the castle of Woodstock, with sir Henry Bedingfield as her gaoler.

On the road, according to the old chroniclers, she more than once tried her favourite trick of gaining time by delaying her arrival. At one place where she was to spend the night she was anxious to have a match at chess with her host, and another day she declared that her clothes and hair had suffered so much from a storm that she must positively enter a house they were passing in order to set them straight. But Bedingfield was not easy to dupe, and politely insisted on continuing their way.

"Whenever I have a prisoner who requires to be safely and straitly kept, I shall send him to you," she said, laughing, when four years after he attended her first Court as queen.

At Woodstock Elizabeth remained till 1555, writing sad poems about her captivity and doing large pieces of needlework; but towards Christmas a welcome change was in store for her, as Mary, who had been married in July to Philip of Spain, now sent for her to Hampton Court.

Even here her life as a prisoner was not yet over, for she was shut up in her rooms for a week, and never once saw the queen. At length, late one night, she was bidden to Mary's room, and there they had a long talk. Elizabeth was most careful to do and say nothing to vex her sister, and seems to have succeeded, for she stayed as a welcome guest in the palace for some months, taking part in all the amusements, and receiving, not at all unwillingly, the attentions of prince Philibert of Savoy, though she never meant to marry him. With Philip she appears to have been on the most friendly terms, and at a great tournament held just after Christmas she occupied a place next him and the queen. Altogether, as the fears for her own safety gradually melted away, she greatly enjoyed herself, and pleased Mary by sometimes attending the services in her own private chapel, decked out, we are told on one occasion, in white satin and pearls. Early in the spring Elizabeth returned to Woodstock, bearing with her a splendid diamond, worth four thousand ducats, the gift of her brother-in-law.

But no sooner had she gone back to Woodstock than rumours of another plot spread abroad, and as usual Elizabeth was supposed to be concerned in it. It does not seem at all likely that the accusation was true, but Mary thought it safer to have her under her own eye, and sent for her a second time to the palace. Elizabeth must have satisfied her to some extent that she was guiltless in the matter, for Mary gave her a beautiful ring, worth seven hundred crowns, and allowed her to go to Hatfield, though she placed with her, as some check on her actions, one sir Thomas Pope, with whom Elizabeth lived very pleasantly.

The story of the next three years is much the same: repeatedly plots were discovered, and in all of them Elizabeth was accused of taking part—probably quite falsely. Still, it was natural that the queen should be rather suspicious of her, though she often invited her to court, and Elizabeth did her best to set her mind at ease by frequently attending Mass in her company. Indeed, she was the less likely to be engaged in any schemes against her sister as it was quite plain that Mary's life was fast drawing to an end. When free to follow her own way the princess buried herself in books, reading Demosthenes at Hatfield with Roger Ascham, besides studying Italian under Castiglione. They all write enthusiastically of her cleverness, but when Castiglione remarks that she had not only "a singular wit," but a "marvellous meek stomach," we feel either how great was Elizabeth's power of deceiving—or how bad was her judgment.

During these three years also suitors were frequent, and among them her old lover, Philibert of Savoy, was the most pressing. Courtenay, to whom she had for political reasons once betrothed herself, had died in exile at Pavia, so, as far as she herself went, Elizabeth was free to marry whom she chose; but though all her life she liked the excitement and attentions which went hand in hand with a marriage, when it came to the point she could not make up her mind to forfeit her liberty. It was also clear to her that if, during Mary's lifetime, she took a foreign husband, and went to live abroad, her chance of sitting on the throne of England was gone for ever.

At this period Elizabeth made up for the "Seven Lean Years" of her Puritanical garments by clothing herself and her suite in the most splendid of raiment, for which she constantly ran into debt. During the last year of Mary's reign she was constantly in and about London, and once we have notice of a visit of the queen herself to Hatfield, when the choir boys of St. Paul's sang and Elizabeth played on the virginals. Soon, however, the queen was too weak for any such journeys. Philip was away, engaged in the war between France and Spain, and Mary remained at home, to struggle with her difficulties as best she might. She knew quite well she had not long to live, and declared Elizabeth her successor, entrusting to her maid of honour, Jane Dormer, the crown jewels, which were to be delivered to the princess. To these she added three petitions: that Elizabeth would be kind to her servants; that she would pay her sister's private debts, and that she would support the old faith, now established by law; which, of course, Elizabeth could not do, or her throne would have been instantly forfeit. Then Mary died, knowing that she had failed in all she had attempted; and, amidst the welcoming shouts of the English people, the Elizabeth whom you all know was proclaimed queen.

FINIS

A Note About the Author

Andrew Lang (1844–1912) was a Scottish editor, poet, author, literary critic, and historian. He is best known for his work regarding folklore, mythology, and religion, for which he had an extreme interest in. Lang was a skilled and respected historian, writing in great detail and exploring obscure topics. Lang often combined his studies of history and anthropology with literature, creating works rich with diverse culture. He married Leonora Blanche Alleyne in 1875. With her help, Lang published a prolific amount of work, including his popular series, *Rainbow Fairy Books*.

Leonora Blanche Lang (1851–1933) was an English author, editor, and translator. Often going by the name Nora, Lang described her childhood as stuffy and repressed. She married Andrew Lang in 1875, and created many literary collaborations with him. Best known for their series, *Rainbow Fairy Books*, Lang was responsible for translating the majority of the story collections. Her work with fairytales and folklore helped shift the public perception of the stories, championing them to be suitable for a wide audience and worthy of critical praise. This influenced generations of authors, including Arthur Conan Doyle and J.R.R. Tolkien, extending Nora Lang's legacy for centuries.

A Note from the Publisher

Spanning many genres, from non-fiction essays to literature classics to children's books and lyric poetry, Mint Edition books showcase the master works of our time in a modern new package. The text is freshly typeset, is clean and easy to read, and features a new note about the author in each volume. Many books also include exclusive new introductory material. Every book boasts a striking new cover, which makes it as appropriate for collecting as it is for gift giving. Mint Edition books are only printed when a reader orders them, so natural resources are not wasted. We're proud that our books are never manufactured in excess and exist only in the exact quantity they need to be read and enjoyed. To learn more and view our library, go to minteditionbooks.com

Enjoy more of your favorite classics with Bookfinity,
a new search and discovery experience for readers.
With Bookfinity, you can discover more vintage
literature for your collection, find your Reader Type,
track books you've read or want to read,
and add reviews to your favorite books.
Visit www.bookfinity.com, and click on
Take the Quiz to get started.

Don't forget to follow us
@bookfinityofficial and @mint_editions